'46

The   Nineteen   Twenties

THE
NINETEEN TWENTIES

A General Survey and some Personal Memories

by

Douglas   Goldring

LONDON

NICHOLSON & WATSON

Produced in full conformity with the War
Economy Agreement

CONTENTS

PART ONE

A General Survey

PART TWO

SOME PERSONAL MEMORIES

v

ACKNOWLEDGEMENT

My thanks are due to Miss Camilla Rodker, daughter of Mary Butts, for giving me permission to print her mother's letters. D.G.

DEDICATION

TO IRENE RATHBONE

Dear Irene,

I have asked you to accept the dedication of this book, the imperfections of which cannot be more obvious to you than they are to myself, because it gives me a chance of thanking you for a literary comradeship which has now lasted more than a dozen years. Five of those years, 1935 to May 1940, were, as I think you will agree, almost more distracting, from a professional standpoint, than the years of actual war which we have been forced to live through. Without your sympathy and encouragement I don't know how I should have managed to produce anything at all during those frustrated 'thirties.

" Are you writing anything now ? " is the sort of well-meant nit-wit question which, as you may have noticed, the wives of stockbrokers consider a good conversational opening, when they meet authors. They would think us rude or crazy if we were to ask whether their husbands had been broking any stocks lately. All the same, odd as it may seem to those who follow more secure and lucrative avocations, it is the business of the professional writer to write. But how were we and our contemporaries, who had already been shaken up and battered by the Four Years' War, to settle down quietly to our job during the period of Appeasement, when the very ground we stood on was collapsing under our feet ?

Imagination, a critical faculty, a streak of intuition, some human sympathy, a sensitiveness to impressions, a general awareness—all these are a necessary part of an author's professional equipment. Again I ask, how were we to make full use of our faculties and pursue our legitimate aims when the civilization which it should be our life's work to serve, was in process of being destroyed before our eyes ? I admire the fortitude of those of our colleagues who were able to ignore the sabotage of the League of Nations, the disgrace of Non-Intervention and the shame of Munich and live in the pure atmosphere of their own artistic creation. I admire it, but I do not possess it, and it has been a comfort to me to discover that your instinctive reactions to current events have so often been identical with my own. Where authors differ from most of those engaged in purely commercial pursuits is in their capacity for intellectual detachment, in the fact that they are trained to study evidence and analyze motives and are accustomed by the necessities of their occupation to think for themselves. Where they differ from the majority of journalists is that they express their own opinions instead of those of their employers.

In 1930, when we first met—shortly after the death of D. H. Lawrence—it looked as though we could look forward to a period of comparative tranquillity. We had been through quite enough strain and turmoil to last a life-time and now was the opportunity to use our experiences in whatever way our talents or inclinations might suggest. With Germany completely disarmed, as we were assured, the boisterous Mussolini incapable of any serious aggression and the League of Nations, with all its defects, still functioning, at least our national *security* appeared to be impregnable. The moment therefore seemed to many writers a propitious one for exposing the futility and horror of the " Great War." The public, at last, was in a receptive mood. It had recovered its mental equilibrium, after the years of ferment which these chapters describe, and was prepared to face its painful memories and to reflect on them. A whole spate of war fiction and reminiscences, mostly pacifist or bitterly critical in tone, poured down in quick succession. Edmund Blunden, if I remember right, led the way. Then came Richard Aldington whose " Death of a Hero " created a literary sensation and soon developed, as it deserved to do, into a best-seller. You yourself followed, shortly afterwards, with your " We That Were Young," which remains in my opinion by far the best novel of the Four Years' War, written by a woman who served in it.

It was only natural that the bulk of this large output should convey the message : Never Again. After all, nearly a million young Britons had given their lives to secure an overwhelming victory in what was represented as a " war to end war." To the survivors, therefore, it seemed only logical that war should, indeed, be ended. I remember Richard Aldington once saying to me : " I'm still a pretty good shot with a rifle. If any of these damned politicians tries to start another war I'll take a pot at him, even if it's the last thing I do." This was a characteristic attitude of ex-Service men at that time. It was based on the assumption that we still possessed the millions of rifles and the large reserves of machine-guns and heavy artillery the nation had manufactured and paid for, that we had an overwhelmingly strong navy, a larger air force than that of any power that might conceivably challenge us, and that our former enemies were disarmed as well as bankrupt. It was based, moreover, on the knowledge, now historically confirmed, that without the deliberate collusion of the ruling Conservative oligarchy, a collusion which at that period seemed inconceivable, a second world war was an impossibility. Few of us suspected the existence of a counter-revolutionary conspiracy. The financial wire-pullers were careful not to divulge their secret plans for crushing Democracy and erecting bulwarks against Bolshevism. As we are now painfully aware, we were all of us living in a fool's paradise, and when public suspicions began to be aroused, Mr. Baldwin's lips were sealed. (In 1940, after Dunkirk, everyone was asking what had become of our rifles and why we had to use improvised pikes to defend our airfields. It remains an unsolved mystery.)

For as long as my endurance held out I refused, like most other writers, to spend time and energy on current politics. They weren't my job, anyway. As I had lost the inclination to write novels, I devoted a couple of years to a long autobiography which at least enabled me to escape into the past. Under an " enemy " Government, like the one imposed upon us by the bankers' crisis of 1931, I could see no attractions in the future either for myself or for any characters I was capable of creating. As a final, desperate " escapist " effort, I recklessly started a society for preserving Georgian architecture and for a year worked like a slave, at considerable personal expense, as its harassed " honorary secretary ". Even this did not have the desired effect. The progress of the war in Spain blew me out of my Georgian gazebo and made me realize that the issues before us were either an ignominious surrender to the Axis or something like a national revolt to force the Conservatives to keep their promises.

In 1935, in what was called the " Peace Ballot," there had been an overwhelming vote for a strong League of Nations policy—for " collective security "—enforced, if need be, by arms. This gave our Tory rulers a clear and unequivocal mandate to pursue the only course which could have checkmated the aggressors. I shall never forget our feeling of relief when, at Geneva, Sir Samuel Hoare, in clear and ringing words, announced Great Britain's intention of acting upon it. Nor shall I forget our consternation, a few weeks later, after the present Conservative majority had been safely returned to the House of Commons, when we realized that it was only an election speech and that Sir Samuel had come to a secret understanding with Laval the day before he made it.

The war in Spain—the " curtain-raiser " to the present struggle—is, I admit, one of my King Charles's heads. I shall never get over the shock caused me by the realization that almost the whole of our Conservative class, including the sort of people among whom I had been born and brought up, had gone over solidly to the enemy. Its relevance here is that the roots of " Non-Intervention " go back as far as 1919 and that its consequences may flare up into world importance before these lines are printed. As Charles Duff puts it, Spain is " the moral touchstone of Europe." In 1936 it was something more than the " moral touchstone " of the propertied classes in France and England. It was a basic test of the instinctive patriotism—there is no other word

—of the naval, military and diplomatic caste in both countries. Can anyone really believe that there were any individuals in the commissioned ranks of the British Navy, Army and Air Force, in the Foreign Office, diplomatic corps and consular service, who were so ill-educated or naturally stupid as not to realize that a victory for General Franco and his Nazi-Fascist allies meant a crushing initial defeat for Britain and France in the war with the dictators then obviously threatening ? Any schoolboy could see that with Spain under Axis domination our Mediterranean lifeline would be seriously endangered. The most elementary considerations of imperial security thus made it incumbent on the Conservatives—the " patriotic " party—to lend every help in their power to the Spanish Republic and to induce the French to do the same. Instead, actuated as always by financial motives—the City had £40 million invested in Spanish mines and other industries—they lent every help in their power to General Franco.

The honour of our country, during this shameful period, was saved by the real patriots, of every class and political background, from peers to hungerstrikers, who flocked to join the British battalion of the International Brigade. If Hitler had paid more attention to the crossing of the Ebro than to Ribbentrop's reports of millionaire house parties, he would have saved himself some blunders. Veterans of the Spanish war, in spite of all the efforts of Security and Military Intelligence, are still the heroes of the other ranks in the British Army. The fact that Marshal Tito and his lieutenants gained their experience in Spain and that Tom Wintringham, Slater and other International Brigaders trained the Home Guard in the principles of guerilla warfare is as widely known as the fact that Lord Croft, of pikestaff fame, was a fanatical Franco propagandist. After Hugh, my elder son, died of wounds in the Western Desert I was deeply moved, when going through his papers, to find that in a diary for 1937 he reproached himself bitterly for not volunteering to fight in Spain. He was only eighteen at the time and just starting his course at the Chelsea School of Art, but he knew what issues were at stake. His grave at El Alamein bears on it the bald statement that " He gave his life to help save the world from Fascism". Four months after his death, General Eisenhower informed the patriots of France that Admiral Darlan was a Frenchman " worthy of his country's great past."

" Social contacts ", as I expect you also found, were from 1937 onwards, decidedly difficult. The highly-subsidized campaign of Catholic-Fascist propaganda, which represented General Franco as a " Christian gentleman "—even after he was plainly shown to be guilty of the murder of innocent British seamen—seemed to drive a large part of the Conservative class, including the Minivers, almost crazy. The traditions associated with the " old school tie " appeared to have gone with the wind and the Tory mind was in a hopeless state of confusion. It was one thing for the Conservatives, following their natural habit, to denounce all progressive ideas as " arrant Bolshevism," quite another to find them ranged on the side of Britain's external enemies and openly desirous of bringing about her surrender and defeat. It was also startling to discover paragons of public virtue, including pharasaical "Christians", championing brutality and beastliness in their most outrageous forms, including the filthy mental disease of anti-Semitism. To the middle-class public, fed on detective stories and the lies of the millionaire press, Socialists, Communists and other " Reds " were the sort of people among whom our " loyal " police sleuths would almost automatically look for spies, criminals and traitors in league with the enemy. It was a new situation, disturbing to all the most deeply-engrained instincts of British snobbery, when naval and military "high-ups", titled landowners and coal-owners, Conservative M.P.'s, captains of industry, police chiefs, Secret Service men, leading civil servants, masters of fox-hounds and Mayfair young ladies were revealed as fifth columnists and the terms " Socialist " and " Red " became, even in the popular press, synonymous with "patriot". To public schoolboys of my generation, the idea of a distinguished admiral, who had filled the post of Director of Naval Intelligence, having to be locked up ; of the sister of an Under-Secretary of State having to be put under police supervision ; of prominent newspaper proprietors secretly intriguing with our enemies, and of an aristocratic Conservative M.P. having to be arrested and imprisoned without trial would have been simply inconceivable.

One of the effects which the succession of crises preceding the present world conflict had on myself was to force me to reconsider preconceived ideas and to start the process of mental stock-taking, reflection and research of which this book is partly a result. In 1920, when my second boy was born, my overmastering desire, like other fathers, was to make it impossible that my sons should ever have to endure the horrors of another war. No one to whom politics, and all the dreary meetings and conferences they necessitate, are as temperamentally repugnant as they are of me, could possibly have got mixed up with them from any other motive. By the time the war broke out in Spain it was clear to me that the pacifist propaganda of the 'twenties, however firmly based on the solid rock of ineluctable truth, had proved hopelessly inapplicable to existing conditions. The realistic pacifism of the Russians, particularly of Stalin's great Foreign Minister, Maxim Litvinov, seemed to offer the only possibility, short of shameful surrender, of preventing the Spanish war from spreading. " Collective Security", starting with all help to Spain, was Europe's last chance. Only if the Fascist counter-revolution was defeated would there be any hope of safeguarding the kind of civilization in which it would be possible for the human race to accept, and act upon, the doctrines propounded by Mahatma Gandhi, George Lansbury and, at a lower level perhaps, Aldous Huxley, Gerald Heard and Dick Sheppard. Unless the Fascists were crushed, the world must relapse, perhaps for centuries, into a form of mechanized barbarism which would make the Dark Ages a misnomer.

After Hugh's death, when I had finished "South Lodge", I found myself constantly reflecting on the early 'twenties, feeling certain that if I looked back into the past I should find a clue to the jig-saw puzzle of events which would enable me to fit them into a recognizable pattern. I found it, at least to my own satisfaction, in the life and teaching of E. D. Morel.

Some time in 1925 one of Morel's sons approached me with the suggestion that I should write his father's life. I made all sorts of excuses for declining—distrust of my qualifications, lack of political knowledge and experience, lack of time and so forth. Since no one else has undertaken the task, I regret now that I did not have the courage to make the attempt. I might have bungled my job as a biographer, but I should at least have made extracts from Morel's vast collection of documents which would have been of value to the contemporary historian. Morel's investigations of the horrors of " red rubber " and of the conditions of slavery which existed in the Belgian Congo before he put a stop to them, had given him an un-rivalled knowledge of the methods of Big Business and of the political influence secretly exerted by pressure groups, particularly in the department of foreign affairs. This knowledge he subsequently put to good use in his untiring efforts to expose the underlying causes of the Four Years' War. Morel realized that the first " Bastille " to be captured in the people's forward march was the Foreign Office. He realized, what is now generally understood, that financial considerations form the bedrock of the foreign policies of all capitalist countries— even the foreign policy of the Vatican is said to be decided by a group of bankers, industrialists and large land-owners—and his methods of investigation enabled him to give chapter and verse for his conclusions. Had Morel been alive to-day he would have laid bare the reasons why the Foreign Office consistently tries to make friends of our enemies and enemies of all our friends and exposed, in detail, the truth behind the long series of diplomatic manœuvres which aroused so much suspicion. Non-Intervention, the appeasement of Franco, the mysterious intrigues in Cairo and Athens, the Darlan-Giraud-Murphy episode, Amgot, Mihailovitch, our relations with the Argentine Republic, Rumania, the Vatican and the Polish emigrés—these matters which, to-day, disturb the public mind would have been no mysteries to Morel. He would have specified the banks, companies, combines and cartels concerned and stated the amount of capital involved.

I believe it is fair to assume that, in the present situation, Morel would urge it as the first duty of a Socialist Government to set up a Royal Commission of Enquiry into the causes and conduct of the war, with full powers to examine witnesses under oath and to enforce the production of relevant documents.

I am not a particularly facile hero-worshipper but Morel stands out in my memory as one of the few really great men I have been privileged to know. He is certainly one of the few of whom we can say that had he survived another ten years he might have changed the course of our political history. What will happen to us when the present war is ended will depend, in my view, largely on whether the survivors, particularly those who are parents, develop sufficient political intelligence to take heed of Morel's teaching and sufficient energy to act upon it. Let them insist upon an unbiased judicial probe into but one out of a thousand closely-guarded secrets—how Hitler got his minerals and particularly his nickel, to take an example at random—and the rest will follow. Nothing but the Truth can set us free, nor can anything except a full disclosure of the facts we have a right to know so educate the electorate as to give our democratic form of government a chance to recover its vitality.

Forgive me, dear Irene, for addressing you as if you were a public meeting or one of those hard-faced editors who so frequently consign our letters to their waste-paper baskets. This book has fallen, for reasons I found unavoidable when I wrote it, into two halves. So also, you may say, has its author ; but I lay the responsibility for this on the revolutionary period in which we have been fated to live. If my dates had been, say, 1840 to 1910, I could have turned out one of those neat, well-arranged volumes, full of autumn sunshine, mellow reflection and kindly sentiment, which are so deservedly popular in well-upholstered circles. Unfortunately, I was born half a century too late for that kind of thing, and through most of my adult life I have had to travel on a hard seat, in a third-class compartment, with frequent changes, bumps, derailments, and delays. All the same, as perhaps the second half of this untidy work makes clear, I enjoyed myself well enough when the going was good. My memories of the 'twenties are of happy days, when I followed the advice of the poets, gathered roses, sometimes with thorns attached, did many foolish things, never went away early when there was more fun to be had by staying late, travelled far, wrote lots of books, made lots of friends. I took no thought for the morrow—at least until the 'twenties were nearly over—and any regrets I might have felt at being a rolling-stone have long since been dissipated. In the light of what we have endured during the past ten years I can only thank my stars that I had enough sense to enjoy the fullness of living while I had the chance. I never cast myself for the role of a Cassandra, never hungered to address meetings, to write letters to the press, or to indulge in the activities of a pamphleteer. All I asked of Fate and the politicians was to be let alone, not to have my sons seized as cannon-fodder, and not to be deprived of my bread and butter if I worked for it. As these simple requests have not been granted me, I cannot feel answerable for the consequences. It is a pity that, like Ford, I haven't been able to write the sort of books that people like : an even greater pity, for my own satisfaction, that I have never enjoyed enough security to write the sort of books I like myself. But at least I am not conscious of having done anyone out of a job, stood in any colleague's light or failed to boost my betters—even to fetch and carry for them—when the opportunity occurred.

Here, anyway, dear Irene, is a mixture characteristic of our chaotic times ; part tirade, part chuckles, part analysis, part fun and games, part gloomy, part cheerful, part bitter but, at least where faithful friends are concerned, wholly grateful and affectionate.

Yours ever,
Douglas Goldring.

July, 1944.

INTRODUCTION

I

THE period which began on November 11th, 1918, and ended with the formation of the first National Government on August 24th, 1931, referred to colloquially as the " 'twenties," is likely to figure largely in the works of historians as yet unborn. Those of us who lived through this amazing decade and, like the writer of this record, had the fortune to come in personal contact with some of its outstanding personalities in politics, literature and the arts, were much too pre-occupied with the excitements of the moment to be able to stand aside and take a detached view of a drama in which we were all more or less actively engaged. It is only now, in the warring " 'forties ", when England is reaping the results of the lost peace and the spiritual defeat which followed her military victory in 1918, that we are able to view this revolutionary epoch in something like perspective. It was revolutionary not only in the political sense, but also in the fields of art, literature, social life, religion and ethics. As we have, at last, come to realize, politics and religion, art and sex are only different aspects of creative energy, closely interlinked manifestations of the *elan vital*, which cannot, without mutual loss, be kept separate, in watertight compartments.

When the political revolution failed, as much through the inadequacy of its leaders as by reason of the united strength of the forces opposed to it, the ensuing deadness and frustration affected every department of intellectual activity. A creeping moral paralysis spread after 1931, from the top downwards, until, after a series of betrayals, the Government lurched, unprepared, into the Second World War. The national uprising of May 1940 released the dynamic energy of the people. But when the danger of invasion receded, the Conservative oligarchy recovered their nerve, brought the Labour leaders to heel, and resumed control. At the Anglo-American conference held in London in July 1942 — from which Russia, China, the people of Britain and the Free French were excluded — all pretence that we were fighting a " people's " or anti-Fascist war was abandoned under reactionary pressure. Thus the Conservatives again endangered the prospects of an enduring peace, after *our* efforts and *our* sacrifices have given *them* the victory, have made the Third World War appear not only possible but probable, and the third English " revolution " merely a matter of time.

The origin of all these events, present and to come, can clearly be traced back to what took place in the 'twenties. It is precisely this which gives the decade its significance for those who wish to understand the real meaning of the counter-revolutionary conspiracy which has already prolonged the present conflict and bids fair to cheat the Resistance movements in every country, our own included, of the liberation for which they have fought. The " mistakes " made in 1919 have already been made again from the same motives, and, in many cases, by the same people.

II

Human nature being what it is, trivial surface manifestations of revolutionary exuberance will always have a fascination for the average reader. Probably more people are familiar with the erotic adventures of Pauline Bonaparte, the propensity of Parisian ladies for receiving male visitors in their baths and the extravagant costumes of *les merveilleuses*, than with the social and economic changes which took place in France before and after the Revolution. Few, moreover, even today, appreciate the fact that during the height of the Terror, the theatres of Paris were open as usual, life went on much as before, and a large section of the population was only dimly aware of what was happening in the next street. In the 'twenties, a very small handful of Bright Young People secured a great deal of publicity by throwing wild parties and indulging in kindergarten orgies of gin, sex, and drugs, which caused their faces to be printed in the Sunday newspapers. Novelists and " belles-lettrists " have already exploited this material and when anything like " normalcy " returns to publishing, we may be certain that they will do so in the future. " Goings-on " are always fun to read about and the writer does not propose to exclude references to them in a book which aims, above everything, at candour. It should be pointed out, however, that in the 'twenties, as in the 'thirties and 'forties, " serious " vice—such as financial corruption, avarice, treachery and selfish cruelty—was chiefly indulged in by members of the wealthy commercial ruling class, who were exceedingly careful of appearances.

For writers and artists the years of " free living " they enjoyed in the 'twenties (and have never enjoyed since) resulted in a liberation of creative activity which has made the decade illustrious and has already deservedly surrounded it with more glamour than the mauve " nineties." The " nineties ", in regard to their most characteristic products, were, self-consciously, an end, a " fin-de-siècle ". The 'twenties, in spite of the paralysis which afterwards ensued and still continues, will be eventually revealed as a beginning. Bliss was it in that dawn to be alive . . .

One of the curious facts about the English which the present war has brought to light, is the imperviousness of a large section of our people, particularly the middle-class, to the impact of world-shaking events, even when their own country is concerned in them. Not only are there millions of us whom the present war has scarcely touched, there are millions more on whom the last war made no very deep or lasting impression. The history of the 'twenties, exciting, full of movement, struggle, agitation, revolt and suppression though it is, is a history only of an active minority. In the Army, between 1914 and 1918, there were hundreds of thousands of men who never heard a shot fired, large numbers of generals, much-decorated staff-officers and office-colonels, who had the time of their lives, never faced anything more dangerous than the possibility of a hang-over developing into D.T.s and were pensioned and regarded as heroes when the war ended. Similarly in industry, between 1920 and 1930, while agriculture was ruined by the bankers, miners denied a living wage and some millions of skilled artisans forced to languish on the dole, millions more enjoyed a steadily increasing prosperity. These naturally exercised a preponderant influence in their Trade Unions. Mr. Wal Hannington, in his book on the National Unemployed Workers Union, which he founded and directed, is justifiably bitter regarding the lack of support accorded him by the Trade Union Movement, the way in which its leaders ranged themselves on the side of the employers and the readiness with which they betrayed their comrades.

While a handful of the *intelligentsia* welcomed birth control, and Divorce Law Reform, advocated a revised moral code, propounded advanced ideas on sexual ethics, preached nudism, free love, sexual emancipation and the abolition of " Sin," the great majority of the population carried on much as before. If there was an increase in divorce, for most of us marriage remained the desirable way of life. An obstinate majority of husbands continued to prefer their own wives to those of others, while among women the ranks of Mrs. Micawbers were not seriously diminished. The age-old pattern of give and take, squabbles and adjustments, side-slips ignored or condoned and the development of mutual interests in home and children, gardens, pets, friends and social life went on very much as usual. The struggle for power which took place during the 'twenties between the profiteering plutocracy on the one hand and the workers, " idealists " and intellectuals on the other, should be seen against a background of unimaginative inertia on the part of the majority who were fairly prosperous, in safe jobs and reasonably contented.

It is impossible to give any accurate figures as to the number of men and women in England who at any given time take an active part in the Government of their country or in the expression and formulation of public opinion. Just before the present war it was estimated that there were in England 540 millionaires, 80,000 payers of super-tax and about 800,000 taxpayers admitting to an income of between £500 and £2,000 a year. How many boys there are, on an average, at schools technically known as public schools and how many graduates are turned out annually by all the universities put together I cannot pretend to estimate. How many people write books, address letters to the newspapers, take any articulate part in political discussions, or help in local organizations is also anybody's guess. My own belief, for what it is worth, is that if we estimate the propertied classes, the bureaucracy, the professional politicians and the *intelligentsia*— including Socialist spokesmen, Labour leaders and politically-minded members of the working class—at five per cent. of the entire population we shall be somewhere near the facts. The remaining ninety-five per cent., the rank and file, are principally concerned with their pay-packets, their amusements and their homes. Their hearts, we may believe, are in the right place : as people go, most of them are, as schoolboys say, "pretty decent". They are not so easily swayed by headlines as the millionaire owners of national newspapers imagine. They have deep-rooted instincts of right and wrong which are basically Christian. They can respond, by instinct, to inspired leadership. But, in the main, they would rather die than think, and as Bertrand Russell observed, "millions do". They can "take it". For this reason, in writing about the 'twenties or, indeed, any other period of English history, attention can only be paid to the struggle between the handful who own the country's wealth and wield the power, and the handful who have the intelligence, energy and courage to seek to wrest it from them for the benefit of the many. The masses can win wars but will only make history when they become politically educated enough to take part in what may soon be a struggle for their continued existence as free men. Until they make this mental and moral effort— which all our history shows can only be made under educated and financially disinterested leadership—they will remain cannon-fodder without the smallest control over their own fate.

III

This survey of the 'twenties makes no pretence to be an objective historical study. It claims to be no more than a personal record, to which comment has been added in the light of later events which reveal the significance of what preceded them. Even in my own department, that of literature and the arts, I attempt no more than a candid appreciation of the outstanding figures with whom I happened to come into some kind of personal contact, or whose works I admired. These include D. H. Lawrence, A. E. Housman, James Joyce, Wyndham Lewis, the Sitwells, Aldous Huxley, Harold Monro, Ford Madox

Ford, W. H. Davies, Norman Douglas, Siegfried Sassoon, Mary Butts and one or two others, who, for some reason or another, have attracted no public attention. I shall have something to say about the conditions in the publishing trade and in the journalistic profession, as I observed them. In the domain of politics, although I had a ringside view, as a member of the 1917 Club, of much that was going on, I cannot claim a sufficiently complete understanding of all I saw and heard to attempt a dogmatic interpretation of it. I had a slight acquaintance with Ramsay MacDonald, and for a time almost daily opportunities of observing him in intimate surroundings. For two of three years before his death I was on terms of friendship with E. D. Morel. I met Philip Snowden, Arthur Ponsonby, Noel-Buxton, Pethick-Lawrence and others sufficiently often to form a novelist's impression of them. For thirty years I was on terms of affection and intimacy with the late Joseph King, who had a benevolent finger in every progressive political pie and an enormous acquaintance among the leaders of the Liberal and Labour parties. But having a natural detestation of politics and not wishing, even if I possessed them, to develop the qualities essential for a career as a political journalist, I played little active part in any of the movements and controversies in which, as an insignificant member of a group, I found myself involved. I made observations and drew some conclusions which, as they have the negative merit of being "first-hand," I have set down in their place. For the rest, I had my share in the Continental wanderings and wild parties of the international " café-society " in which I found myself and enjoyed days and nights of care-free happiness and gaiety, which I shall never again experience. For a year or two in the 'twenties, the lights were all turned on, Freedom filled us with a stronger sense of intoxication than any of the potations in which we indulged, and Hope, Freedom's lovely sister, inspired us again with a rapturous delight in living. In the succeeding decade, we found ourselves under a reactionary Government—less harsh than those of Italy, Germany and Franco Spain—but cold, clammy, deadening and frustrating. This Government was the enemy of Freedom everywhere —in Spain, in Russia, in France, in Italy, in Germany, no less than in England. And as Freedom was taken from us, Hope hid her face. The 'twenties were followed by years of alarm and despondency for all those who had been fortunate enough to glimpse some of the happiness that life was capable of affording.

IV

Among the things which wrecked the " revolution " of the 'twenties, apart from Ramsay MacDonald's leadership, was the narrow sectarian cliquishness and inverted snobbery of the official Labour Party. Among those educated at public schools and the older Universities there is a kind of freemasonry which holds them together, in spite of their divergencies of opinion. They may be Conservatives, Liberals or Socialists, but they all talk the same language, pronounce it in the same way and recognize each other by these signs when they meet. The Roman Catholics of all classes have the nexus of their Religion : so also have adherents of the extreme political creeds, Communism and Fascism. Nothing seemed to bind the Socialist leaders together except their self-interest, their innate fear of Socialism and their common distrust of those members of their Party who took their Socialist principles seriously. Their cliquishness was then, and still remains, almost unbelievable to the man in the street. Socialist journalism in the 'twenties became an organized racket, a fact of which any writer from outside who attempted to muscle in was quickly made aware. A novelist who introduced progressive ideas into his books for the purpose of holding up a truthful mirror to his age could rely on being judged on his literary merit by *The Times Literary Supplement* and other organs of the " capitalist " press. In " Socialist " weeklies, if not completely ignored, he was apt to be treated as the rector of a rural parish might treat an itinerant preacher who set up his soapbox outside the parish church. Even professional journalists who wrote for the Left, like H. N. Brailsford and Mrs. H. M. Swanwick, were driven from papers which they brilliantly edited by the Committees employing them. In 1923, the owners of *The Nation* killed H. W. Massingham's great weekly, and thus destroyed his life's work, precisely at the moment in our political history when it was most important that it should continue. For sixteen years it had maintained the highest standards of honest political journalism and its loss was a disaster. Authors, attracted to the Left, who would gladly have sacrificed pecuniary gain to advance the cause of Socialism among a middle-class audience, received no encouragement from the class-conscious Labour bosses.

The jealousy shown by the Labour leaders of the " bourgeois " was only equalled by their sycophantic attitude towards what they regarded as the Top Shelf. Whenever an Old Etonian tie appeared in the 1917 Club Ramsay MacDonald used to purr and beam, while the presence of any titled personage sent him into an emotional dither. Small wonder that the progressive and, in the broadest sense " liberal " section of the professional middle-class, without whose support Labour has never had a chance of establishing itself as the dominant political force, resented its rebuffs, gradually realised that it was not wanted and found itself largely disenfranchised in 1931 and 1935. Only when the out-of-date nineteenth century terms " Labour " and the " Workers " are discarded and a United Socialist Party of Great Britain emerges can we hope for a progressive and truly " national " Government representing all classes of the people. In the years to come, all of us will be " workers " who are not parasites.

Several useful and entertaining books have appeared during the past ten years which give a general view of the principal political events, movements in art, literature and the stage, changes in social life and economic developments during the first decade after the Four Years War.   Among those I have profitably consulted are " Just the Other Day " by John Collier and Iain Lang ; " Ourselves : 1900-1930," by Irene Clephane and " The Long Week-End," by Robert Graves and Alan Hodge.   The authors of these books have had access to the files of newspapers, Hansard and a mass of other documentary material required for the compilation of a contemporary history.   Their researches have been of the greatest use to me in jogging my memory, in starting trains of thought and reminiscence and in supplying facts and details about things I had either forgotten or never knew.   For the most part, however, this book is a first-hand account of one man's observations, impressions and experiences during the period with which it deals.   As such, it suffers from obvious limitations.   The writer has been forced, throughout, to obtrude his own personality.   The eyes with which he looks back on the past are his own grown older ; and the comments and criticisms he makes on what he sees, in the clarifying light of time—with its gift of reflection and the increase of knowledge which time brings to all but the mentally inert—are his own no less.   If the reader still objects that there is too much " ego," I bid him ask himself how otherwise could a book like this, on so complicated a subject, be composed with any degree of modesty or intellectual humility ?   To attempt an entirely impersonal survey of the nineteen twenties, to indulge in the generalisations, based on accurate scholarship and the comprehensive study of all that others have said, which the professional historian finds unavoidable if he is to be concise, is far beyond my capacity.   Not only would it require gifts and qualities which I do not possess : it would also necessitate access to libraries, which I am at present denied,* and more years in which to make use of them than I am likely to be granted.   Moreover it would require a different impulse, a different temperament and a different habit of mind from those with which I happen to be blessed or cursed.

* While this book was being written the London Library was forced to suspend its postal service as a result of enemy action.

PART I
A GENERAL SURVEY

CHAPTER ONE

THE COUPON ELECTION

I

WHEN the fumes of the champagne they had consumed to celebrate the victory won by " the Boys " had cleared from their brains, the big shots of Britain's financial oligarchy woke up with all the symptoms of a hangover. Wherever they looked they saw clouds gathering and breakers ahead. It was obvious to them that the transition from a war economy to sound finance and uncontrolled free enterprise would require the most careful handling if the masses—including " the heroes " now clamouring impatiently for demobilisation—were to be kept under proper restraint. The Russian Marxist Revolution was an open and visible threat to the established order. If the Revolution was not quickly sabotaged, if " Bolshevism " was allowed to spread among the working classes of the defeated Central Empires, there would be no safety in the future for the Conservative Party and the bankers, stockbrokers, monopoly capitalists, cartelists and power politicians who direct its policy. An additional headache was provided by the crack-brained but infectious idealism of President Wilson, with his " fourteen points "—which had now served their purpose—and his projected League of Nations. It was a good thing to have the world made safe for " democracy ", provided only that the unofficial dictatorship of the Bank of England and its associated groups was not threatened or interfered with. India and Ireland must be dealt with firmly, regardless of American criticism, and the Left Wing pacifists prevented from weakening the strong arm of the Government by recalling pledges which had only been given from motives of expediency. Similarly, though the " gallant lads " must, of course, be patted on the back, the rewards promised them would have to be scaled down to what was practical at the moment. We must, they wisely reflected, always cut the

1

A

people's clothes in accordance with the amount of cloth we feel
inclined to spare them.

The position of the " captains of industry ", though they would
have been indignant had anyone suggested it, was not unlike that
of professional cracksmen who have just brought off a sensational
coup.   Many of them had made fortunes by trading with the
enemy through Sweden and Holland.   Others had cornered
most of the available shipping and held the country up to ransom
at the height of the U-boat campaign.   During the years of
crisis and emergency, when the issue of the war hung in the balance,
it had been easy enough to rob the nation's till and hand back the
money to the Government in exchange for interest-bearing bonds.
The trouble now was how to salt down the swag, " square the
police "—that is to say, the handful of politicians acting in the
public interest—and secure a Parliament guaranteed to ask no
awkward questions.

After the Armistice, the personal prestige of Lloyd George
equalled, if it did not exceed, that of Winston Churchill after the
Crimea Conference.   The astute Tory wire-pullers realised
that the mood of national rejoicing and the popularity of the
Welsh wizard—the man who won the war—might not last
indefinitely.   Lloyd George himself required a mandate from
the people to strengthen his hand at the peace conference.   It
was essential to capitalize these assets while the going was
good.   They therefore decided to hold a snap election before any
substantial number of the armed forces could record their votes.
The task of getting the Right Men into the new Parliament was
facilitated for Sir George Younger, the popular Scotch brewer
who was the Conservative boss, by the fact that when saving his
country Lloyd George had disintegrated the Liberal Party and
produced a state of chaos in the opposition camp.   The device
of sending " coupons " only to those who had supported the
Government in the Maurice debate, had the effect of excluding
from the House of Commons men like Asquith, Reginald
McKenna and Sir John Simon.   The country was too exhausted,
mentally and spiritually, to take much interest in the election and
the poll was unexpectedly low.   In spite of the fact that only
5,121,359 voted for the Coalition, as opposed to 4,600,000 against,
the Coalition members secured no less than 478 seats and thus
had a huge majority.   Most of them were Younger's nominees,
and were aptly described as " hard-faced men who looked as
though they had done well out of the war."

Although the campaign was largely fought in the consti-
tuencies on such slogans as " Hang the Kaiser " and " Make
Germany Pay ", the policy outlined by the Coalition Government,
when it went to the country, was calculated to make a wide appeal.
It described as " our first task " the conclusion " of a just and
lasting peace " in order to establish " the foundations of a new
Europe that occasion for future wars may for ever be averted."
Other points were " the provision of land for soldiers ", the
" promoting of scientific farming, the housing of the people
[homes fit for heroes], the development of the Empire and active
measures to ensure employment for the workers of the country."

That Lloyd George's intentions were, on the whole, statesmanlike and that with adequate Parliamentary support he would
have carried out much of his programme, must be assumed from
his record. Unfortunately, he had to reckon with the hostility
of Lord Northcliffe, then owner of the *Times*, whose request to
be made one of Britain's delegates at the Peace Conference had
been very properly declined. In revenge, Northcliffe collected the
signatures of 370 Conservative M.P.s to a telegram, despatched
to Lloyd George in Paris on April 10th, 1919, urging him to
make the terms imposed on the enemy more severe than those
foreshadowed by the Armistice. Among the Northcliffe partisans
were several who later came into prominence as " Men of
Munich ". It is scarcely surprising to find among them Edward
Wood, now Lord Halifax, Sir Samuel Hoare, Lord Croft, Lord
Moyne (Guinness) and Sir Douglas Hacking. The object of
the Northcliffe intervention was to pile on Germany a crushing
load of Reparations, payment of which was out of the question
without the most careful economic adjustment, skilled handling
of the complex political situation and above all the reduction to
impotence of the Prussian Junkers and the officer caste. Lord
Northcliffe's friends, owing to their terror of Bolshevism, had no
desire to make life impossible for the Junkers on whom they
already looked as potential allies.

II

After the successful conclusion of the war, Lloyd George's
political genius seems to have been temporarily in abeyance.
His position was, moreover, complicated by the fact that he had
the support only of a handful of Liberals, most of his majority
being composed of profiteers, some of whom he had been forced
to bribe by titles. These " honours " were showered on big

industrialists in return for their patriotic collaboration—at a price—in the production of the munitions without which our armies would have suffered defeat.   K.B.E.s abounded—Cardiff was appropriately nicknamed the " City of dreadful Knights "— and men whose surnames stank concealed them under titles which recalled the chivalry of Feudal England or the poetry and romance of Highland glens.

Against a background of demobilisation riots, strikes, wrangles and intrigues at Versailles, guerilla warfare in Ireland, massacre in India, sabotage in Russia, profiteering in flats and houses and rapidly mounting prices for essential commodities, the clever cads who had preferred cash to glory indulged in a veritable orgy of expensive pleasure-seeking, while shell-shocked heroes and disillusioned workmen looked on with apathy, contempt or, as in the case of the miners, rising anger.   " The interest on six thousand millions of pounds ", wrote C. F. G. Masterman, " is paid out annually to some, as the result of the taxation of all ; those some spend it all, to the envy of all.   Most of it represents profit made by the war, in a period of national necessity.   In face of these facts and emotions, England cares little for the League of Nations and is indifferent to the recovery or the ruin of Europe."

Mr. Compton Mackenzie, whose memory is the admiration and envy of his brother writers, has thus described the squandermania which raged in London after the Coupon Election.   The country was infested with avaricious men " in key positions " who, as he points out, " grew richer than before from the prizes that fell to them from the disposal of the mass of surplus material accumu- lated by the new Ministries for the prosecution of the war.   A serious scandal was once or twice imminent ; but the thieves of politics and big business, nervous of the discontent beneath the surface, by not falling out defeated the efforts of honest men to expose them.   The merchant service might have lost men by enemy action, but the shipping industry had thriven on it, and there was hardly a magnate who had not waxed fat as a lobster on corpses.   To the Banks and the insurance companies which worked loyally with big business, the greater part of the country and even of the Empire was now in safe pawn."

Of the political situation he observes that at " almost every by-election the uneasiness created by the Coalition Government was noticeable in labour victories or tumbling coalition majorities; but the deepening corruption of public life was not fully apprehended in the glitter of superficial prosperity. Louder than the boom of the guns was the boom of business, as it set about creating the new world which the politicians had promised but found themselves without the imagination, the energy, or even the common sense to direct".

In the first two years of the Coalition Government, among the people most severely hit were members of the middle class—particularly writers, journalists and artists—and various professional types with a public school "background." These carried on a desperate but, for a time, unavailing struggle to maintain even a semblance of their former standard of life. Ex-officers in particular were reduced in many cases to the direct misery and ex-officer organ-grinders, cabmen and railway porters became familiar objects of compassion.

By contrast, the working class, " the great body of England ", did well out of the short-lived post-war boom. Writing in 1922 Masterman notes that they " successfully struck for higher wages during the months of plenty succeeding the war. They are having a bad time, and have unsuccessfully struck against reduction of wages in the months of penury which have followed". As early as March 1919 the unemployed numbered over a million and the system of doles had to be instituted in the following month. Much hardship was caused to all except the well-to-do by the premature removal of price regulations and controls, at the instigation of the big combines. Margarine was decontrolled in February, 1919 ; meat, butter and sugar coupons were abolished in the following August and the cost of living soared to 110 points above the 1914 standard. In the same month there was a police strike, which caused the propertied classes the utmost alarm. When the railway men came out in September, the strike was treated as a revolution, Haig was put in command of the home forces and middle-class volunteers promptly rallied to the side of the Government, as they did again during the General Strike of 1926. The miners, as usual, got a particularly raw deal. Men taken from the mines had formed the mainstay of the famous 46th North Midland Division, which " achieved the impossible " by crossing the St. Quentin Canal and breaking the Hindenburg Line. Their gallantry, in the hour of their country's need, failed to soften the hearts of their employers. The Sankey Commission, which Lloyd George had forced upon the miners' leaders, reported in favour of nationalization which was one of their primary demands, but this solution was rejected through the operation of

the same " pressure groups " as caused its rejection during the
present war. The man who had made the world " safe for
democracy " was forced to become the leader of a class struggle
in which all the resources of the State were mobilized against
the masses of the people by those who had betrayed and robbed
them. All projects for post-war reconstruction were abandoned
or whittled down to almost nothing. The colonies were left
undeveloped, farmers were ruined by the repeal of the Corn
Production Act and the removal of State support, agricultural
wages slumped almost to the level of the dole and " homes fit for
heroes " became a bitter jest. Not long after the appointment of
Mr. Montague Norman to succeed Lord Cunliffe as Governor of
the Bank of England, the policy was inaugurated of pouring
millions of pounds of British money at high interest into the
Central Empires, to rebuild their towns and re-equip their
industries for another war, while the common people of Britain
and her colonies, after an enormous expenditure of blood and toil,
starved and languished amid uncleared slums. Those fortunate
enough to have jobs spent their surplus wages watching hired
teams of football players, or indulging in such anodynes for the
nervously exhausted as hard drink and fornication.

III

While shell-shocked ex-officers, disillusioned, jobless, impoverished and often homeless " intellectuals " and other members
of the professional middle-class who would normally have constituted a body of informed public opinion, were pre-occupied
with their personal problems, the most astonishing events were
taking place on the world's stage. Direction of foreign policy,
subject to Mr. Lloyd George's improvisations and " intuitions ",
was entirely in the hands of the financial oligarchy which has
retained control over it ever since. The suppression of the
democratic forces liberated by the war, both at home and abroad,
was—and remains—their paramount aim. Horror of what Mr.
Winston Churchill, in a lapidary phrase, described as " the foul
baboonery of Bolshevism " swept over the entire Conservative
class. As Dr. Esme Wingfield-Stratford records in his book
" The Harvest of Victory", " the least suspicion of sympathy with
Lenin—or even the courtesy of pre-fixing his name with a
' Monsieur '—was enough to brand anyone as a socially undesirable personage." In the middle and upper classes, the word
" Bolshevik " became the worst term of abuse which could in

decency be applied to any human being. In regard to Mr. Churchill's obsession, Dr. Wingfield-Stratford suggests that " his ideal solution would have been, instead of disarming the German host, to have enlisted it in a fresh war or grand European crusade against England's former ally." This view was widely held by high officers of the Army and Navy, and contributed to the half-hearted way in which the work of disarming Germany was undertaken. Over a hundred million pounds of British money was wasted in supporting the ex-Czarist generals Denikin, Wrangel, Yudenitch and Admiral Koltchak. British troops, enlisted to fight for "Democracy", were sent to Archangel and the Caucasus, and secret agents were let loose to blow up bridges and otherwise hinder the establishment of the new régime. The exploits of Sir Paul Dukes and others, though now rarely referred to in England, are doubtless recorded in Soviet school-books. In April, 1919, Mr. Lloyd George received the intelligence, pre-sumably from Secret Service agents, that Bolshevism was already rapidly on the wane and breaking down " before the relentless logic of economic facts". That, today, the Soviet economic system is still a complete failure from the standpoint of " sound finance", is apparent to all. It is equally apparent to all that the kind of "failure" which produces homes, security, maternity benefits and education for the masses, and a mighty army to protect them, is preferable to the kind of orthodoxy which produces slumps, unemployment, semi-starvation, recurrent wars —and millionaires.

In a sudden access of Liberalism, Lloyd George announced that " we cannot interfere, according to any canon of good government, to impose any form of government on another people", although we were in fact interfering. In May 1919, it was jubilantly announced by Conservative wishful-thinkers that Koltchak would reach Moscow in a few months and Petro-grad in a few hours. Lenin and Trotsky had different views.

While the British were non-intervening in an attempt to impose financial rectitude on the U.S.S.R., American reactionaries, with more skill and more success, were destroying the newly-won freedom of the Hungarian peasants and workers in the interests of the Hungarian landlords. How they did this was first re-vealed by Mr. T. C. C. Gregory—chief lieutenant of Mr. Hoover in his relief organization, who was in charge of Central and Eas-tern Europe—in three articles which appeared in an American periodical, The World's Work, in April, May and June 1921.

The gist of Mr. Gregory's complacent admission of treachery to
the starving Hungarians, in which he was assisted throughout
by a British Military Commissioner, whom he genially described
as "a sportsman and a gentleman", was given in a timely article
by Mr. H. N. Brailsford in *The New Statesman and Nation* of
January 8th, 1944. As Mr. Gregory proudly claimed, Hoover
"was feeding and succouring Balkanized Central Europe, only
as an incident in the fight he was making to throw back the wave
of Bolshevism". Relief, moreover, was run from first to last on
strictly commercial lines and every pound of food and every piece
of material distributed had to be paid for. According to Mr.
Gregory, Hoover exhibited "an almost ruthless use of power"
and proved himself a "real dictator".

The folly and ineptitude of the Government's treatment of
Russia was surpassed by their brainless brutality in Indian and
Ireland. During the war, when India's loyal aid was badly
needed, the Liberal Jew Edwin Montagu, speaking for the
Government, had made a declaration to the effect that it was
intended to develop self-governing institutions by stages, "with
a view to the progressive realization of responsible Government
in India as an integral part of the British Empire". This was
held by Indians to mean that India was at last to take her place
as an equal partner in the British Commonwealth of Nations.
The Montagu-Chelmsford Constitutional Reform Law of 1919
was the usual stingy and half-hearted compromise, which created
the unworkable and makeshift system known as "dyarchy".
Any good it might have done was counteracted by the massacre
at Amritsar and by the hated Rowlatt Act, which gave the
British Raj powers to detain suspects without trial. 1919,
however, saw the emergence as national leader of that remarkable
Indian saint, Mahatma Gandhi.

General Dyer, the soldier responsible for firing on a crowd which
had illegally gathered in the Jallianwala garden at Amritsar—
also for leaving the killed and wounded without succour, and
compelling Indians to crawl on their hands and knees past a
spot where some roughs had beaten up a woman missionary—
was a type of military fanatic which we are now inclined to regard
as exclusively the product of Nazi Germany, Fascist Italy and
Franco Spain. Graziani's massacre of the Abyssinian élite
after his entry into Addis Ababa, though a more cold-blooded
affair, was an action of the same order as Dyer's.

The Amritsar massacre annoyed the more responsible members

of the British Cabinet and even stirred the exhausted and apathetic British public into some show of indignation. Dyer was court-martialled and presented with his bowler hat as a result of the trial. The rage and bitterness caused by his crime might have died down had it not been for the provocation of Indian feeling provided by the class of Englishmen with whom Indians came most frequently in contact. The House of Lords disgraced itself by vindicating General Dyer, after his court-martial, while the readers of the *Morning Post* subscribed to present him with a tip of £26,000, to console him for the abrupt end of his military career.

The typically " Nazi " methods which characterized the rule of the British Conservative class in India in 1919, and have been intensified during the present war, were applied—with no backing from the British people—in the attempt to hold down Southern Ireland. The credit for organizing the semi-military force known as the " Black-and-Tans " is usually given to the Lowland Scottish police boss, Sir John Anderson, who became joint-secretary to the Lord-Lieutenant.

Had opinion in the United States permitted the continuance of the Irish guerilla war, there is little doubt that the Black-and-Tans would have crushed the Sinn Feiners, made a wilderness of Southern Ireland, and called it peace. The full story of the Black-and-Tan activities was told, soon after the struggle ended, by General F. P. Crozier, Henry W. Nevinson and other eye-witnesses. Their books—painful reading to those who believed that even the horrors of war could not turn English " gentlemen " into savages—reveal how the "methods of barbarism", later associated with Mussolini, Hitler and Franco, originated. There seems little doubt that Mussolini closely watched the proceedings of the irregulars and some of their devices, such as shooting prisoners "while trying to escape", were adopted by his black-shirts in their campaign to suppress Italian liberty. Since imitation is the sincerest form of flattery it is not to be wondered at that Mussolini quickly became popular with British Conserva-tives. Even Sir John Anderson could not have made Italian trains run more smoothly and punctually than the Duce.

IV

If the average middle-aged Englishman was asked what he recalled about 1919, he would probably talk about the housing shortage, the difficulty of finding a job, the high cost of eating and

still higher cost of drinking, and possibly, if the subject was congenial to his interlocutor, his sex experiences. Of public events
his impressions would almost certainly be vague. The sinking of
the German fleet at Scapa Flow, the Peace Treaty, the failure to
"Hang the Kaiser" and to punish the war criminals, the Victory
Day pageant, the strikes and the general discontent might have
left some memories behind them, but it is unlikely that he would
make any references to India or be able to give any details about
the troubles in the sister island. India was a far-away place of
which the ordinary non-political Englishman knew little or
nothing, and cared even less, while Ireland was a " question "
which it was not his business to solve. It is tragically true that
at no time was it more important for public opinion to be on the
alert than in 1919 and the succeeding years, yet at no time has it
ever been more apathetic and indifferent. The reason for this is
obvious. Not only were many of the most active spirits, who
would normally have led and directed political criticism, dead
and buried, but millions of those who survived were mentally,
spiritually and nervously exhausted. The British race was, in
fact, tired out after four years of suffering, bloodshed and prolonged effort. Many ex-soldiers were still feeling the effects of
military discipline and inclined to leave everything to
the high-ups. In the public schools, blind obedience to authority
had been inculcated for generations, and no amount of disillusion, cynicism or despair gave ex-officers of the public
school type the moral or mental energy to rebel against it. The
Welsh wizard was at the head of the Coalition, but the Conservatives, "the gentlemen's party", had a substantial majority
in the House of Commons. They would rather beg in the street
from other, more fortunate, " decent fellows", than have any
truck with "Bolshies", pacifists and, generally speaking, the
lower orders. So it came about that the very small group of hard-
faced men, and the professional politicians who carried out their
wishes, had things all their own way. The political Opposition—
Socialists, trade unionists, and independent Liberals—grumbled,
protested, agitated. No doubt they represented a numerical
majority of the population but, badly led, split into factions and
without the support of the press they were, at the essential period,
impotent to affect policy.* All they could do was to " let off
steam ".

* This generalisation should be qualified by a reference to the "Jolly George"
incident. The dockers who refused to load this ship with munitions intended for
use in Poland against the U.S.S.R. undoubtedly " affected policy."

The horrors of the struggle in Ireland, the Amritsar massacre and Dyer's crawling order, affected the writer with all the more dismay and shame because he was convinced that the tragedies then being enacted were not willed or desired by the English people, most of whom were entirely ignorant of what was happening. Typical of the *informed* and uncorrupted Englishman was the indignation expressed by Henry W. Nevinson. In his book " Last Changes, Last Chances," he records how on his return to London from Ireland in Mid-October 1920, " a small party of us paraded Parliament Square with placards and posters bearing appropriate inscriptions such as ' We English Protest,' ' Stop Reprisals,' and ' Terrorism is not Government.' " I was a member of the " small party ", on this memorable occasion, and walked immediately behind " Old Nev ". The poster which he carried was one which bore the words " We English Protest". Never shall I forget his scarlet cheeks, his white imperial, his large serviceable brown shoes of the kind known as " beetle-crushers", his solemn, honest, distressed and kindly face.   Nevinson was one of the last " English gentlemen ", using that term in the ethical sense understood and respected by the Victorians.   He was the uncompromising foe of those "British interests", defence of which is the only form of " patriotism " understood by Conservative politicians, the City and the Foreign Office, and the courageous champion of the true interests of the British people.   The great abstractions—justice, freedom, decency, public honour, gener-osity, tolerance—belief in which has been for so long the life-blood of the English tradition, were bedrock realities to Henry Nevinson.   He took a grim view of the exploitation of the loyalty and heroism of the masses—their willingness to die for " King and Country "—by men who played the war game, with the impassivity of chess-players, to amass private fortunes, enlarge their spheres of influence, and, by creating reservoirs of cheap labour, to pile up dividends for privileged shareholders.   " Old Nev", last of the old guard of English humanists, spent his life "protesting".   Few of the younger generation of public school and university trained " gentlemen " took much notice of him in the 'twenties.   Hidebound by a form of class education which had lost its original inspiration and developed no new ideals, they saw nothing in " the old school tie " except a means for their own advancement at the expense of less favoured competitors. Nevinson may have to wait long for his statue.   Eventually, perhaps, some street, at present called after a speculating jerry-builder, will be re-named " Nevinson Street ", and men will think it an honour to live in it.

Throughout the Irish troubles and Indian disturbances, it was clear to the most casual observer that the Lloyd George Coalition Government did not have the English people behind it. The English, at least outside a small but dominant section of the propertied class, are naturally kindly, dislike injustice and brutality and believe in the precept " live and let live ". For the people of the sister island they had, and have, a warm sympathy and liking.   This is shown by the fact that since the middle of the nineteenth century sentimental Irish ballads—even songs which, like " The wearing of the green," have a strong anti-British political bias—have enjoyed widespread popularity among the common people.   Today, in the sixth year of a war largely against political Catholicism, in which Southern Ireland, owing to its memories of "the troubles", has maintained a non-belligerent neutrality, " Where Irish eyes are Smiling " and " Rose of Tralee " are rapturously encored in Hampshire public houses. English people living at what are politely called " the lower income levels " have, in fact, never willingly " oppressed " the Irish nor, except perhaps in the Cromwellian era, have they been party to any of the crimes which stain the pages of Anglo-Irish history.   To an Irish friend, who was inveighing against " you bloodthirsty Englishmen "—he mentioned the names of Generals Maxwell and Tudor, Mr. Lloyd George and Sir John Anderson— I took occasion to point out that not one of these gentlemen was any more " English " than he was himself.   I reminded him also of " Old Nev's " poster, "We English Protest".

If a handful of politicians mismanaged Anglo-Irish relations between 1914 and the establishment of the Irish Free State, now Eire, it is equally true that only an infinitesmal minority has had any say in the government of India during the past two centuries. If all the bankers, industrialists and shareholders, all the bureau-crats and army officers, all the professional politicians, and all the protesting Left Wing intellectuals who have played any active part in Anglo-Indian, Anglo-Burmese, or Anglo-Malayan affairs could be rounded up and put under house arrest, ample ac-commodation could be found for the whole of them in South Kensington alone.   If we compute that they amount to one half of one per cent. of the population of this island, the estimate would probably err on the side of liberality.

From the Coupon Election of December, 1918, to the present

year of grace, the writer has tried in vain to discover one action on the part of the Conservative oligarchy that has not been prompted by a determination to suppress democratic progress in the interests of property and profits. If this charge seems too sweeping, let the reader investigate the columns of Hansard for himself and see if he can contradict me. This indictment obviously does not include the record of individual Tories, like Viscount Cecil and Winston Churchill. Lord Cecil's devastating revelations in his autobiography "A Great Experiment" and Mr. Churchill's pre-war speeches, shed a clear light on the nature of the Party machine which reduced them both to impotence. The former was soon forced into resignation and had to watch the destruction of his life work, and the deliberate sabotaging of the only international organization by which collective security could have been enforced and maintained. The latter was kept out of office during the nine years in which he could either have made the outbreak of war impossible, or the rapid defeat of our enemies a foregone conclusion.

V

One of the results of the Coupon Election was to leave the political police and the Secret Service in the undisturbed control of the Caucus. This network of spies formed a discreet private army, too strong to be cleaned up by Ramsay MacDonald during his brief terms of office, even if he had the desire to do so, which had as its main objective the task of keeping tabs on "revolutionaries", and, in particular, preventing them from infiltrating into the public services. "Revolutionaries", from the Home Office and Foreign Office standpoint, were any individuals or groups of individuals who indulged in political controversy which might result in a Conservative defeat at the polls. Ranging from mild Liberals, and gas and water Socialists, to Communists and unemployed recalcitrants, everyone was a "Red", and therefore liable to be included in a list of dangerous persons, who expressed any views in conflict with those of the Carlton Club. If, after the termination of the present war, the heads of the Home Office and the Foreign Office are required to give evidence on oath and produce their files and dossiers, it is safe to say that the public will be staggered by the facts a cross-examination will reveal. To take an example, I have it from a reliable source, and believe it to be true, that the police dossier concerning that highly respected "revolutionary" Sir Stafford Cripps was not destroyed until he became a member of the War Cabinet ! As many are now aware, the victimization of anti-Fascists in the British army by " Security " and Military Intelligence has been carried to extraordinary lengths since 1939 and still continues.

Early in 1919, I got some inkling of how the Conservative gestapo works when I attended a luncheon given by a wealthy supporter of the Labour Party in a large restaurant in the Strand. Most of the guests were pacifists of one sort or another, concerned with the idea that the first requirements of the Peace Treaty was not "to end peace " but to make future wars impossible. Among those present, if I can trust my memory, were Bernard Shaw, George Lansbury, Joseph King, Arthur Ponsonby and Robert Dell. Aldous Huxley, whom I then met for the first time, was certainly there. The conversation, or what I heard of it, could not have been more innocuous or less " revolutionary", at least as regards "saying it with bombs". In spite of this, the waiters nearly spilt the soup down our necks in their anxiety to hurry back to make notes, for Sir Basil Thomson's benefit, of our harmless chit-chat. Joseph King told me later that while visiting a friend of his, High Sheriff of one of the home counties, he was astonished to be shown a typed account of the proceedings at this innocent private gathering. Today, thanks to the educative influence of the Vatican, General Franco and Sir Oswald Mosley, the eyes of the public have been opened. If there are any people among us in traitorous contact with enemy agents we all know where to look for them. It will not be among the Reds !

VI

The reader will hardly need to have his attention called to the fact that such "unity", as exists in England—whether "national", party political or religious—is of a temporary and artificial character, imposed by outside circumstances. When the Soviet army has completed its defeat of the Nazi *wehrmacht*, with the aid of the Anglo-American forces, and the official war on which we are now engaged has been ended by " unconditional surrender", many already prophesy that the real war, the war between reaction and progress—between socialism and fascism—will soon break out with renewed severity.

In 1919 the fact that there are " two Englands " was already apparent to outside observers, even if it was imperfectly realized by a middle class which lacked political intelligence and failed (as it still fails) to be conscious of the fact that it holds in its hands the balance of political power. At moments, during the 'twenties, the " real " England—on which, owing to its traditions, the hopes of all progressive Europeans are still partly based—managed to break through the crust of Tory domination and give proof of its existence. Even in the dark days of 1919, one of the leaders of the Russian Revolution issued a proclamation in Lenin-grad which it is heartening to recall. "On all fronts", the pro-clamation read, " you meet the hostile plots of the English. The counter-revolutionary troops shoot you with English guns. In (White) depots, you find supplies of English manufacture. The prisoners you have captured are dressed in uniforms made in England. The women and children of Archangel and Astrakhan are maimed and killed by English airmen with the aid of English explosives. English ships bomb our shores . . . but even to-day, when we are engaged in a bitter fight against Yudenitch, the hireling of England, I demand that you never forget there are two Englands. Besides the England of profits, violence, bribery and blood-thirstiness, there is the England of labour, of spiritual power, of high ideals, of international solidarity. It is the base and dishonest England of the Stock Exchange manipulators that is fighting us. The England of labour and the people is with us."

To-day, we have the confusing spectacle of the England of labour and the people, toiling, sweating and shedding its blood in the same cause as that for which our Soviet allies—to whose heroic exertions we owe in such large measure our continued existence as a free nation—are victoriously fighting, while the conduct of the war remains under the control of the England of profits and Stock Exchange manipulators, which was directly responsible for its outbreak. The root cause of this unnatural situation can be traced back directly to the Coupon Election of December 14th, 1918. In the struggles, set-backs, betrayals and temporary defeats of the nineteen-twenties we can at the same time find reason for hoping that the " England of labour, of spiritual power, of high ideals, of international solidarity " will ultimately emerge triumphant.

CHAPTER TWO

THE DEATH OF SOCIETY

I

THAT the Four Years War effected very great changes in the manners and morals of the (perhaps) three per cent. of the population of Great Britain who enjoyed an income of £400 a year and upwards, is admitted by everyone old enough to remember the England of 1914. The complications of the caste system which prevailed in England up to that date were also considerably modified. The idea that the social structure underwent the fundamental alterations which seemed apparent to contemporary observers like C. F. G. Masterman (who will be quoted later) has, however, proved an illusion. Class divisions survived all the shocks to which they were subjected and the class structure of English social life has remained to this day almost unimpaired. The "death of Society", which so many deplore, has been a spiritual decay rather than a loss of material wealth or political power.

Up till the Coupon Election, which inaugurated the "class war" now rapidly approaching its culmination, the common people believed that the aristocracy, although parasitical and reactionary, was, in times of national emergency, conventionally patriotic. It fought for "King and Country", it provided officers for the Army on whose self-sacrificing heroism the masses of the people had safely relied. On the whole, in spite of its addiction to pleasure and its indulgence in amiable vices—qualities which aroused more envy than malice, more admiration than censure—it acknowleged obligations of public service and accepted its responsibilities towards the lower orders, whose interests, especially in the domain of foreign affairs, it undertook to defend. With the appearance in Russia of what we should now term an "ideological" menace to the whole financial foundation of the Established Order, the British governing class dropped its traditional role of patriotic leadership and became increasingly international in outlook. Property owners, frightened and on the defensive, looked abroad for allies against the rising tide of "Bolshevism", strengthened their connections with the American and Continental manipulators of international finance, dispensed with Victorian ideas of public service and morality, and closed their ranks for the protection of privilege and profits against the claims of insurgent democracy. Families which had grown rich in the eighteenth century by stealing the common lands from the humble and industrious population of rural England—and had educated their sons, for several generations, in " public " schools, stolen from the village scholar for whose benefit they had been established and endowed—found it advisable to overcome their snobbish prejudices and join forces with the new families which had acquired wealth by profiteering. This process, in greater or less degree, had been going on for a century or more. The only change in the 'twenties was that the pace was accelerated.

Before discussing Masterman's observations on the plight of the British " pluto-aristocracy " in 1922, it may be worth while to consider how the different social strata into which the swarming population of London is divided, appeared to an intelligent Scot, some twenty years after the battle of Waterloo. In his book " The Great Metropolis " (1938), James Grant takes a poor view of the upper ten thousand.

" Who ever finds them the planners of any scheme for ameliorating the condition of humanity ? " he asks. " A meeting is called to assist in procuring the emancipation of West India slaves ; Exeter Hall is full : there are 5,000 people present. Among this number how many of the nobility are there ? Lord Suffield perhaps is in the chair. You look around to see if you can perceive any other members of the aristocracy : you look in vain. . . . It is the same in the case of all other enterprises of humanity and benevolence ; you will never find them originate with the aristocracy ; you will never find them supported to any extent by the nobles of the land . . . they live in a circle of their own ; all beyond that circle are persons unworthy of their notice." Even in 1838, however, the rich could not entirely dispense with the company of artists and writers who, then as now, had the knack of conferring fame, or at least publicity, on their wealthy patrons. " A literary man," says Grant, with some bitterness, " who has raised himself to distinction, is asked to the table of " the great " on precisely the same ground as Madame Malibran, or any other celebrated singer, is invited. It is not from respect to the individual himself, or from admiration of his commanding talents ; it is because of the amusement his wit or conversational powers afford. . . . Let such a person's popularity only decline —which is a very common case in the literary world—and see

B

how the aristocracy will treat him.   Not only will their doors be shut against him, but they will pass him by in the streets without even deigning to give him the recognition of a nod.   If he is reduced to poverty, as literary geniuses often are, they would not bestow on him even a shilling to keep him from starvation or the workhouse. . . ."   In this department at least, some changes in aristocratic behaviour were noticeable in the 'twenties, when it became the fashion for titled or " old Etonian " journalists to push into an already overcrowded profession and rob the needy even of their Grub Street jobs.

Grant defines the middle classes in the London of his day, as " those families whose annual expenditure exceeds £250 or £300 a year and who have no accident of birth or station in society which would justify us in ranking them among the higher classes."   For these families, the more commercially successful of which have since risen in the social scale through the agency of the Victorian   public schools, Grant had a high regard.   " The middle-classes," he says, " taken as a body, are excellent members of society.   They may indeed be said to be the benefactors of their species.   The great majority of the many humane and benevolent enterprises which are at once the glory and happiness of our country, have their origin among and are supported by, those who move in the middle sphere of life."   He adds that they are " more virtuous, both in regard to their public and private conduct, than the aristocracy", refers to their outstanding intellectual and scientific achievements and blames them only for apeing " their betters."   In regard to the common Cockney, however, Grant's Scotch prejudices tend to obscure his judgment. He blames their addiction to gin, which he calls " blue ruin", is obviously baffled and disconcerted by their ability to maintain their cheerfulness " amidst so many and such great privations", and observes, almost with indignation, that " nothing short of absolute starvation can depress the spirits of the lower classes in the Metropolis, or render them discontented with their station in life".   Coming from a land of secret whisky drinking and puritanical prurience, he is appalled by the fact that " sexual intercourse obtains among these to a most frightful extent.   You will not, perhaps, meet with one young man in a hundred, who has passed his twentieth year, who can plead innocence in this respect."

While the main outlines of class characteristics and distinctions, noted by Grant in 1838, were still traceable in 1914, a new type, invented by Dr. Arnold of Rugby and his numerous imitators, had risen in public esteem and left its impress on English social life. This was the " Christian gentleman", recruited in almost equal numbers from the families of " barbarian " squires and newly-rich " philistine " manufacturers and professional men. Described in the simplest terms, the Victorian " gentleman", whose function it was to set a high standard of morality, patriotism, personal honour, modesty, integrity and disinterested public service, was the exact opposite of everything we know about General Franco and his British admirers. Although the schools which turned out the finished product, by their Conservative political colouring and inculcation of a blind obedience to " those above", have since, in some cases, degenerated into breeding grounds of Fascist *herrenvolk*, prior to 1914 they gave England a privileged class of which it had every reason to be proud. The Four Years War destroyed it as a coherent social and political influence : its virtues and traditions were maintained—as the glorious year 1940 indicated to our enemies and allies—by the broad masses of the people of Britain.

The genius of a race comes to full fruition and finds expression, now in one class, now in another. In the course of our long history, barons, Tudor adventurers and parvenus, the eighteenth-century landed aristocracy and the Victorian gentry have all had their periods of greatness. Today, in England as in Russia, the common people have come, or are coming, into their own, and it is through them that our native genius will be released for the benefit of mankind.

II

In 1922 when C. F. G. Masterman published his study of " England After the War", it was natural that he should exaggerate the damage inflicted on the middle and upper classes of English society and underestimate their capacity to re-form their ranks and hold their own. The best of the younger generation of the privileged had been killed, maimed or ruined. Tens of thousands of families, formerly in comfortable circumstances, had been bereaved of their sons and heirs, while high taxation and financial loss forced a large number of owners of stately homes to sell their estates, their pictures and their furniture to Canadian, American or native profiteers. All this was " news", which must poignantly have affected Masterman, since it was on people like himself, and on the social circles in which his life had

been spent, that the burden of suffering and loss fell most severely.
Wise after the event, we can now see that this burden, as in the
present war, was very unevenly shared.   The bulk of the propertied and professional classes, although suffering some dis-
comfort and temporary loss of income, soon recovered from their
country's ordeal.   They " gave " their sons of military age,
framed their photographs and heaved an occasional sigh, but
had plenty of growing boys and girls to fall back on.

In the early 'twenties, the proportion of the population which
had borne the whole burden of the struggle, which had poured
out its blood with no thought of profit or reward, was exhausted,
bled white, indifferent to everything except football matches,
clean sheets, and the primary reliefs and satisfactions.   Those who
had done well out of the war, through large profits, high wages or
cushy jobs far from the danger zone, held not only all the strings
of power but also had all the untapped strength and energy to
pull them.   In wars, the scum of a population rises to the surface,
and it usually remains on top after they are over.   This was the
case in England after the Coupon Election.   But, with the worst
will in the world, the politicians could not force their surviving
cannon fodder into fresh adventures.   " To-day," says Masterman, " any attempt to rekindle the conflict, under any conditions, for any cause, would be strangled at birth.   Any statesman
or government which essayed a second war of conscripted soldiers
would perish in the revolution which he would have created.
The people would not only not fight against Bolhevik Russia,
or for the imposition of territorial rearrangements in Europe, or
against alleged insult or attack upon British interests or British
honour. . . . You could not raise a conscript army to retain
India, or Egypt if they " rebelled."   You could not raise an
army, except by bribery at enormous expense, to prevent Ireland
becoming a Republic."   The prevailing disillusion weighed
down even some of the most high-minded and intelligent of the
" intellectuals " who had survived the slaughter.   Masterman
quotes an unnamed " prose writer " who expressed his hopeless-
ness in terms which many to-day might feel tempted to endorse.
" I would gladly share in the optimism of other soldiers of the war,
for the man is to be envied who can still put his faith in the
" masses of Englishmen," or find satisfaction in working for a
League of Nations or League of Youth.   The War has demon-
strated in a manner most painful that human nature does not
change ; that fear and greed, its governing principles, are in-

eradicable, and are fundamental conditions of existence. . . .
The prospect of a League of Nations would be amusing if it were
not a travesty of a cherished ideal ; the wild beasts will be
forming a League next and requesting the lion and tiger to be
joint presidents. . . . I think that the hopes of all ex-soldiers,
who hope at all, are centred in the Labour Party and we watch
with anxiety the coming struggle between Labour and ' the
tragic comedians ' who now misgovern the British Isles. But
the fate of those who have endeavoured to realize any great ideal,
and they have usually been men to whom the idea of violence
was abhorrent, fills us with despair. There is now a minority of
intellectual people . . . some of whom suffered persecution and
imprisonment during the war ; there has always been such a
minority fighting for truth ; there always will be, and they will
pay for their efforts, and expiate the fact of their existence as
Christ Himself and thousands of others have done. . . . Theirs is
a thankless and a hopeless task. It will bring them happiness
while they retain the illusion of its utility ; but those of them
who lose their illusion would have been more fortunate had they
never been born."

In view of the resumption of political power by members of the
" old " aristocracy, which took place during the years in which
the ex-cavalry officer, Viscount Margesson, was patronage
secretary and Chief Whip, it is curious to note that in 1922
Masterman believed that the aristocracy had " vanished". Even
the hated " cavalry generals "—whose blunders the official
historians could not wholly conceal—were not, as a caste, either
much diminished in numbers or deprived of their control of the
military machine. In 1944, the Government engaged in fighting
Fascism is headed by a Duke's grandson, and includes men like
Lord Halifax, the Dukes of Norfolk and Devonshire, Colonel
Stanley and Sir Samuel Hoare, the House of Commons is packed
with bearers of what are called " historic names", and all the
highest commands in the Army are, as usual, in the hands of
Irish generals. When, in February 1944, the electors of West
Derbyshire revolted against having a Feudal representative forced
upon them by the Tory machine, and returned a local cobbler's
son to Parliament, the fact was so remarkable as to cause consternation in the Conservative Central Office. In Masterman's
view, however, " the Feudal system " by 1922 had " vanished
in blood and fire, and the landed classes were consumed". He
considered this a " mournful ending to a great tradition". It is

evident, to-day, that the landowners, as a class, suffered far less than he supposed. " In the useless slaughter of the Guards on the Somme, or of the Rifle Brigade in Hooge Wood," he wrote, " half the great families of England, heirs of large estates and wealth, perished without a cry . . . often through the bungling of Generals." If the fine flower of a generation of young patricians was mown down and destroyed, as was undoubtedly the case, the families which had produced them were soon able to repair their losses. Their powers of assimilation, through marriageable daughters, enabled them to re-gild their coronets with newly-created wealth, while the influence of social prestige on snobbery enabled them to get a firm footing in big business and thus to consolidate and increase the political authority which their long experience in the art of governing had given them. It was obvious to the astute controlling brains of our hereditary aristocracy that if the pre-1914 social structure was to be maintained the value of the existing bloodstock, however decadent, polluted or venereal it might have become, must not be allowed to depreciate in the matrimonial market. The accumulated assets of the " best people " consisted in many things besides family portraits, old masters, romantically historic names and the glamour attaching to such heirlooms in the eyes of the new millionaires. The possession of wealth for many generations had given the ruling families an enviable ease of manner combined with an unself-conscious arrogance which education in the charm schools of Eton and Harrow, followed by Oxford or Cambridge, had made acceptable to the lower orders. As actors and actresses on the stage of high life they had an hereditary skill, experience and poise, which made newcomers, particularly those cashing and crashing in from Canada and the United States, feel painfully inferior. In addition, they had a thorough knowledge of all the pleasures which life can afford to those to whom money is no object. Money, as they proceeded to demonstrate—on terms— is no use unless you know how to spend it. They were " sports-men", skilled in hunting, shooting, fishing and racing and no less proficient in middle-class recreations like cricket, golf and tennis. Some even patronized the arts and, for publicity purposes, made useful connections with literature, the stage, the ballet, music, painting and sculpture. Their international social affiliations, through their long control of diplomacy, were well-established, far-reaching and financially important. Many had a fair command of foreign languages, possessed friends and relatives of their own class in Rome, Vienna, Paris, Madrid and even Berlin, and could order dinner impressively in any capital city in the world. Before the end of the 'twenties, so completely welded were the old families and the newly rich that a superficial observer might have believed that nothing had changed. The " pluto " aristocracy of England had lost nothing except its *raison d'être*.

III

If Masterman's lamentations over the collapse of the Feudal aristocracy have proved to be premature and exaggerated, so also have his observations about the sorry plight of the bourgeoisie, particularly the public-school-and-university-trained professional class to which he belonged. Of these, the best of a whole generation had undoubtedly been killed, physically or morally maimed, disillusioned, or financially ruined. Rupert Brooke had uttered the swan song of a doomed band of public schoolboy patriots who were to be wiped out, after his death, at Passchendaele, on the Somme, in Gallipoli. Their code had prevented them from joining in the scramble for paper money and reserved occupations, like the commercial middle-class and the bureaucracy. They had, instead, flocked to the recruiting stations and scrambled for death with glory. It seemed that their code and their traditions had died with them, and that the post-war world had no place for the embittered, impoverished and often unemployable survivors. Writing of the middle-class " gentry " Masterman observes that " it is this class, not the big capitalists, who really paid for the war. It includes the writers of books and the journalists, most hardly hit of all. . . . Everywhere in Europe it is perishing—in Vienna, Berlin, Moscow, even among the victors in Paris and Rome. It is the class which maintains any intellectual life, although intellectual activities do not absorb the energies of most of it. It is the class in which the old Puritan religion still dominates. . . . It is this middle-class—John Bull less stout and complacent—which everywhere, from the clergyman or civil servant or medical man at the top to the small shopkeeper or the clerk in his particular city at the other end of the scale, is being harrassed out of existence by the financial after-consequences of the war". In particular he bewails the fate of the *intelligentsia*. " The class which makes ideas and diffuses knowledge is the class which is perishing of hunger and cold. . . . But the lawyers and nobles (who govern England) with their later additions of as yet unennobled profiteers, have never seen so much value in the assistance of an intelligentsia, or any reason to waste money on its support. So the *intelligentsia* which is interested in public life now goes largely to Labour and identifies itself passionately with Labour ideas : to be received, however, with far more distrust and much less welcome than if it had retained its position ' in its own class,' or found some other outlet for its energy."

Masterman failed to foresee the recuperative power, energy and adaptability not only of the *intelligentsia* but of the main body of the professional middle-class, though as an enlightened Liberal politician he rightly deplored the subservience of the latter to their social superiors and their fear and hatred of the masses. " It (the bourgeoisie) will never break its allegiance to the powers above in order to unite with the powers below. Even in perishing, it will still wave the old banner of anti-Labour, and still be wishful to provide volunteers to ' blackleg ' every tram or railway or coal or municipal strike". This prophecy proved accurate in the General Strike of 1926, when the " old school tie " bourgeoisie rallied to the Government standard and kept the essential services running by supplying " blackleg " labour. They had, even in their direst period of want, little animus against the profiteer. " From the lairs in which these men are hiding, too proud to show their poverty, they contemplate the non-fighting profiteer, offering such a display of reckless and luxurious expenditure as the world has rarely seen. Yet they take it all ' lying down.' For the profiteer has only to mention ' Bolshevik ' and the middle-class scurries off to its dilapidated home." Crushed by landlords with their " repairing leases", forced to pay more for basement flats than their parents had paid for large houses with gardens and tennis-courts, inarticulate, without any power of combination or political intelligence or courage, the middle-classes yet continued to vote Tory.

Had I been writing about the class into which I was born, in 1922, instead of 1944, I should no doubt, have echoed Masterman's gloom. Of my school friends seven out of ten were killed, maimed or thrown on the scrapheap. The one I cared for most, after being wounded and decorated, gassed himself in despair. My own circumstances were at least as precarious as Masterman describes. But looking back over twenty years, with the knowledge gained from some experience of English provincial towns and villages, it is apparent that this lamentation was premature. The struggle of the Conservative middle-class, " the gentry", for " the bare maintenance of any semblance of its accepted standard of life", was not, as he supposed, a " losing one", but, by the end of the decade, completely successful. If their ranks had been diminished by the death of the noblest of their youth and the impoverishment, below the genteel standard, of many families of modest patrician ancestry, they were soon more than replenished by a horde of newcomers whose sons had been turned into gentlemen in accordance with the Victorian formula, by the public schools. Of these Masterman observed : " It is to be feared that the public school which had been the special preserve of feudalism has learnt little and forgotten little from all the experiences of war ; and that in these great institutions, the new profiteers who desire their children to be made gentlemen, are destined to squeeze out the descendants of a forlorn and bankrupt feudal system." This is no more than romantic nonsense for, apart from Eton and two or three other ancient foundations patronized by the landed aristocracy, the public schools in the Victorian era were the special preserve, not of feudalism but of the middle-classes newly-enriched by the Industrial Revolution. They now became the special preserve of the profiteers newly-enriched by the Four Years' War. Meanwhile, it was untrue to suppose that as types, the lawyer, the doctor, the clergyman, the bureaucrat, the professional soldier, sailor, manager, technician, or rentier were " harassed out of existence". Some were, but most suffered neither loss of income, nor of social prestige. The English system of class education made the position of the gentry unassailable, by reserving for them all the most lucrative positions in the professions and the public services. And since this education had an almost exlusively Conservative political bias, it made them into a disastrously effective " bulwark against Bolshevism", that is to say against any kind of democratic progress. Conditioned as they were by their public school training, to blind subservience to the authorities who controlled jobs, preferment and commercial " openings", they became, as " Non-Intervention " proved, allergic even to elementary patriotism, and accepted, without criticism or comment, anything with which the Tory leaders and the Press thought fit to dope them. Paradoxical though it may seem, the Conservative middle-class, although the most politically ignorant and prejudiced, was and remains the great opinion-forming section of the community. Ideas were funnelled through to the " gentry " from the " high-ups", with the greatest of ease and were adopted by them and passed on to their inferiors as gospel revelations. Not even Labour leaders are more readily influenced by toffs or have a more engrained respect for the titled than the middle-class Conservative. When Colonel Semaphore spends a night in his London club he is charmed to discover, after a chat with his friend Lord Sharepusher, what all the members of " our class " are thinking. On his return to his town or village, he expounds these views to the vicar, the lawyer, the doctor and any other gentry or near-gentry with whom he may come in contact. These, in turn, delighted to be able to parade their intimacy with the Colonel, pass on the Tory gospel to the butcher, the baker, the farmer, and the clerk. Thus large sections of the population, without going through any process of personal ratiocination, were " softened up " to receive their matutinal directives from the " national " newspapers and the B.B.C.

The alarming growth of unemployment, after the first pre-liminary post-war boom, played into the hands of the Con-servative industrialists by " conditioning " millions of black-coated workers to whom the loss of their jobs meant a sentence if not to death, at least to semi-starvation on the dole. Men drawing comfortable salaries were soon tempted to acquire not only their jerry-built villas, but cheap cars, wireless sets, furniture and other amenities, on the " never-never " system. With each new obligation they became more and more the slaves of their employers. " Very well, Mr. Smith, I'm sorry. But if you are not satisfied, *you know your remedy*." This familiar phrase, trans-lated into plain English, meant " another word from you and you'll find yourself on your backside in the street". Mr. Smith may have been a hero at Mons, but he became a terrified rabbit when he thought of his " little palace " at Colindale, his Kozy Kot at Wembley, or the overdue instalment on his Austin Seven. Who, indeed, shall blame him ? Politically, this proud citizen of a land which he had " made safe for democracy " by his own exertions, became the subservient echo of his boss.

Had the " boss class " who, with all their faults, were as English as anyone else, thought it worth while to go in openly for new-fangled stunts like Fascism, their black-coated employees would have lined up obediently in their thousands to buy their coloured shirts. As it was, " democracy", when controlled by the Conservative Caucus, under the direction of high finance, served them perfectly. Their party owned practically the entire press and, except for two brief interludes, the conditioned employee and his rural equivalent—the farm labourer, liable to be turned out of his picturesque hovel if he voted against its owner—supplied them with substantial majorities in the House of Commons.

During the 'twenties a horrifying sub-human suburban type came into existence which was genially depicted as the " little man", by the cartoonist Strube. This odious homunculus and his revolting wife—ignorant, stupid, a moral craven but easily capable of being infected with mob-hysteria—exemplified one of the worst of the economic consequences of the so-called " Peace."

IV

The 'twenties witnessed the beginning of that collapse of the moral sense, capacity for leadership and instinctive patriotism in the higher social classes, which was finally revealed by the outbreak of the Franco rebellion. That was the supreme test of England's " gentleman tradition". How the real " gentlemen " of England—men of the same type as those who carried on during the Blitz, fought the Battle of Britain and were not defeated after Dunkirk—rose to the occasion forms part of the immortal story of the International Brigade. How the Conservative ruling class, who arrogated to themselves the title of gentlemen, failed their country when the test came, is revealed in the squalid history of Non-Intervention.

People who still believe that there were any British naval or military officers, any Foreign Office " experts", Secret Service men, diplomats or consuls, any Conservative politicians or financiers who did not realize the threat to the security of our Empire and its communications implicit in an Axis victory in Spain are capable of believing anything. Any intelligent fourth-form boy armed with a map could follow the strategical ideas behind the dictators' actions. As for the Foreign Office, to keep Spain " within the British zone of interest " had been one of the cardinal points of British policy for upwards of two centuries, until Neville Chamberlain, Anthony Eden and Lord Halifax reversed it. Faced with the choice of two conflicting alternatives—loyalty to their country or loyalty to what they supposed to be their financial and class interests—the Conservative gentry, as Hitler and Mussolini anticipated, unhesitatingly chose the latter. Our sons in the fighting services have been paying for over four years the penalty for this betrayal.

What the Tory financiers did for Hitler was frankly acknowledged by him after the outbreak of the present war. " The victory of the Reds", announced the Nazi-controlled radio in Prague (March 1941), " would have placed Spain within the British zone of influence. The triumph of the Nationalists freed Spain of the tutelage of the English and Italy from the danger of encirclement". The Rome radio was even more candid. After giving a full list of the supplies sent to Spain and stating the number of Italian troops co-operating with Franco's forces— facts of which, at the time, Mr. R. A. Butler, on behalf of Lord Halifax, strenuously protested his ignorance, in the House of Commons—the speaker went on to say that had the Spanish and Abyssinian wars not taken place, " Britain would have succeeded in keeping the world on her side against Germany and Italy. In fact, those two wars, conducted by Italy, were an important preliminary to the present war. . . . The one liberated the Spanish peninsula from democratic influence, the other resulted in the destruction of the League of Nations, which was *only a means for the realization of democratic ambitions.*"

That Fascism was a logical development of the violently anti-democratic bias of the Conservative financial oligarchy was made clear by the late Lord Rothermere when, through the columns of the *Evening News* and the *Daily Mail*, he was endeavouring to secure support for Sir Oswald Mosley. Sir Thomas Moore, now Conservative M.P. for Ayr Burghs and formerly a member of the Council of the Anglo-German Fellowship, stressed this point in an article published in the *Daily Mail* on 25th April, 1934. "Surely," he wrote, " there cannot be any fundamental difference of outlook between the Blackshirts and their parents the Conservatives ? For let us make no mistake about that parentage. . . . It (the B.U.F.) is largely derived from the Conservative Party."*

V

Looking back on the seething and exciting 'twenties in the fifth year of a war resulting from the inability of the progressive elements in the nation to close their ranks and produce the leadership which might have crushed Fascism at birth, we may well regret the mistakes that were made and the opportunities that

* Quoted in " The Trial of Mussolini," by " Cassius."

were missed. If history is on our side, as we are bound to believe, the forward march may nevertheless seem exasperatingly slow. What the 'twenties achieved was to clear the ground and to plant the seeds of new ideas. Up till 1914 the class system, based on the possession of property, was generally approved by the nation, because it was bound up with an acceptance of responsibility on the part of the privileged and an acknowledgment by them of their obligations. Middle-aged people, brought up in middle-class surroundings, remember the days when wealth was considered meritorious and poverty conveyed a moral stigma. The " poor " were divided into the " deserving poor " and the undeserving, discontented and " workshy " poor. All the rich, on the other hand, were " nice " people, more or less, and if they had had money for two or three generations, they were very nice indeed. The 1920's changed all that. So many " captains of industry", so many pillars of the social system had either increased their wealth or amassed new fortunes out of the blood of the young that money stank in the nostrils of decent citizens. It stank the more because of the callous indifference of the profiteers to the fate of the starving ex-servicemen whose valour had enabled them to make it.

Throughout the Armistice years, when such was the abundance of food that whole cargoes of oranges were thrown into the sea to prevent a glut, tons of fresh herrings were used as manure instead of being distributed and acres of vegetables were ploughed back into the soil, the newspapers were full of stories of human suffering, revealed in the police courts. In cases which concerned rack-renting landlords—I remember one in which a man with a wife and five children was charged 16s. a week for a damp basement room, so infested by rats that he had to stay awake to keep them from gnawing his children's faces—the name of the victim was always given in full, but the name of the guilty landlord invariably suppressed. The prevalent starvation neither aroused the shame of the politicians responsible for it, nor touched the consciences of their Conservative supporters. After 1940, the comfortably-off, who were forced to accept evacuees from the slums, recoiled in horror when they were confronted with the results of their own selfishness. They could not make the excuse that they were ignorant of what sort of homes their Party considered " fit for heroes", or that they had not realized that the " hunger strikers", whose pitiful appeals they disregarded, were, in fact, hungry. The feeble pretence that these men were " Reds", exploited by Bolshevik " agitators", could not be maintained in view of the harrowing stories which the newspapers found it impossible to suppress. The following paragraph, a cutting from the *Daily Herald*, may be taken as characteristic of the Armistice years, when the men who have since sabotaged every plan for post-war reconstruction, created famine in the midst of abundance in order to maintain an artificial price level. It is headed : " Starving Man Collapses in Court."

" A man who appeared at Chesham, Bucks, police court yesterday, on a rate summons, collapsed twice through lack of food.

" It was revealed that his wife was ill, that his four children were starving and that he had lost everything he possessed— except a mattress.

" The rate was remitted.

" The case had been adjourned so that the police could verify a statement made by the man a fortnight ago, in which he said : ' My wife and children are starving. We have not got a bit of food or coal in the house. She and the children are at home starving now.'

" Superintendent Neal said yesterday :

" ' The man's story is perfectly true. He is penniless. All he has is a mattress.'

" ' It is only the fact that my wife is too ill to be moved that has kept a roof over our heads,' —— told the *Daily Herald* last night.

" ' My one hope is that I shall be able to get a job, for which I have an interview to-morrow.'

" He looked tired and ill. Playing round his feet were his three younger children. His elder daughter, aged 14, contributes the family's only income, 10s. a week out of her 12s. 6d. wages as a cashier."

The misery revealed in the human story quoted above, a misery which prevailed in greater or less degree among a large section of the working classes all over the country, was, as is now generally admitted, to a considerable extent the outcome of the return to the Gold Standard in 1925. It is one of Mr. Winston Churchill's most valued characteristics that he " knows nothing about finance", but it was unfortunate for the country that this ignorance should have been regarded by his Party as qualifying him for the post of Chancellor of the Exchequer. As Chancellor, he faithfully followed the expert guidance of the all-powerful Governor of the Bank of England. Thus resulted the paradox that, while the public was ceaselessly subjected to propaganda about the alleged wickedness of "Bolshevism", the appalling social consequences of "sound finance"—the economics of restriction—were visible to all unprejudiced observers. It is hardly surprising, in view of what occurred between 1925 and 1931, that the recent (1944) Bankers' Conference at Bretton Woods has aroused widespread misgivings. If, as Dr. Paul Einzig and others have asserted, the plan there formulated results in another crucifixion of the masses on "a cross of gold", the economic consequences of the forthcoming peace settlement may be even more disastrous than those of its predecessor.

The moral responsibility for the starvation and unemployment of so many thousands of ex-servicemen, in contrast to the vast wealth accumulated in the hands of the few, lies at the door of the ruling financial oligarchy, the professional politicians who served them and the members of the "top shelf" who supported them. The whole British social system was on trial. It proved itself devoid of conscience, corrupt and almost as indifferent to the people's sufferings as were the French aristocrats before the Revolution. The appearance of hunger marchers in the streets of London was a sign and a portent which indicated—to those who could read what it foretold—the approaching dissolution of an order of society already doomed.

CHAPTER THREE

THE LEAGUE OF NATIONS

THE main subject of European controversy throughout the 'twenties was, naturally, enough, the Treaty of Versailles and its eagerly-watched offspring, the League of Nations. The debate may be said to have continued without cessation ever since the terms of the Treaty were first published. The extent to which its provisions made the outbreak of World War Two inevitable is a point which has recently been argued with renewed violence. Versailles, perhaps, has more defenders in 1944 than it had in 1924.

How many thousands of books have been published in all languages about the League and the Treaty, how many billions of words they contain and how many tons of paper have been used in their manufacture is beyond computation. In England the principal conflict was between the "idealists"—mostly

Socialists, pacifists and religious-minded people who believed in the dawn of a new era and saw visions of a world set free from recurrent trade wars—and the " realists " who based their arguments on the belief that human nature never changes, that facts are facts and that the way to treat a beaten enemy is to knock him out so effectively that he can never hit back.

Clemenceau, Foch, even Pershing were uncompromising " realists", as were some of the best brains among the younger professional soldiers of all the Allied nations. President Wilson was the dominating figure among the " idealists", who endowed him with qualities which he, unfortunately, did not possess, while Lloyd George, displaying the traditional British skill in improvization, attempted to make the best of both worlds and nearly succeeded. In the light of recent events, those " realists " who prophesied that " the Junkers will cheat you yet", have scored heavily. Francis Francis, in his brilliant book " Our Ruling Class " (1922) expressed with great clarity and insight the views of many intelligent and patriotic British officers. " The Peace of Versailles," he wrote, "has placed so little restraint upon the future development of Germany, in fact has left her with such enlarged scope in this respect, that the Great War is merely interrupted, its recrudescence merely a question of time. . .. The war threatened the existence of Governments, the fatuities of the Peace Conference threaten the permanence of civilization. Once more, German duplicity and dishonesty, the prospect of a renewed German menace, are the disturbing factors in European politics". French realists like Clemenceau, Foch and Poincaré, whom the " idealists " of the 'twenties, inflamed with a passionate desire for international reconciliation, regarded as unspeakable villains, had no illusions. As we are now painfully aware, if the capitalist system had to survive, they were right. Even pacifists as well-informed and clear-sighted as Robert Dell and E. D. Morel underestimated the validity of the French arguments and greatly exaggerated the possible dangers of French military predominance on the continent of Europe. In the latter error, which they shared with President Wilson, Lloyd George and the British Foreign Office, they were led astray by misjudging the character and temperament of the French people, placing too much con- fidence in the Weimar Republic, and failing to grasp what the British financial wire-pullers were really aiming at. There are depths of duplicity which even the most experienced investigators of secret diplomacy find it difficult to credit.

If the " idealists", from whom many of the essential facts were hidden, built up logical arguments which later turned out to be unsound, at least their basic contention will prove to be as true tomorrow as it was yesterday. They maintained that there could be no durable settlement, no hope of lasting peace, without a new economic policy ; they believed and asserted that so long as the peoples of the world remained under the yoke of international finance and monopoly capitalism, recurrent wars were inevitable. This basic contention, one of the foundation stones of Socialist theory, stands today unquestioned and unchallenged by anyone who can genuinely claim to be opposed to Fascism. When Mr. Churchill blandly informs us that as the war goes on it becomes " less and less ideological", and when he hands bouquets to the most unspeakably vile of the Fascist dictators, he is merely admitting that the war aims of himself and his Party are quite different from those of the masses of his compatriots who are providing the blood and toil, the tears and sweat. If the war is not " ideological", if it does not result in the emergence, in this country, of a planned economy, Victory, when it comes, must prove as great a fraud as it did in 1918. It will result not in Peace, but in another Armistice, which is unlikely to be of as long a duration as the last one.

The redeeming feature of the Treaty of Versailles was, as even its critics admit, the establishment of the League of Nations. In spite of the multitude of obstetricians, the reluctance of the mother to perform her natural functions and the rivalry of the wet-nurses, the child was weaned and had reached adolescence before the wicked uncles slew it. Could it have grown to manhood ? Could it have developed into a League of Peoples and brought about, by mutual agreement, the economic changes necessary to avert the present conflict ? No one can read Viscount Cecil's autobiograhpy, " A Great Experiment", a judicial and authoritative history of the League from its inception to its ignominious collapse, without coming to the conclusion that it might have succeeded had British big business permitted it to function. Lord Cecil's record leaves little doubt that it *could* have been made an effective instrument for preventing aggression but for the deliberate sabotage of British Conservative politicians acting under the influence of " pressure groups". Its bitterest opponents were the manufacturers of war material and the " anti-Bolshevik " Bankers' combine, who saw in it a menace to their long-term plans.

The first challenge to the League's authority came in 1923, when Mussolini made his wanton attack on Greece. It was successful through the intervention on the Duce's behalf of Baldwin and the ineffable Lord Curzon. The Italian Navy had not been remarkable for its offensive qualities during the Four Years' War. Mussolini inaugurated his new era by ordering one of his ships to bombard the " fortress " of Corfu which had been dismantled for fifty years and was then being used as a children's orphanage. The naval officer responsible for carrying out the Duce's orders was petrified with fear at the possible consequences of his action. He need not have worried. Mussolini was already the protégé of the British ruling class and the League was forced to register its first humiliation. It suffered many others, at the same hands, but survived them—until Sir Samuel Hoare delivered the final lethal blow—because millions of decent people in all the countries represented, regarded it as Europe's only defence against the wild beasts of international finance.

The foundation and rapid growth throughout Great Britain of the League of Nations Union showed how eagerly ordinary English people responded to the practical idealism of Viscount Cecil, Professor Gilbert Murray and other enthusiasts. The L.N.U. quickly acquired a large and active membership, but as it was not organized as a political party it was able to assert no effective political influence. Throughout the 'thirties Britain was entirely in the hands of a thinly-veiled Tory dictatorship, which relied on a majority obtained by means of the grossest deception and ignored or defied public opinion. After the " Peace Ballot " —the nearest approach to a plebiscite this country has ever known—when nearly eleven millions voted for a strong "League of Nations " policy, which nearly seven millions agreed should, if necessary, be enforced by arms, the Tories pretended to accept this expression of the people's will. Sir Samuel Hoare was put up to make his famous election speech at Geneva. No sooner had the necessary majority been secured—the majority which controls the present House of Commons—than the pledges given to the electorate were dishonoured.

Whatever may have been the defects of the League, however justifiable may have been the criticisms levelled against the Treaty of Versailles, the fact remains that no war in English history was ever more clearly avoidable than the one which droke out on September 3rd, 1939. Unfortunately, it is not bossible to exonerate Transport House of a large share of the blame. Even after the first shots had been fired in Spain, in July 1936, it was not too late, by bold and straightforward action on the part of the Opposition leaders, to rouse the country to revolt. Alas, they completely failed to rise to the occasion. It was, however, in the 'twenties that the seeds of the subsequent débâcle were sown. Coming events, for the unfortunate few who were gifted with the torturing quality of imagination, cast their shadows before them.

The League was sabotaged and the Money Power of Britain, in collaboration with what is now known as Vichy France and with the support of Wall Street, developed its plans for collaborating with the Axis in what was hoped would prove a crusade against " Bolshevism". The essence of the conspiracy, in England as in France, was to compel the people of both countries to accept subservient collaboration with the " anti-Bolshevik " dictators by leaving them without arms for their defence. The plan was only upset by the revolt of the British under Churchill's leadership, the Channel, Polish intransigence and Hitler's impatience. Had the Poles agreed to a " second Munich", as Bonnet seems to have expected, our fate might have been sealed. It would, however, be premature to suppose that the Money Power has altered its plans for making as much of the world as can be kept outside the Soviet sphere of influence safe for " sound finance". To-day the same financial dictators, actuated by the same motives, are intriguing to rob the anti-Fascist patriots of Italy, Belgium, Greece, Spain and even France—not to mention those of Great Britain—of the freedom earned by their heroic efforts. Before the Second World War has dragged to its end, it may be that the first shots in the Third World War have already been fired.

One of the unfortunate results of the League was to perpetuate the use, by journalists and politicians, of the " personified State". Whatever was said or done at Geneva by the representatives of a Government temporarily in power, was said to be done by " France", " Britain", " Poland " or " Brazil", as the case might be. This was a perpetuation of the Foreign Office habit of thinking of nations in terms of their figureheads and leaving the populations concerned totally out of account. A line from a comedy of the 'twenties amusingly satirized this propensity. " Have you heard," says one of the characters, " Dolly has promised to give us India—isn't it grand ? " For the uninitiated it may be explained that the Prime Minister, Lord Adolphus So-and-So, had promised to make the speaker's husband Viceroy of India. An example of this practice, put into disastrous action, has recently been revealed in connection with Greece. To maintain friendly relations with " Greece", for strategical reasons, has been a cardinal point of British foreign policy for at least a century. The procedure adopted by Mr. Churchill and Mr. Anthony Eden to keep " Greece " friendly has been to bolster up a detested alien monarch, who acquiesced in the establishment of a Fascist dictatorship, and to use British troops and the British Navy to quell a revolt of the Greek patriots who fought with us so gallantly at El Alamein. The fact that a courageous and patriotic race who, since the days of Byron, have regarded the English with special esteem, may be alienated for generations by these proceedings does not disturb the calm of Whitehall. After all, the Greek guerillas are not on the " social register", while the Greek monarch, his relations and his entourage are—very much so.*

Robert Dell, who spent the last years of his life as a " Geneva correspondent " and whose warnings about Hitler's real intentions went unheeded by many of the Left—myself, I regret to acknow-ledge, among them—until the war in Spain revealed them, spent years inveighing against references to the " Personified State." The present war, except in the case of the U.S.S.R., has reduced the practice to an absurdity.

CHAPTER FOUR

THOSE UNITED STATES

I

IF the 'twenties may be said to have been " the American decade " as far as England was concerned, the prospects of an " American century " may well discourage the most philoprogenitive of Europeans from continuing to struggle for survival. The results of President Wilson's belated belligerence in 1917, which owing to the official hush-hush policy have only recently been realized by any large section of the British public, are worth considering today because of the light they throw upon current events. Behind a smoke-screen of moral uplift and bogus generosity, the United States emerged with collossal financial profits from a

---

* Written six months before General Scobie's arrival in Athens and all the events which have resulted from it.

struggle in which the American forces engaged had only played a very minor part. That British good nature managed to survive the shocks to which these facts would normally have subjected it, can be ascribed to a variety of causes. In the first place, the "idealist" utterances of Wilson and his messianic posturing deluded not only British pacifists but, to use his own phrase, "the plain people" of every nation which had suffered by the war, into believing in his power to inaugurate a new era and in the capacity of his country to assume the moral leadership of a distracted world. In the second place, all the facts which might have led to some modification of this widespread wishful-thinking were carefully concealed from the British public. In the third place, as Masterman pointed out, those who had borne the burden of the war were too exhausted and apathetic to care very much what happened provided they had pay-packets and enough to eat. Individual contacts with American citizens were usually agreeable and fostered the legend, invented by the press and by the politicians, that the United States was on the whole well-disposed towards this country, although there was no historical justification for any such belief.

Francis Francis, writing in 1917, after over twelve years spent in many different States of the Union, strove in vain to dispel this illusion of American amity towards Great Britain. As he points out, unconscious as we are of any animosity against Americans, we have always found it difficult to credit the fact that they fail, as a whole, to reciprocate our desire for friendship. "For a very long while," he writes, "British Governments and the British people have courted the friendship of the United States. Either we have given way in any disputes between us, or offered to settle them by arbitration. We have submitted to a good deal of ungracious treatment at the hands of American politicians. We have allowed "twisting the lion's tail" to become a consecrated rite in America. . . . On the sole occasion within recent years when the United States was at war, we stood by her and discouraged interference in the struggle by certain European Powers. In fact, we have acted ostentatiously as her first line of defence. That, at any rate, has been the position we have occupied in the calculations of the rest of the world. Is there any other explanation of the fact that, with their immense wealth practically undefended, the Americans have been left undisturbed, unthreatened even, for so many years in a world that was armed to the teeth? England had but to stand aside, and a

European coalition against the United States would soon have
given her trouble. . . .   There has never been the least acknow-
ledgement from her for the service rendered to her by our Navy,
nor has it been allowed to modify her sentiments towards us. . . .
Led by her confined political outlook to believe that she herself
was unassailable, and that in seeking her friendship we merely
sought to strengthen our own position, she never has been able
to meet our overtures in the spirit in which they were conceived.
At the same time, she has permitted a false statement of such
history as mutually concerns us to be taught in her schools and
proclaimed from her platforms.   Her politicians have used the
bad blood thus engendered in America as a leverage in their
Party contests.   Whenever any movement to improve our
relations has arisen, the United States' Presidents, Senate, Congress and public opinion, as though some Machiavellian intrigue
threatened, have hastened to suppress it.   Consequently there
never has been a time in the past when a war with Great Britain
would not have been far more popular with Americans than one
with any other power."

Francis points out that while we have done all that a self-
respecting nation could do to establish better relations between
the two countries our efforts will always be unsuccessful so long
as Americans are not furnished with an impartial version of our
joint history.   " We should have little to fear from the revelation
this would be to them. But if histories, like hymns of hate, are
sown, good-will will not be harvested."

Writing before President Wilson reluctantly abandoned his
profitable neutrality, Francis pointed out certain facts which
somehow escaped the attention of Mr. Andrew Mellon when the
time came to discuss war debts.   " The present war is of the same
vital importance to the United States as to ourselves.   Our
interest in it is only a little more immediate than her own.   If
we are fighting for our existence, hers depends upon our victory.
The defeat of the Allies would leave the United States face to
face with a ruthless world-power, immeasurably stronger in
armaments than herself, and representing everything that she is
diametrically opposed to in principle.   Not only would Germany
then control the navies of Europe, she could safely utilize the
forceful body of her adherents entrenched within the Republic. . . .
With so much of the world's liquid wealth in American hands,
Americans would have to arm to the teeth to protect it against a
victorious Germany.   Would they allow a non-military neutral

to retain the monetary profits of the present struggle ? The idea is incredible. And yet, because of an altogether groundless hatred of England, Americans have allowed German propaganda to obscure the origin and objects of the war to such an extent that her Government dare not side with the nations actually defending her. . . . Those who doubt that whatever is active in American feeling with regard to the war favours Germany rather than the Allies, have only to remember that so long as Germany was winning, the United States made no efforts to interfere. They have only to consider what her action would have been had Great Britain, France, or Russia been guilty of the atrocities committed by Germany". Francis gives a long and shocking list of German war crimes and observes that " the country which claims to lead civilization has uttered no protest". He goes on to point out that " the United States is under obligations to both France and Russia ; our attitude towards her in the past has practically relieved her of the cost of armaments ; from Germany she has had nothing but exploitation and insults. In view of these facts does it not seem to be infatuation for Great Britain to continue in her belief that she can establish really friendly relations with the United States ? . . . These considerations, much as we may deplore them, need not excite bitterness on our part. Americans never have concealed their sentiments towards us. They are not to blame if we have been foolish enough to misinterpret them. It is, however, time that we took a more practical view of the situation between us. Policies of obsequiousness and animosity alike are futile". Francis, writing with the excusable bitterness of a patriotic English soldier, observes that " so long as Germany was winning, America was silent. Only when Germany began to weaken did she propose peace, and then it was to be a " peace without victory", or detriment to Germany. It still is uncertain whether her influence will not be used to save Prussian militarism from annihilation, and thus inevitably renew the reign of arma- ments and terror in Europe". To this comment, written in 1917, he added a footnote in 1922. " No longer is there any un- certainty on this score. The disaster has occurred." There follows this clear-sighted and prophetic utterance : " And if the United States is instrumental in restoring the German menace to Europe, what effect will this have on her own position ? Sooner or later she will find herself face to face with Germany as a world power, hostile to her. For Germany is incapable of friendship. She only courts accomplices, who eventually become her victims. The United States is not invulnerable. Her peoples are not yet homogeneous, but an agglomeration of different nationalities, animated by differences in tradition, character, temper, which, laboured by skilful German propaganda, might easily be used to divide them in a crisis. Her Monroe Doctrine is not an impregnable physical barrier, but a declaration of her will, which Germany has always desired to challenge. If at any time in the last decade the Allies had chosen to intimate to Germany that they were not disposed to thwart her ambitions in South America, she would have found there the outlet she required, and this war might have been postponed indefinitely. But for Great Britain, this probably would have occurred. And still the bulk of Americans sympathize with Germany and have no word to say in Britain's favour."

If slanging the British while using the British Navy as her first line of defence has been the only discernible foreign policy of the United States for the past hundred years, it must be admitted that the type of diplomat sent to Washington by the Foreign Office to conduct our affairs and the patronizing attitude of British politicians towards their so-called "American cousins" have largely contributed to this regrettable situation. What Francis Francis wrote nearly thirty years ago, is even more true to-day when only extreme candour on the part of British spokesmen can counteract the unimpeded stream of American abuse. "Subservience and flattery destroy respect ; they never conciliate and though there is scarcely a man in England who would not welcome better feeling and a better understanding between ourselves and the United States, our politicians have no mandate from the people to grovel for it. . . . By their attitude of servility towards the United States, our leaders only earn contempt, and beget restiveness here."

What sort of an " ally " President Wilson was, is made clear to the present generation in Leopold Schwartchild's admirably documented volume " World in Trance " (1943). By the middle of 1917 Wilson had already developed his plan to exert pressure on France and Great Britain, to force them to obey his orders. Like President Roosevelt in the present war, whose private instructions to such " personal representatives " as Admiral Leahy, Mr. Myron Taylor, Mr. Robert Murphy, and Archbishop Spellman have been concealed alike from Congress and from the press, Wilson sent a " personal representative " to Paris in the shape of Colonel House who was accountable to nobody but himself. The correspondence which took place between them was only published long after the events concerned. " When the war is over," Wilson wrote to House, " we can force them (his Allies) to our way of thinking, because by that time they will, among other things, be financially in our hands, but we cannot force them now." Coming from the Messiah who roused the people of Europe by demanding the abolition of " secret diplomacy " and insisting on " open covenants openly arrived at", this instruction to his Paris watch-dog seems as peculiar as Colonel House's reply to it. House wrote : " I would suggest that you quietly diminish the transport of troops, giving as an excuse the prevalence of influenza or any other reason but the real one—I would also suggest a little later that you begin to shut gently down upon money, food, and raw material. I feel confident that we should play a strong hand." This revelation of methods which are second nature to American politicians, and have certainly been followed, as Mr. Stettinius has admitted, in the course of the present war, does not appear to have aroused any adverse comment in the United States. In England, criticism has to be qualified by the doubt whether British politicians have, at least in relation to the U.S.S.R., shown any more squeamish regard for loyalty and honour. Colonel House's personal code and his sense of decency were, fortunately, of a higher grade than the President's. In October 1918 the Germans, with a thorough knowledge of Wilson's character and pro-German outlook, were astute enough to make a personal approach to him on the subject of peace conditions. House's advice was that Wilson should have " no private correspondence with the Germans", and promise only " a consultation with the Allies". What Wilson decided on was no consultation with the Allies and only private correspondence with the Germans. The Allies watched the proceedings from a distance with considerable anxiety and some justifiable annoyance in view of the wholly disproportionate contribution made by the United States to the approaching victory. " The French casualties at this period were over 1,300,000 dead, and 4,000,000 wounded. The corresponding British figures were 900,000 and 2,000,000. America's tribute to Moloch was less than 2 per cent. of the total". Nor was America's aid in other departments anything like what, for the purpose of deluding the British and French people, it was cracked up to be. True, America's contribution in money, foodstuffs, raw materials, shipping space and certain types of munitions had been enormous—so was the bill afterwards presented for them—but her failure on the decisive points, tanks and planes, was complete. In February 1918 Pershing cabled Wilson that there was not a single American-made plane in Europe and two months later tanks were still regarded as a new-fangled curiosity in the U.S.A. Foch, in July 1918, told Pershing of the urgent need for tanks, but none were forthcoming.

In view of these facts the threats of open hostility against Great Britain and France, made first by House on the President's behalf, and subsequently by Wilson himself, if the American peace plans were not accepted, were the more disturbing.   On one occasion, the President got as far as having his bags packed to leave Paris.   On another, House told Clemenceau that if he did not comply with Wilson's demands " the question would then arise whether America would not have to take these matters up directly with Germany and Austria".   Clemenceau said : " That would amount to a separate peace between the United States and the Central Powers."   " It might", replied House.

When Lloyd George demurred to Wilson's views about the right to blockade in time of war, he was told that the United States would start a battle of armaments by building a Navy of unprecedented size, if he raised objections.   In regard to the German Army, Wilson certainly wished it to be made too weak to make another stand against its adversaries, but he wanted it to remain strong enough to be able still to threaten them.   The Allies must be kept in check by the fear that if America withdrew from the common cause, they might again have to face German arms alone.   He explained to House that " it is certain that too much success or security on the part of the Allies, will make a genuine Peace settlement exceedingly difficult, if not impossible." Inspired by a commendable idealism—by a desire shared by millions of German Socialists as well as by the masses of suffering people throughout Europe, to get rid for all time of the scourge of war by removing its causes—the British pacifist leaders pursued a line of argument which would have been wholly justified had it been built on a foundation of fact.   Unfortunately, the truth was concealed from them as it was from everybody else and the Official Secrets Act was employed to confirm them in their ignorance.   Not only were they totally mistaken in the character and real aims of Wilson, but they were equally unaware of the secret aims of Anglo-American reaction in regard to the Weimar Republic, of the recuperative power of the Prussian military caste and of the validity of the French demand for security. It was in regard to France that they chiefly misled their innocent and enthusiastic disciples, of whom this writer was one.

II

In 1922 the Conservative financial oligarchy thought it safe to dispense with Lloyd George whom they had always disliked and whose popularity as the " man who won the war " had now served its purpose. The opportunity came when the masses showed a marked disinclination to be involved in another war with the Turks, at Chanak. Getting rid of Lloyd George meant also getting rid of his vote-catching election programme with its references to land for soldiers, " homes fit for heroes", jobs for all, and suchlike unpractical nonsense, which the Conservative profiteers, at least, had never taken seriously. The successful crushing of the coal and other strikes had removed their fears both of revolutionary labour and of the demobilised servicemen. They felt strong enough to come into the open and govern as a Party, instead of under the camouflage of a national coalition. Accordingly they withdrew their support to the Government on October 20th, Lloyd George resigned, Bonar Law became Premier in his place, and the country found itself once again with a Conservative Government, after an interval of seventeen years.

For some reason, which has never been satisfactorily explained, a Conservative First Secretary to the Treasury of whom the general public had, until then, never heard, was promoted to the high office of Chancellor of the Exchequer. Two months later, it fell to this inexperienced minister to proceed to the United States for the purpose of funding the British War Debt. With him on this mission went the newly-appointed Governor of the Bank of England, Mr. Montague Norman, and his " American adviser", a certain Dr. Sprague. That the negotiations would prove to be " sticky " was shown by the hostile reception given in America to A. J. Balfour's statesmanlike suggestion that there should be an all-round cancellation of war debts. Great Britain had already made a generous gesture in this direction by wiping off many millions owed to her by the Allies. Not the least of the advantages of Balfour's proposal was the fact that it avoided, as between nations which had made sacrifices in a common cause, any danger of an association between blood and book-keeping.

The famous " Balfour Note", addressed in August 1922 to the French and Italian Governments, contained the following passages :*

" . . . In no circumstances do we propose to ask more from our debtors than is necessary to pay our creditors, . . . but all will admit that we can hardly be content with less.   For it should not be forgotten that our liabilities were incurred for others, not for ourselves.   The food, the materials, the munitions, required for the immense naval and military efforts of Great Britain, and half the £2,000,000,000 advanced to the Allies, were provided by internal borrowing and taxation. Unfortunately, a similar policy was beyond the power of any other European nation.   Appeal was therefore made to the United States ; but . . . it was only on our security that they were prepared to lend it. . . ."

As usual, the United States exacted the uttermost pound of flesh from their beloved English " cousins".   When France, Belgium and Italy came to make terms at Washington, a large part of their debts was written off and the interest on the rest was only about half what was requested from Britain.   Our struggles to keep up payments in gold to our rapacious creditors hastened the economic collapse which occurred six years after the settlement.

To the average English mind, the discrepancy between the amount of blood shed by the British to defeat Germany and that shed by American citizens was so immeasurably great as to make any question of our *owing* anything to the United States utterly unjust.   If anything the United States was clearly in Britain's debt, not Britain in hers.

As Wall Street had entered the war during its closing stages with the very practical motive of defending " the American pocket-book", the United States Government did not share this view.   The Americans, as much of their press comment and the subsequently published Wilson-House correspondence made clear, did not regard their hereditary enemy as an " ally " in any accepted sense of the term.   On the contrary, they regarded Britain as a decadent commercial rival, with a collapsing Empire, whom, as H. L. Mencken stated in the *American Mercury*, it was desirable to put " in a plain and incurable second place".   In order to accomplish this they followed the stereotyped procedure

* Quoted in The Twenty Years Truce, 1919-1939, by Robert M. Rayner, 1943.

of American banking and big business towards a firm in difficulties. First they demanded a usurious annual tribute ; afterwards they raised an unscaleable tariff wall to prevent Britain from selling her goods in the American market, and thus obtaining the money to pay it. Between these two events, the funding of the Debt and the imposition of the Hawley-Smoot Tariff, the situation in Germany made any prospect of " squeezing the Hun till the pips squeak " a fond illusion.

What actually happened when Stanley Baldwin found himself face to face across a table with the American millionaire, Andrew Mellon, we shall probably never know, unless, perhaps, Lord Baldwin is using his retirement to write his memoirs and chooses to reveal it. According to a story which had wide currency at the time Mr. Mellon, following the usual practice in big business interviews, remarked that none of the other debtor nations would get better terms than those he proposed. These, roughly, were that the British taxpayer should pay the United States £1,000 millions in interest on the debt of £900 millions contracted by our Allies under a British guarantee. Lord Baldwin is, rightly or wrongly, supposed to have behaved like the perfect Harrovian gentleman, to have " high-hatted " Mr. Mellon by accepting his word without argument and signing on the dotted line. The rate of interest proved to be twice as high as the rate subsequently negotiated with France and eight times as high as Italy's rate. There is no evidence that it ever occurred to Baldwin to mention our dead or to refer to the 390 days during which the American forces in France bided their time, and were only saved from being taken prisoners without firing a shot by the stubborn resistance of the French, English and Dominion troops. Although the Baldwin agreement ran counter to all the instructions he had received, Baldwin announced on his return, to the ill and horrified Bonar Law, that he had pledged Great Britain to the settlement. Before he died, Law admitted to Lloyd George how much he regretted that he had not resigned sooner than approve the terms which Baldwin had arranged. Lloyd George's comment on the deal was that it was " in the nature of a negotiation between a weasel and its quarry."

Had Baldwin belonged to any other Party except the Conservatives this unfortunate blunder, at the outset of his ministerial career, would have led to his retirement from public life. The Tory Party, however, follows rules of its own which no one outside its ranks can profess to understand. (During the present

war so many discredited politicians have been rewarded by
elevation to the peerage that the House of Lords has been irreverently
nicknamed " The Chamber of Horrors.") On May 21st, 1923,
after Bonar Law's resignation, Baldwin became Prime Minister. " I
suppose it had to be Baldwin", was Bonar Law's depressed comment.

That there was a good deal behind the debt settlement which
was never revealed to the public may be taken for granted. In
the fifth year of the Second World War, for the outbreak of which
the United States must bear a large share of responsibility, all
the negotiations which have taken place between the two countries since it started remain wrapped in profound mystery. Not
one ray of light penetrates the veil of official secrecy.

To return to Lord Baldwin and his debt settlement, the safest
guess is that it had Mr. Norman's approval and was considered
by him a necessary first step towards Britain's return to the
Gold Standard, which took place with such disastrous effect in
1925. During the second MacDonald administration a Socialist
M.P. told the writer that he was present when Mr. Norman was
induced to attend a private meeting of Members in a Committee
Room of the House of Commons. Whenever a question was put to
him concerning the effect of the financial policy of the Bank of
England on the general export trade of the country and on the
unemployment figures, Mr. Norman, according to my informant,
invariably tittupped : " It's no good asking me *that*. I am not
an economist. I'm a banker." From this we may, perhaps,
assume, that Lord Baldwin, when in the United States, did exactly
what our financial dictator told him to do and that his promotion
to Prime Minister followed. " It *had* to be Baldwin."

Anyone possessed of a modicum of commonsense, or any
knowledge of elementary psychology, could have predicted that
Baldwin's stretching out of " hands across the sea " to our
" American cousins " far from making them love us more would
only have the effect of exacerbating their contempt, suspicion and
dislike. One of the first signs of this was the publication of a
letter addressed by Mr. Andrew Mellon to the President of
Princeton University, which gave such a distorted version of the
debt situation that Winston Churchill, then Chancellor of the
Exchequer, was induced to make a public reply. No notice
was taken of it, officially. Meanwhile, anti-British outbursts,
on the lines of : " wae won the wr for them, didn't we ? " and
" they hired the money, didn't they ? " continued to be a popular
feature of a large section of the free and uninhibited American

press. This sourness of temper towards Great Britain was reflected in the American note on the abortive Anglo-French naval understanding—which one London newspaper referred to as "firm but friendly "—in President Coolidge's valedictory speech on resigning office, President Hoover's election addresses, and in press comment on such minor episodes as the sinking on the high seas, by a United States cutter, of the rum-runner *I'm Alone*. District-Attorney Tuttle's curious enquiry into the *Vestris* disaster produced a nation-wide explosion of anti-British hysteria, while " Big Bill Thompson's " injunction to the blameless King George V to keep his snoot out of Chicago City raised a howl of delight in the boot-leggers' capital. Wall Street imperialism found an able exponent in Mr. Ludwell Denny, a European correspondent and conference observer, whose book " America Conquers Britain " had the success its title alone would have secured it. Mr. Denny's theme was that his country was destined to "own the world". In oil, in aviation, in hydro-electric power, the United States, he pointed out, was steadily gaining predominance. " What chance has Britain against America," he asked, " or what chance has the world ? " He summed up the real reason for America's continued expenditure on armaments in a sentence which, if he read it in prison, must have delighted Adolf Hitler. " If Britain is foolish enough to fight us, she will go down more quickly, that is all." Even the pacifist and radical New York *Nation* quoted in a review of this book Walter Page's observation that " she (England) will be our colony before she is done ; not in name but in fact." The dollar imperialists were already casting covetous eyes on portions of the colonial empires of their former allies, Britain and France. In particular the British West Indies and the French islands of Martinique and Guadaloupe excited their cupidity. Publicists openly looked forward to the time when we should have to cede our West Indian possessions in order that they might be turned, in the interests of American " security", into bases for the United States Navy. In the early 'twenties Mr. William Randolph Hearst had already discovered that the batteries of Bermuda were pointing menacingly at New York.*

* According to the *New Republic* of June 26th, 1944 (quoted in the *New Statesman and Nation*, of August 19th, 1944) the dispute between President Roosevelt and General de Gaulle arose " from the fear of the President that certain French Colonies may one day be a military menace to the U.S.A. He demands that these Colonies shall be ' inter-nationalized '—a term which the article does not define. The colonies in question are Martinique, French Guiana, Dakar, St. Pierre et Miquelon and even Indo-China." De Gaulle naturally refused.

The effect of America's open hostility to this country, after her repudiation of the Treaty of Versailles, on the politicians concerned with defending our interests, was to make them grovel for America's " friendship " in precisely the same way as they subsequently " appeased " the Axis. Without any reciprocal advantage, our rulers made concession after concession, accepting every rebuff with meekness and discouraging adverse comment in the British press. The reason for all this can, no doubt, be traced back ultimately to the bankers, to fear of Bolshevism, and to the considerable pickings to be got from the flood of American capital that was pouring into stricken Europe.

On the infiltration of American money into Great Britain, our press was silent. Obviously the rapidly expanding cinema industry was largely in American hands, but it was from an American periodical that the writer happened to discover quite by chance that a certain Mr. Harley C. Clarke, of Chicago, had gained control of the Gaumont British Picture Corporation and its allied companies. This Mr. Clarke was also revealed as being president of the all-American company which had obtained control of the Greater London and County Trust, Ltd., which supplied light and power to parts of London, Birmingham and other cities. It is worth while noting that among the English directors of this American-controlled trust were Lord Birkenhead, Sir Austen Chamberlain and Sir L. Worthington-Evans.

III

On the British masses American sourness during the post-war years made no effect whatever. Not one Englishman in a thousand knew or cared what the great United States was saying or doing. The terms of the debt settlement were meaningless to a nation long inured to " financial nonsense " by the astronomical figures of war expenditure. The strident American claims to have " won the war " were regarded with genial amusement by ex-servicemen, mingled with the Englishman's habitual contempt of those who do more boasting than fighting. Some ill-humour was shown when Mr. Pussyfoot Johnson arrived in London to preach Prohibition, but this was soon forgotten when a crowd of boisterous students accidentally put his eye out. Apart from this incident, the process of Americanization, owing to the public apathy, met with no attempt at opposition. Never was there a time when any foreign country had such a vogue in Great Britain as the United States had during the 'twenties. The more the

Yanks disliked us, libelled us in their press or humiliated our statesmen, the more we loved them. If it is true that we hate those we have injured, it is equally true that we tend to forgive and make excuses for those whom we have always regarded as friends. American dance music, American plays, American architecture, American novels, American movies—even at the expense of our own struggling industry—American slang, American business methods, American gangster crime, American drinks and American divorce all became the rage. So much so that the few cultivated Americans, who visited the land of Shakespeare in search of "traditional England", were horrified to find it "Americanized."

Anglo-American contacts, owing to the geographical position of the two countries, have always been limited in number and generally speaking Americans in England and Englishmen in America have tended to meet people of like interests and similar outlook to their own. There may perhaps be fifty thousand American citizens (out of a hundred and forty millions) who have a fairly intimate acquaintance with a corresponding number of Englishmen. If we select from these—admitting that the figures are guesswork—some ten thousand Americans of both sexes who belong to the worlds of scholarship, art, literature and journalism, and start to generalize about Anglo-American relations from the warm friendships and happy intermarriages which have resulted from their contacts with an equal number of English people of the same kind, we shall have no fears about the future friendship of the English-speaking nations. Cultivated Americans of liberal views, as all are aware who have had the privilege of knowing any, have the most charming manners of any people in the world and, like the real élite everywhere, are rarely rich. Unfortunately, they dislike politics and have little political influence.

As if inspired by the deliberate intention of keeping the ordinary citizens of both countries from meeting and fraternizing, the ruling cliques on either side of the Atlantic made it a practice to keep a sharp watch on incoming liners and to pounce on their innocent passengers before they had a chance of making contacts outside their charmed circle. As a result of this manœuvre there hardly can be found in the world two large agglomerations of " plain people " more utterly ignorant of each other than the inhabitants of Great Britain and the United States. For this unfortunate state of affairs the enormous transference of material wealth from Europe to America, and the resulting enrichment of millions of rather crude American citizens and corresponding

D

impoverishment of an equal number of cultured Europeans was largely responsible.

The fact that Americans accord " social prominence " chiefly to wealth, material success and publicity value, their national inability to form stable and disinterested relationships with their fellow humans, male or female, and their Republican veneration for titles, made transatlantic visitors to our shores eager to accept the proffered aristocratic embrace. They had the money, could make the best hotel reservations and could surely expect to contact the " best " people. Quite a few—though by no means all—of our " best " people, their rapacity sharpened by high taxation and by the losses sustained during the war, were only too ready to trade their assets for what they considered an appropriate amount of dollars. Everything they had was for sale, at a price, beginning with their marriageable sons and daughters. Many a globe-trotting millionaire discovered that a week-end in a " stately home ", apart from the danger to health from draughty passages and cold bedrooms, was one of the most expensive diversions which England had to offer. Little old ladies, laid up (as you might say) in lavender, quickly developed a skill in hawking phony old masters which many a Bond Street dealer might have envied. Even literary visitors from the Great Pure Republic were not free from the national obsession of " success-snobbery " —a vice with which they very quickly infected post-war London— and sought the acquaintance only of such authors as they were pleased to consider " worth while ". An example of the American attitude to the London literary scene was afforded me in 1927 when I made a brief excursion to New York and Boston. An American boy was introduced to me at a party, in my capacity as " visiting English author ", who had, it appeared, literary ambitions, based on the sale of two or three articles to magazines. His occupation was that of a bank clerk. His English equivalent would, if lucky, be earning about £5 a week, would have as his highest " ambition " admission to the local tennis club and his ideas of foreign travel would be limited to spending his annual fortnight's holiday in France or Belgium as a conducted tourist. The young American had been able to save enough dollars to spend a month in England and, as a would-be writer, he was determined not to waste his time. He produced, therefore, a list from his pocket, containing about fifty names of British authors, to whom he proposed to introduce himself on arrival, and consulted me as to whether there were any he should strike out as being unworthy of his attention. The first three names were G. B. Shaw, H. G. Wells, and Thomas Hardy. . . .

To this nice, clean, upstanding boy, coming from a nice lower-middle-class suburban home, the idea of condescending to make the acquaintance of any young Englishman of his own occupation and station in life simply did not occur. He was interested only in National Monuments, in outstanding " personalities " who were, from his standpoint, " worth while ". I have no doubt that, on arrival in London, he was lavishly entertained by the type of English people who laid themselves out to pounce on American visitors and even found many of the writers on his list flattered by being called upon, willing to accept him at his own valuation and ready to give him enough signed copies of their books to enable him to defray the expenses of his holiday.

The only Americans who, so far as I was able to observe, ever really got " inside " England and met the " real English ", were the few thousand scholars, genuine men of letters, artists, journalists and cultivated people, to whom I have already referred. Many of these found their way into our Bohemian circles, settled down in picturesque cottages in English villages, learnt to appreciate our country pubs, stayed in our University towns, made use of our libraries, and in a number of cases made successful English marriages.

If there was no English boom in the United States in any way to be compared with the boom in Britain enjoyed by imported American films, jazz and other transatlantic crazes, American publishers showed commendable reciprocity in their dealings with English authors. But for the then wide-open American market, many English writers would have suffered far more severely from the prevalent post-war poverty and insecurity than was actually the case. Transatlantic hospitality was lavish and largely un-discriminating. Even third-rate scribblers, gifted with enough effrontery, found themselves able to sign contracts for profitable lecture tours. It is improbable that more than one in a thousand of these explorers saw anything of the " real " America, beyond the eastern fringe of Europeanized cosmopolitans.

The dominance of the American market in the domestic economy of our authors during the 'twenties, had the natural effect of creating a one-way traffic in literary treacle. The fact that the American publishing trade, largely built up during the nineteenth century out of the profits derived from piracy, owed something to the British literary profession did not detract from the gratitude of writers for being, at last, given a square deal. This agreeable situation unfortunately failed to survive the Wall Street crash.　The market then lost by the more deserving writers, not in the best-seller class, was never recovered.　To-day (1944) while some $27\frac{1}{2}$ per cent. of the scanty supplies of paper on which English authors have to depend for their living, is devoted to the production of books by Americans, many of which are trash, only $2\frac{1}{2}$ per cent. of American publications are of British origin. American interest in what the British people are thinking about international problems, in their reactions to the war, in what they are really like, appears to be non-existent.　Even highly intelligent American journalists, like Virginia Cowles, can come to our shores in a moment of crisis in our history and record her contacts with " Loelia Westminster and her brother Sysonby " as if they were really important.　If the English scene suddenly and visibly changes, as well it may, and all the familiar dolls and puppets are shoved unceremoniously into a cupboard, America will be as much aghast as it has been at the revelation that Vichy is not France.　Both the " White Cliffs of Dover " and Ye Olde Hollywood Englande, populated by patriotic baronets and obsequious yokels, will be revealed as celluloid fantasies, no more true to life than Mickey Mouse and Donald Duck.　If our publicists were allowed by the press lords to " answer back ", whenever American journalists indulge in hymns of hate at our expense, the present relations between the two countries would be on a far healthier and more hopeful basis than any but fools imagine it to be.　The way to American friendship, as Francis Francis pointed out nearly thirty years ago, is not by the path of " masterly understatement " or dignified silence, but by bold, combative, candid and good-natured retort. " Expediency " and appeasement have never yet paid a dividend or earned our banker-dominated Foreign Office anything except a long and dreary succession of kicks in the pants.

To attribute only to " appeasement " the dumb or servile attitude of the British press during the 'twenties towards the United States is perhaps over-simplification in view of what has occurred since 1942.　In the 'twenties, both liberal Americans and English progressives found themselves under the rule of governments whose principles they distrusted and whose actions they condemned.　It was consequently a matter of major importance to the reactionaries in both countries—then as now —to prevent as far as they could any free exchange of opinion between the intelligent and " idealistic " sections of their respective populations. Had the English been fully informed of the views prevalent among liberal Americans regarding British rule in India, to take an example, it would only have heartened those of the Left in this country who were agitating to give India Dominion status and increased the bonds of sympathy between democrats on both sides of the Atlantic. Similarly, if English Left wing opinion about the execution of Sacco and Vanzetti had been given a wide currency in the United States, American liberals, who fought so gallantly to secure the acquittal of these unfortunate men, would have been encouraged by realizing that the " real England " was on their side. A recent example of the sinister forces still at work to prevent the masses of anti-Fascist Englishmen from making contact with the millions of anti-Fascist Americans, was provided by the Darlan episode. Month after month the " Washington correspondents " of English " national " newspapers, suppressed the outburst of criticism in the anti-Fascist American press and only cabled extracts from the articles of Wall Street spokesmen. As a result a situation of extreme tension arose between the Allied nations, which only died down when it became evident that the pressure of American criticism, of which the English people had been studiously kept in ignorance, had modified the anti-Gaullist attitude of the State Department. The dangers inherent in the artificial barrier erected by the reactionaries to prevent any free interchange of public opinion between the two countries was stressed by Mr. Wendell Willkie in a speech which has, unfortunately, so far had but little effect.

If the American people learnt nothing about the real England during the 'twenties, the English were subjected to a flood of insidious propaganda about the United States which gave them an utterly false conception of that country and its inhabitants. Many Americans have protested that no nation in the world has ever been so misrepresented and vilified by a section of its own people as the United States has been by Hollywood.

The financial stranglehold obtained on the nascent European film industries by American capital, while it led to some technical advances in the mechanics of film production, such as the development of " talkies " and " technicolour ", had a disastrous effect on the minds and morals of the masses, particularly in Great Britain, the Dominions and the Colonial Empire. The new form of entertainment had such a widespread popular appeal, was so cheap and so quickly became easily accessible to all by the rapid development of " super-cinemas ", that a vast uncritical public readily accepted whatever in the way of film dramas was offered · to them.   Some of it was good ; but the outstanding genius of Charlie Chaplin and one or two others was more than counter-balanced by an incredible flow of garbage which, though sexually " pure ", from the American Roman Catholic standpoint, was profoundly immoral and demoralizing to populations whose traditional standards of civilized conduct had already been undermined by war.

In China we are told that the Japanese aggressors have been deliberately destroying all Universities, schools and cultural centres and at the same time attempting to undermine the moral stamina of the Chinese by promoting the sale of pernicious drugs like opium and heroin.   In France, the recent Nazi practice, with a similar object in view, is stated to have been to encourage pornography and sexual licence among the young.   It may reasonably be doubted whether these totalitarian policies have had a more deteriorating effect on the populations subjected to them than Hollywood films, crooners, and the baser sort of hot music have had on the English   A censorship of taste, had such an office been established, must have excluded at least 90 per cent. of the American films shown in our big cities and provincial towns.   The worst sufferers from the mental and moral infection were the " flappers " to whom Lord Baldwin accorded the privileges of adult citizens.   No doubt he rightly calculated that a body of nit-wit voters, easily swayed by hysteria, false values and synthetic glamour and incapable of thinking for themselves, would be a valuable asset to his Party.

A reasonable measure of protection, provided preference had been accorded, in view of their artistic merit, to the pictures made in Russia, France, Germany, Sweden and one or two other countries, would have given the British motion picture industry a chance to develop a native idiom, in competition with the best Continental productions.   Instead, no attempt was made to withstand the pressure of American finance or to enable the British people to protect themselves from the debauchery of the public taste by Hollywood propaganda.   Such censorship as was set up, by the industry itself, was concerned only with politics or with the cruder aspects of sex.   Gangster films " glamourizing " American crime were passed for general release, while continental pictures of outstanding artistic merit were either cut to pieces or banned altogether. Early Russian materpieces of cinematography, such as " Potemkin " and " Tempest over Asia ", were banned from public exhibition not, however, by the " Board of Censors " but by the Home Office. (That the same reactionary influences which operated to prevent the British public from seeing Russian films in 1927 are still at work, behind the scenes, in 1944, is indicated by the fact that Russian war films, sent for exhibition in this country, have been practically boycotted by the distributors, while a picture called " The Chetniks ", which represents Mihailovitch as the Yugloslavian patriot leader, has been released for general exhibition in English provincial towns. The Hemingway picture of the Spanish Civil War, " For Whom the Bell Tolls ", was emasculated of its political significance under pressure applied by General Franco and American Catholics.)

IV

As a footnote to this chapter it may be permissible to reprint here some passages from an article I wrote just before Ramsay MacDonald's futile visit to President Hoover, which a Sunday paper had the courage to print on August 11th, 1929. The captions were " Why Grovel to Uncle Sam ? Frank and healthy criticism far better than a cap-in-hand " Hush-Hush Policy." It was a solitary utterance, although the editor would not have printed it had he not known that it expressed what millions of Englishmen were thinking.

" Why do most of our newspapers and public spokesmen keep on grovelling to America ? " is a question which numbers of common-or-garden Englishmen have asked themselves in puzzled bewilderment during the past ten years.

The "authorities", the "people behind the scenes " and other wiseacres may know the reason. But to Tom, Dick and Harry, who have, when let alone, any amount of goodwill towards the American people, but no convinced belief in their moral and cultural superiority to the rest of mankind, it seems humiliating and unnecessary. It certainly does nothing to advance the cause of Anglo-American friendship.

Up to the time when President Hoover took office one could hardly open an English newspaper without reading such headlines as " Washington Annoyed ", "American opinion irritated ", " American Suspicions Aroused ", "American business man gives England advice."

" An American visitor to our shores, who finds that in regard to Anglo-American controversies most of our papers either rush to the assumption that Great Britain has no case, or else are clamorous with their reticences, can hardly be blamed if he gets an entirely wrong impression of the real state of English public opinion.   Our hush-hush policy prevents that frank and healthy exchange of ideas and criticisms which, to judge from their own journals, the American people understand and respect.   In a way, the proud but eloquent silences of the English Press regarding America are as insulting to the American people as the fawnings and tail-waggings of our " cousinly-love " school of writers are insulting to the British. . . .

There are certain outstanding facts about America which, to do them justice, the Americans themselves state openly and honestly in their papers and do their best, though without success, to get into our heads.   In the first place, America is a *foreign* country. The Anglo-Saxon element only barely predominates there.   Masses of her population, which is now almost as mixed as that of Europe, have names ending in "itch", "koff", "oulos", and the traditions, ideas and habits of mind which go with such terminations.   English politicians who persist in thinking of America in terms of an ex-British colony, who talk about " blood " being "thicker than water", and delude us into supposing that America has some special affection for this country, only still further inflame the already highly sensitive American nationalism against us.

The Americans came into the European war simply and solely as debt collectors.   They entered it, when Wall Street pressed the button, with the utmost astuteness, at precisely the right moment for themselves, and secured the maximum of spoil with the least possible expenditure of blood.   Since that time, to quote Mr. H. L. Mencken, they have " put England on board wages."

Our treatment by America since the Armistice has been in essentials little different from that which a fairly tolerant Power might be expected to accord a defeated enemy.   Her policy has been, again to quote the editor of *The American Mercury*, " to put England in a plain and incurable second place " in European affairs, as a prelude to putting her in this subservient position throughout the world."

After referring to the strong body of progressive opinion in the United States which had, up till then, kept the sabre-rattling Imperialists of Wall Street in check, the article goes on to point out that the world had, unfortunately, had " abundant evidence during the past ten years that the real power behind the American throne is vested in a gang of financiers whose policy is selfish, grasping and materialistic. We cannot forget how quickly the well-meaning Wilson, after he had served his purpose in bamboozling the war-distracted peoples of Europe with his lofty moral sentiments, was shoved on one side by Wall Street. . . .

Taking a long view, it is impossible to dissociate the plans of the " big navy " group in America from the economic policy displayed in her recent proposals to build her tariff wall still higher, while at the same time preparing, on a scale hitherto unprecedented, to dump her goods on Europe and the British Dominions.

This policy, which means a lowered standard of living for the working classes of nearly every European country, has done more to advance the idea of a United States of Europe than anything that has happened for centuries. As the Italian representative observed, in guarded language, at the recent International Labour Conference at Geneva, the United States are " developing a vast economic invasion of other countries solely from the point of view of North American interests, and in an atmosphere outside the economic policy of the League of Nations and the social policy of the International Labour Office. . . ." A generation hence, if the United States succeed in forcing the principal nations of Europe into an economic union to resist her commercial rapacity, England may be found once again filling her historic role of maintaining the balance of power. American prosperity, marvellous as it is, clearly holds within it the seeds of its own decay."

The slump in American prosperity thus predicted began a few months after this article appeared. Ten years later, after preliminary trials of strength in Abyssinia, Spain, Austria and Czechoslovakia, Hitler began his attempt to create a United Europe, with the vast wealth of the American continent as his ultimate objective. The common people of England rejected the Conservative policy of collaboration—which had gone so far as the discussion of a loan to Nazi Germany of £1,000 million of British money—denounced appeasement and forced the Governing clique to fight not only for their own survival as a free people but in defence of the United States. What their reward will be, since the political development of the United States is fifty years behind that of England, France and other progressive European countries, and her immediate political future, is, at this writing, unpredictable even to Americans, no one can attempt to foretell.   Mr. Churchill has blandly informed us that we are " going rolling along with America " ; which America does he mean ?   The America of Wall Street reaction- aries, which appears to be heading for inflation and possibly civil war, the America of far-sighted statesmen and " idealists " like Mr. Henry Wallace, or the liberal, reasonable and generous America which President Roosevelt and Mr. Wendell Willkie seem to represent ? He does not, cannot, know ; nor do we ; nor do the best-informed and most enlightened American citizens. We can but hope for the best and take heed of the danger signals.

CHAPTER FIVE

THE NEW MORALITY

I

UP till August 1914 there were still many young women of the middle and upper classes who could truthfully assert that they were " mere children " when they married and learnt the facts of life only when their husbands initiated them.   A few months later such children might find themselves being de- flowered on the benches of dim-lit railway waiting-rooms by boys whose expectation of life was often a matter only of days, if not of hours.   Moral precepts were quickly consumed in the flames of pity and love and the maiden, if opportunity came her way, gave herself gladly to the young warrior about to die. Hundreds of thousands of girls, till then preserved in cotton-wool wrappings of gentility and innocence, joined the W.A.A.C.'s or trained as nurses and became V.A.D.'s, and were thus suddenly, by the tide of war, brought face to face with its realities of suffering and destruction.   Mingled with all the horror of those years, there was a strange and terrible beauty, a beauty born of self- sacrifice, heroism, comradeship and the blossoming and fulfilment of youthful passion in the very jaws of death.

What followed when the unnatural strain, excitement and nervous tension of the war was relaxed was natural, inevitable, easily predictable and, in the long run, probably good.   Dr. Freud's psycho-analytical theories, which had been promulgated before the war without attracting much attention, now became the rage among the intellectuals and psuedo-scientific jargon

about " repressions ", " complexes ", " escapism " and " psychological compensation " was employed to explain phenomena
which anyone of commonsense might have anticipated. Only
fools could have supposed that women could be employed to do
men's work and share men's perils, without being accorded the
rights and privileges of equal citizenship. As women are nothing
if not practical, their first claims to emancipation were less concerned with the vote, which was granted them by stages without
any further agitation on their part, than with the abolition of
their social, sexual and economic disabilities. Having been
subjected to much the same physical and emotional stress as men,
they demanded, after the Armistice, the right to indulge in what
had hitherto been regarded as exclusively male relaxations.
Put in a crude form, it was useless to tell a woman who had
driven a heavy lorry for a hundred miles that it was immodest
of her to go into a pub and order a pint of beer at the end of her
journey. It was equally useless to keep up the " fallen woman "
nonsense if she chose to satisfy her natural appetites without
benefit of clergy. In a word, she became sexually adult and the
terms " boy friend " and " girl friend " registered a wholesome
change of outlook, without affecting the general pattern of human
behaviour, which in regard to sex relations, never fundamentally
changes. For the majority of women, in the 'twenties as in
every other period, marriage, motherhood, professional activity
or hard physical labour continued to absorb creative energy and
thus to make what is technically known as " virtue " the desirable
and appropriate way of life. The difference between the
'twenties and preceding generations was less a matter of behaviour
than of the prevalent mental attitude towards " sex expression ".
The younger generation of those who chose the path of virtue,
and were lucky enough to find jobs or husbands, became less
censorious about their sisters, especially as many of them had at
one time or another exercised their newly-accorded right to
sow wild oats. The point should, however, be stressed that if
post-war emancipation established the right of woman to behave
as an adult and to do as she pleased with her own body, the result of
this freedom did not necessarily prevent her from being any less
wifely and maternal than her grandmother. Except for the rich,
who can always afford the time to be " immoral ", sentiment as
well as economic necessity made the home worth defending by
those fortunate enough to have a roof over their heads and
husbands capable of paying the rent. On the other hand, owing

to the housing shortage and the lowered standard of living for the middle-classes, family limitation became a necessity.

As if in answer to prayer came the publication of " Married Love ", by Dr. Marie Stopes, which by popularizing a safe and easy method of contraception, laid the foundations of a new morality. As was to have been expected, the attitude of the established churches, especially the Roman Catholic Church, towards Birth Control, was violently hostile and reactionary. The sheep in this, as in so many instances, were more enlightened than the shepherds.

It was natural that after four years of senseless massacre in which the young were killed, while their parents, if in commerce, grew rich from their slaughter, there should be a revolt against the Death Worship, later revealed as the animating principle in Nazi-Fascism, and a corresponding demand for the right to live and love. The pioneers of the new morality turned a critical eye on " Sin "—the great Victorian aphrodisiac and lynch-pin of the now decaying social system—and, as regards the natural act of love-making, abolished it. Copulation, far from being coarse and disgusting, far from being a deplorable triumph of man's Lower Nature over his nobler instincts, was, they asserted, the most inspiring and the most spiritually healthgiving of human joys. It was, in fact, a Good Thing, like singing, dancing, sunbathing, swimming and taking wine with friends. But even Good Things must be used in moderation and with due respect for human rights. The new moral code, which supplanted " Sin ", after an experimental period of trial and error—usually referred to by the pre-war generation as " unbridled licence "—was therefore based principally upon man's duty to his neighbour. It became, in effect, an enlightened interpretation of the principles laid down in the Church Catechism. The new morality was designed to protect the individual from the anti-social effects of mere selfish indulgence, thus safeguarding what Edward Carpenter called " Love's coming-of-age ". The young man who obeyed the injunction to love his neighbour as himself could, clearly, do nothing to injure her mind, soul, body, social life or economic position. Thus the sins to be shunned by those desirous of living the good life were such actions as bringing unwanted children into the world, transmitting venereal disease, destroying homes, ruining lives, tampering with adolescents of either sex and condoning prostitution. The abolition of prostitution, as women were quick to realize, involved the discarding of the Victorian fetish of

virginity.   The existence, after the war, of some two million
"surplus women", made Victorian ideas on this subject, in any
case, no longer tenable.

Since writing the above, I have come across a passage in
"Brought Out in Evidence : an Autobiographical summing-up",
by William Bowyer, which to some extent corroborates my general
conclusions about the new ideas of sex morality which gained
prevalence among the *intelligentsia* of the 'twenties.   Among
most Socialists and all feminists, however, there was the strong
dislike of all forms of prostitution, to which I have referred.

" I had no scruples about fornication in itself," Mr. Bowyer
states, " only about deception and desertion.   These were immoral, sins against the Charity I believed in ; the rest was only
tribal law gone sour.   Immoral rather were the uncharitable
censoriousness and prudery that wished to deny the right of free
and equal men and women to take pleasure in each other's
bodies, whether they were the same or the other sex.   Seduction
involving deception was plainly a sin, but this was not, and to
indulge a natural appetite with a woman whose profession it was
to give it the completest satisfaction would involve no infraction
of any law I believed in, any more than eating or drinking for
pleasure. . . . I could not forget the cynical remark by a former
college that the only difference between the virtuous ones and the
others was that the others were cleaner and knew their job."

To the attitude of mind betrayed by the remark Mr. Bowyer
quotes, the free-loving idealists—or perhaps sentimentalists—
would have taken strong exception.   Their point of view was
more clearly expressed in Miles Malleson's play "The Fanatics",
which was produced with considerable success in 1927.

A necessary concomitant of what I have called the " trial and
error " period, was a new freedom of discussion among the
advanced of both sexes, of what had hitherto been regarded as
forbidden topics.   Woman, as " comrade", claimed the right
(however much her good taste might preclude its exercise) to
share men's jokes, use his vocabulary, and drop the pretence that
her physical desires, appetites and satisfactions were radically
different from his own.   Women sat on juries with men, and
judges had to resign themselves to their insistence on listening to
the evidence in scabrous cases, instead of leaving the Court in
a ladylike manner.   Moreover, since women and children are the

chief sufferers from venereal infections, intelligent women began to take a lively and active interest in hygienic questions which they had previously been discouraged from studying. Exhilarating draughts of fresh air blew in through the cracked panes of many respectable Victorian windows, dark cupboards were unlocked and all the closely-guarded secrets of Victorian pornography revealed to amused and irreverent inspection. Oral tradition tells us that Lord Tennyson, behind a row of calf-bound eighteenth century theological works, had an extensive collection of "curious" books. His contemporary, Monckton Milnes, Lord Houghton, author of an instructive little poem called "Shadows", also had a large library of " curiosa " in which the youthful Swinburne is said to have browsed with exciting, if deplorable, consequences. When " Sin " was dangerous and had to be concealed under a thick cloak of outward respectability, it was highly enjoyable and lent a gambler's zest to life, since to be found out was to be socially ruined. Once brought into the open and inspected by the young with cynical amusement, it quickly lost its glamour. At a party given by Bright Young People in the early 'twenties, the writer heard a Mayfair lovely read aloud, amid shouts of girlish laughter, passages from the works of Krafft-Ebbing and Havelock Ellis which she had just unearthed in the library of her grandfather, a retired major-general of extreme respectability. Her grandmother, had she been present, would have endured an agony worse than death.

The more serious-minded and idealistic of the post-war generation busied themselves not only with questions of hygiene and family limitation, but with the sex-education of children and adolescents. During the 'twenties, the auto-erotic indulgences common to both sexes, and in themselves natural and harmless, began at last to be treated by advanced parents and school-masters in the light of commonsense. The bugaboos of shame and fear, which haunted so many Victorian children and had such pernicious psychological effects on them, were dissipated by sympathy and understanding. Those in charge of the young ceased to be "shocked", abandoned humbug and inculcated continence more by an appeal to reason than by threats of hell.

Since no one but a doctor or a scientist, with the necessary data at his disposal, can set up to write a sexual history of his time with any claim to authority, the most that a mere layman can do is to record general impressions, based on his own experiences and observations.

II

Fashions in behaviour, as well as mental attitudes, are largely affected by two numerically small classes : the class which has the most money to spend and absorbs most of the social limelight, and the class which creates ideas, concerns itself with the arts and disseminates knowledge.   For a period during the 'twenties —the period of " unbridled licence "—the two became very much mixed up and formed together a Bohemia which touched Mayfair at one extremity and Bloomsbury and the Provinces at the other. It was populated both by the products of public schools and Oxford and Cambridge and by those of elementary schools and provincial universities, by " degenerate " young aristocrats and by intelligent and insurgent youth uninhibited by any social background, by disillusioned ex-servicemen out only for fun and games, and by Socialists and pacifists, out to save the world from human bondage.   It contained among its literary leaders bourgeois Etonians like Aldous Huxley, hereditary aristocrats like the Sitwells, detached and sardonic satirists like Wyndham Lewis, messianic geniuses like D. H. Lawrence, and a whole host of sub-Huxleys and sub-Lawrences of both sexes.   It contained co-educationists, Morris-dancers, vegetarians, teetotallers, professors of Economics, drug-takers, boozers, Socialists, gossip columnists, playwrights, Communists, Roman Catholic converts, painters and poets—some bearded, some beardless—actors, actresses, politicians, playboys, idealists and cranks.   From this emancipated group, from their sayings and doings and from the novels they wrote about themselves and each other, a stream of new and iconoclastic ideas was disseminated among the educated and half-educated masses.   As art, sex, religion and politics are indissolubly intermingled, it may be presumed that these ideas had a stimulating effect on the minds of a large section of the population, though what influence they had on the sex behaviour of the average young person must be a matter for conjecture.   It seems safe to assert that as regards normal sexual intercourse a great deal of deleterious hypocrisy and humbug went out of fashion.   I have not seen statistics regarding prostitution and venereal disease but I should be surprised to learn that they had not fallen to an appreciable extent, between 1919 and 1939. The harder working sections of the community, the great majority of wage and salary earners, naturally observe a decent reticence about their private lives.   No one, however, can fail to be aware that it has now become quite usual for respectable engaged couples to live together before marriage, with excellent results on their health, morals and prospect of future happiness.   The " companionate " union—which if unsatisfactory becomes a "trial trip", to be terminated without hard feelings—has become an established feature of our national life, although to mention the fact may provoke the usual uproar.   Parents, for the most part, now make a virtue of necessity and leave the young to manage their own affairs, supplying advice and first aid only when asked for them.   In cases where the authorities, in their blindness and folly, penalize civil servants, school teachers or bank clerks for daring to marry, the victims of such interference may dispense with the ceremony in order to keep their jobs but rarely regard themselves as under any moral obligation to refrain from letting nature take its course.   Laws and regulations affecting the liberty of the subject, which are contrary to the moral conscience of the community, are invariably evaded.   The succession of bad governments imposed on Great Britain during the 'twenties and 'thirties, led to a continuance of Dora's evil progeny, which had much the same effect, in regard to the manufacture of crime and the corruption of the police, as Prohibition had in America.

The much publicized amorality and " free love " of the 'twenties was a godsend both to reactionary politicians and the churches.   To the former, it gave their campaign against " Bolshevism " a cloak of moral uplift which went down well with the class which subsequently admired the Christian gentility of General Franco.   To the latter, it provided an excuse for neglecting the duty they owed to their country and their God, of rebuking spiritual wickedness in high places.   While Bishops foamed with righteous rage at the idea of naughty boys and girls copulating on Wimbledon Common, they turned a blind eye to such matters as our rulers' conduct towards Ireland and India, to the housing scandal, the Means Test and the shameless treatment of the miners.   Their cowardice, though it was by no means universal—the Church of England, thanks to the efforts of a group of enthusiastic young clergymen has, on the whole, an excellent record in regard to housing—did much to bring organized religion into disrepute.

As a footnote to all the hubbub and commotion about the sexual freedom, " licence " and—in the case of a small handful of Bright Young People—" shameless debauchery " of the 'twenties, we can at least record one salient fact. Never, within the memory of anyone now living, has Britain produced a finer generation of boys and girls than those begotten between 1915 and 1925. The young men who fought the Battle of Britain and, when at last they were provided with adequate arms and reasonably competent leadership, won victory after victory, were conceived by parents who had fought for Freedom and were inspired by Hope. How Freedom, particularly the free expression of ideas in books and newspapers, was shackled, how hopes withered, under the blighting rule of the Conservative oligarchy, are the salient features of the history of the Armistice Years.

What may be history's final verdict on the 'forties, no one can at present predict. All we can be sure of in this country is that the flood of liberating ideas let loose in the early 'twenties have germinated and taken root, awakened the minds and consciences of many millions of our compatriots and will eventually decide the issue in their favour. The " new morality " forged in the 'twenties was not merely a matter of sexual ethics but comprised a re-statement of the age-old creed of Humanism. Though many of its most ardent adherents have rejected Christianity, few can deny that, as Dr. Sun-Yat-Sen once pointed out, the basis of Western Humanism, new or old, rests upon the revolutionary teaching of Jesus Christ.

CHAPTER SIX

The Cult of Gentility

I

FOR a few marvellous years in the early 'twenties, as I have already remarked, the younger artists and intellectuals, and their associated girl friends had their uninhibited fling. The writer looks back on them as the happiest in his life. To revert to jargon, they were years of " psychological compensation " for what preceded them. I pity those of my colleagues—however rich and illustrious they may be—who were either too old or too young to enjoy them.

Writers of my age and generation have suffered under severe handicaps. Two major wars in one lifetime, apart from their economic consequences for what is humorously regarded as a "luxury profession", have been too much of an emotional strain for any except the major talents or those protected from the

E

harsh winds of adversity by what are called "private means". My natural inclinations, if a personal illustration may be excused, lie in the fields of scholarship, historical research, travel and the appreciation of architecture and the plastic arts. Had I belonged to an earlier generation, I could have followed my predilections with pleasure, profit and possibly some small degree of public approval. I should have had the necessary leisure to cultivate the polished prose style required of contributors to the more distinguished reviews, and, at the end of my life, I should have had the thrill of looking on at a world war without having to take any active or dangerous part in it. Finally, I should have died after witnessing my country's triumph, secure in the belief that a new era of peace and prosperity had dawned for a distracted world. It would be surprising to find what a large number of Victorian authors managed to survive into the 'twenties, were it not for the known fact that life, or at least the desire to live, can be prolonged by curiosity. Curiosity is, perhaps, the one quality which all writers share in common. Marie Corelli, Hall Caine, Mrs. Humphrey Ward, Stanley Weyman and dozens of other "Old Gods", as Mr. Malcolm Elwin calls them, managed to linger on to see what happened and, let us hope, died very contented with what they thought they saw. Those of us who were in the early 'thirties when the war ended had to carry on our professional activities amid the wreckage of the past, but under the moral obligation, imposed by *l'honneur du métier*, to do what we could to prepare the way for the future. Weeds grew apace in the Waste Land, rank growths of greed, corruption and brutality, but the flowers and the fruit trees native to the soil still contrived a precarious blossoming. In order to protect them we were forced to become politically-minded at the expense of our art.

Amid the disillusion caused by the years of massacre and muddle, the profiteering by the commercial classes and the apparent lack of any " ideological " gains and compensations for so much suffering and loss, there were grounds for hope, even excuses for joy. As regards its conduct by the Government, World War One was at least comparatively clean. Lloyd George and his Cabinet had honestly tried to win it and, in spite of mutual jealousies, incompetence and occasional acts of sabotage by the naval and military mandarins, they had succeeded. The mephitic odours of treachery in high places which have already poisoned World War Two, prolonged it unnecessarily and made so many Conservative Fifth Columnists fearful of its end, were not sufficiently apparent to cause widespread perturbation or revulsion in the public mind. Thousands of young lives had been uselessly sacrificed by incompetent generals, but no one suspected the brass-hats of not being "on our side". Like its many predecessors, it was a national war, fought against an aggressive and powerful enemy nation, and while it continued there was no fundamental difference in aim between the leaders and the led. In consequence it did not stink, except in the nostrils of a handful of Pacifists and Reds, and those who died in it only died in vain because they were subsequently betrayed. There seemed no reason, in the early 'twenties, to believe that Great Britain and the world would not, at last, be set free from the scourge of recurrent conflicts. There was no reason, then, for thinking that the wreckage of the four years' struggle would not quickly be cleared away and a new and better Britain built on firm foundations. The Armistice was soon followed by an outburst of creative energy. The idealists, free at last to raise their voices, shouted their ideals from the housetops, and actually believed that the cautious middle-aged careerists in the Labour Party shared them. The younger generation, as events proved, fatally misjudged the power, the astuteness and the solidarity of the old. But, in the few years which elapsed before the General Strike was first provoked and then crushed—with a completeness which set back the political clock for twenty years—we had our glimpses of "the dawn". Looking back, I would not exchange those years of penury and excitement for decades of sheltered ease in any Ivory Tower. Love, laughter and the fullness of living are worth more, in youth, than hours in libraries and the creation and propagation of ideas one fondly imagines to be one's own are more satisfying to the soul than the subsequent discovery that everything that can be thought has been thought before, that everything that can be said has already been expressed. That the act of giving birth is a mere repetition of a familiar process, does not diminish a mother's joy in fulfilling her natural function, and giving birth to ideas is a natural function of the writer.

II

What divided the Bohemia of the Intellectuals in the 'twenties, after their too brief period of solidarity, good-time-seeking and general high jinks, was the power and influence of Money. At first, those who made money out of the war were regarded by all decent people as the scum of the earth, as undeniably they were and are. No one had any money in 1920 except the profiteers. Admittedly, the war ruined the best people and exalted and enriched the worst. The worst, however, seemed singularly indifferent to the opinion of their betters. Having all the cash, they were able to buy up the things which cash procures, which, barring what may be called "imponderables", was soon shown to be pretty nearly everything. Their sons went to Eton and Harrow, to Oxford and Cambridge, joined the smartest clubs, went into politics or into the Foreign Office, and married into the " old " families. Their daughters were " finished " at expensive schools, quickly acquired a Mayfair accent and the art of spending. They smoked "the cigarette that bears a lipstick's traces", they bought "the air-line tickets to romantic places". Some of them patronized literature, the theatre and the ballet, bought the pictures of promising young painters and even slept with them. The profiteers owned almost all the Press, and therefore employed most of the journalists, while a few planted their sons in the publishing trade. As Money had control of the Government machine, it controlled all the Government jobs. Ambitious young men from the universities quickly discovered on which side their bread was buttered and who buttered it.

To the newly-enriched whose overmastering determination was to get back to 1914 "and all that", and thus to cover up the origins of their wealth, the activities of the iconoclastic writers and avant-gardist painters savoured of Bolshevism and were naturally anathema. Since they could not suppress the D. H. Lawrences, they encouraged, by all the means in their power, a sounder school of fiction which upheld what they were pleased to regard as "the old, sane values". What those values really were was ruthlessly revealed by the publication of a novelette called "The Young Visiters", written by a precocious schoolgirl of nine who, in her home, had evidently imbibed British snobbery in its purest form.

" ' You can help me perhaps to be more like a gentleman,' said Mr. Salteena, getting rather hot. ' I am quite alright as they say, but I would like to be the real thing ; can it be done,' he added, slapping his knees.

" ' I don't quite know,' said Bernard. ' It might take a good time. I can give you a letter to my old pal, the Earl of Clincham . . . he might rub you up, and by mixing with him you would probably grow more seemly.' "

Mr. Salteena calls on the Earl and confesses he is not a gentleman.

" ' Well, my man,' said the good-natured Earl, ' what I say is, what does it matter, we can't all be of the Blood Royal, can we ? '

" ' No,' said Mr. Salteena, ' but I suppose you are.' Lord Clincham waved a careless hand. ' A small portion flows in my veins,' he said, ' but it does not worry me at all, and after all,' he added piously, ' at the Day of Judgment, what will be the odds?'

" Mr. Salteena heaved a sigh. ' I was thinking of this world,' he said."

In a letter to his " old pal ", Bernard observes of Mr. Salteena that he is " not quite the right side of the blanket as they say. In fact he is the son of a first-rate butcher, but his mother was a decent family called Hyssopps of the Glen."

Undoubtedly some of the secret motives and attitudes of the post-war rich were unconsciously satirised by Miss Daisy Ashford, and much of the popular fiction of the 'twenties, even of the sophisticated sub-Huxley school, showed as much awareness of the " old sane values " as Bernard and Mr. Salteena. Etonian Salteenas, though adopting a slightly contemptuous and superior attitude, were careful to stud their novels with " thorough ancestors ", " sinister sons of Queen Victoria ", and Earls of Clincham. P. G. Wodehouse cleverly preserved the sane values while making them funny. The novels of Gilbert Frankau, Alec Waugh, G. B. Stern, Angela Thirkell and Dennis Mackail, to mention a few deservedly popular names, are interesting for the light they shed on the way best-sellers helped to maintain and develop the pre-war association of property with class distinction. Meanwhile, the new cosmopolitan café-society—the Rolls-Royce-Ritz-Carlton world—was both castigated and " glamourized " by popular playwrights like Noel Coward and Somerset Maugham. As the decade drew to its close, more and more writers and journalists were caught, conditioned and tamed and the economic situation of those who continued to aspire to " independent thinking " became increasingly difficult.

The word "propaganda", the dictionary meaning of which is " association, organized scheme for propagation of a doctrine or practice ", was seized upon as a term of abuse for Left Wing authors who were certainly not " organized ", had no " associates " and merely expressed, as individuals, what they believed to be true. So loud was the outcry against these so-called " propaganda novels " that no one noticed the fact that ninety per cent.

of the commercial fiction approved, pushed and publicized by the Money Power and its press, was in fact " propaganda " for all the pre-war social values, for owners of "old school ties", for really " nice " people, for the Colonel, the Squire, the diplomatic attaché, the Foreign Office clique, and the titled bureaucrat. It was, in short, reactionary "propaganda", aimed at encouraging snobbery, stimulating fear of Bolshevism in the middle-classes and, in the event of a class war, preventing them from siding with artists and the unwashed common people who " kept their coals in the bath tub."

Even the purveyors of "whodunits", the manufacture of which soon became a large and profitable industry, usually laid the scenes of their murders in manor houses, complete with butlers, footmen and titled guests, and often made their Scotland Yard detectives either graduates of Oxford University or nephews of peers.   The types most favoured as villains were artists, Bolsheviks or " long-haired " poets.   As I frankly confess myself a 'tec story addict, I open a characteristic example, just borrowed from the library, to illustrate my point.   The hero is a young doctor, Donald Crombie, who has been struck off the register for some incredibly noble (but illegal) operation.   He is a hundred-per-cent. he-man, rugger-player, skier, strong, clean, etc.   In Switzerland he meets Allegra, who has just inherited a useful £600,000 and is staying at the same hotel at Mürren.   She is also a good skier, but nevertheless, from Crombie's standpoint, gets into a Bad Set.

" ' You don't like them (the Bad Set) ? ' Allegra asks.   ' Oh, be frank.   Why don't you like them ? '

" ' I prefer not to go into details,' says Crombie.   ' There is a particular man here .   Don't you realize that his name is mud in decent people's ears ?   He may possess genius, but that doesn't excuse other things.   Allegra, be careful.   Don't alienate yourself from all that is decent through sheer impulse.' "

The genius whose name is mud turns out to be a painter, and with him is a poet, " whose lines never scanned, and whose meaning was about as clear as mud . . .   It was astonishing that in an hotel in which there were some two hundred guests, the vast majority of whom were charming people, Allegra should almost instinctively gather to herself the wildest elements."

There was " the artist Lacoste, who worked on Surrealist lines and was a rage in Paris and London ".   Crombie subsequently hears from a fellow-guest who has a friend " in a high position at

Scotland Yard", that Lacoste is "absolutely a wash-out. All kinds of things take place in his studio". No doubt, if I were to read on, I should discover that Lacoste and his poet friend were secretly in league with Moscow and notoriously addicted to such nameless horrors as the Russian ballet. The habitual denigration, by novelists who designed their goods for the Conservative middle-class market, of artists, poets and other members of the *intelligentsia* was a natural result of the struggle for the soul of the younger generation which raged throughout the 'twenties. Allegra was not exceptional in being bored by "charming people" and instinctively gathering to herself "the wildest elements". In the battle of the "two Britains", there were constant defections from the Conservative ranks into those of the intellectuals, who, for the most part, had thrown in their lot with the masses and turned Left in politics. The artist, the novelist of ideas and honest freelance journalists who sought to express the truth that was in them, without regard to the financial consequences, exercised a powerful attraction over the idealistic young, particularly as the Bad Sets they had a habit of forming were infinitely more amusing than the Good Sets which plutocratic post-war hostesses endeavoured to establish. It was maddening to the new peers to see their sons and daughters deserting the social altitudes to which they had so painfully struggled for admission, for the delights of artistic "café-society" and the squalid pleasures of "Bohemia". No wonder the Fascists of the future, the fawning admirers of Mussolini—and, when they emerged, of Hitler and Franco—feared and detested all these subversive influences. No wonder the well-paid lackeys in their publicity department—the tamed press man and popular fiction writer— played up to all their prejudices. No wonder, in the 'twenties, the names of Aldous Huxley, Siegfried Sassoon, D. H. Lawrence, James Joyce, Richard Aldington and their like, were "mud" in the ears of the respectable. Even the present writer can claim as one of the few heartening incidents of his career the fact that a wealthy cousin, pillar of the suburban middle-class, forbade his children ever to bring one of his books "into the house."

An enormous fillip to the propaganda organized by the Conservative ruling class in favour of bogus gentility and against the liberating ideas of the "New Morality", was provided by the establishment of the British Broadcasting Corporation, under the control of an able Scotch engineer, a son of the manse, who was educated at a minor English public school without proceeding to a major English university. Of Lord Reith's organizing ability there can be no question. Unfortunately, combined with this was an almost morbid veneration of the " old school tie " and its genteel conventions which, owing to the strength of his personality, he was able to impose on his staff.

In the early Savoy Hill days I used to visit a friend employed by the B.B.C., who had to be in attendance after dinner although he had practically nothing to do till midnight. To mitigate his boredom, he used to give small parties, and as liquor was strictly forbidden on the premises, the guests arrived with half-bottles of Haig, which we drank out of tooth glasses. When the party broke up, it was the practice to carry away the empties and put them behind the seats of the taxis which took us home. My friend, who had to be dressed in a white tie and tails, was provided with a retiring-room, complete with looking-glass and dressing-table, to which he repaired before saying his piece. This occurred at twelve o'clock, when he had to go to the microphone and announce : " That concludes our programme. Good-nate, evrabuddy. Good-nate." Not only were the announcers made to dress the part of "gentleman", but they were expected, as regards their private lives, to conform to standards of a quasi-monastic asceticism. To counteract any tendency on the part of the staff to adultery, fornication and loose morals, a remarkable system of snooping and gestapo-like espionage was established of which Mr. Lees-Smith, a former Postmaster-General, revealed particulars to an astonished House of Commons.

Irritating to the public as were the Scotch sermons, the talks in Gaelic, and all the plugging and publicizing of crude Lowland uplift and religiosity, the final insult to English listeners was "B.B.C. Variety". In spite of the wealth of professional talent available—we have only to imagine what C. B. Cochran would have done with this department, if he had been given a chance—the direction of the programmes was entrusted to amateurs whose only qualifications seemed to be the possession of " old school ties " and university degrees. As a result, entertainments were provided more insipid than anything ever heard outside a charity concert got up by a curate in a parish hall. A girl I knew once got a temporary job with the B.B.C. as an " applauder " at these grisly performances. At signals given by the " applause mistress", the girls had to laugh heartily at jokes by " cross-talk comedians " which were already stale in the far-off days of the Moore and Christy Minstrels. She was paid ten shillings a day and told me she had never endured so much to earn so little.

As a great many highly talented men and women managed to get jobs under the B.B.C. umbrella—though not always to keep them—the programmes quickly improved. Certain things were done superbly well, and indeed it would be easy to write a column in praise of selected activities of the B.B.C. without being either fulsome or departing from the truth. This does not alter the fact that there was, and is, something like a cancer at the heart of the Corporation, caused by its repression of what, to the reactionary controlling minds, are dangerous thoughts, by its cult of bogus "refanement", and its fixed determination to turn its artists and its intellectuals into *bureaucrats*.

Whether the legendary figure of "Admiral Carpendale" ever existed, or was merely a fictional character, invented by dismissed members of the staff to describe the kind of "interviewing officer" who assisted Lord Reith to weed out aspirants to the fame-conferring "mike", I cannot pretend to judge. "Carps", at any rate, was credited with insisting on a sort of Quarter-deck discipline, confining his crew as far as possible to officers and gentlemen. Wags used to relate that his first question to Little Tich (or some equally famous comedian) was what public school were you at?

I was reminded of these fabulous stories of the 'twenties when, after I had bombarded the B.B.C. for employment during the present war, they at last summoned me to London and went through the motions of considering my application. It occurred to me, in my innocence, that although of an advanced age—I was only fifteen years younger than our septuagenarian Prime Minister—I might be considered still capable of performing some menial task, of a literary kind, which would set free one of the junior members of the staff for military service. The room into which I was ushered contained long trestle tables at each side, lined with members of the interviewing committee. At a table crossing the two ends sat the Chairman, with my dossier in front of him. The applicant faced him, with two "psychologists" or snoopers, on either hand, who could watch his reactions without being observed. I had anticipated that I should be put through my literary and journalistic career but, tc my amazement, the Chairman started by reading out the name of the preparatory school (fortunately a good one) which I had attended at the age of ten! The job for which I was being tested was simple sub-editing work of the kind which my younger boy, Patrick, was doing without much difficulty at seventeen. They seemed dubious of my being able to learn the somewhat elementary task required of me, and one of the younger " examiners " genially remarked : " You know, Mr. Goldring, you wouldn't really much like coming to an office regularly every day." To which I replied that, if it came to that, my two sons hadn't very much liked leaving their jobs and getting into uniform at the beginning of the war. As the greater number of the Committee appeared to be of military age, this remark must have blotted my copy book for my application was rejected. I felt rather as Tich must have felt when cross-examined by " Carps."

What would have given the *intelligentsia* its chance in the 'twenties would have been the multiplication of new periodicals under the control not of their proprietors but of their editors. This would have provided them with new markets and the possibility thereby of appealing to a wider public. Unfortunately for England, the profiteers had no interest either in keeping intellectuals alive, or in permitting them to disseminate their opinions and, as has already been noted, the number of existing periodicals, instead of increasing, was sensibly diminished. As papers got fewer and circulations larger, much of the character and guts of those which survived were overlaid by commercial considerations. The advertising revenue had a restraining effect on editorial policy which, in any case, was more and more dictated by proprietors. The effect on the journalists who managed to retain employment when staffs were broken up and scattered was to increase their technical efficiency at the expense of their intellectual integrity. They were highly paid, their standard of living went up, and those who became " star turns " received a great deal more personal publicity than under pre-war conditions. Those who were " literary " became, like the staff of the B.B.C., bureaucratized. They joined expensive clubs, eschewed "vehemence", since they had no fire in their bellies or faith in what they wrote, and cultivated that " genius for understatement " which Victorians like Charles Reade and Scawen Blunt would have regarded as a polite name for moral cowardice. The only writers they dared to slate were those unable to answer back.

Reviewing, at least in the more influential newspapers, fell largely into the hands of a group of well-paid author-critics, who developed an astonishing degree of mutual admiration, automatically praised each other's masterpieces and boycotted, as far as possible, the avantgardists and iconoclasts. "This practice", says E. F. Benson, in his book "As We Are", "initiated by Arnold Bennett, of authors doubling with their own work that of regular and professional critics, has become a very general institution. Some, like him, having attained eminence as novelists, brought their prestige to bear on their new function; others sought to overscore their failure in the creative line by critical acidity; others, by a continual diet of novels, hoped to build themselves up into writers. Between them there came into being a ring of critics, all of whom were fairly prominent authors (or at least have tried to be) who can hardly help looking with a favourable eye on each other's works, aware that when their new books come out, favourable eyes will be turned on them, and they will be certain of a ' good press.' "

To the living literature of the 'twenties, the author-critics and their associated gangsters did all the harm they could. They encouraged the genteel fiction, written for the profitable middle-class market, which they themselves turned out, either ignored or sneered at the work of writers like Ford Madox Ford, James Joyce, Wyndham Lewis, and D. H. Lawrence, fell over themselves in their eagerness to applaud the literary efforts of the " socially-prominent "—who entertained lavishly—and failed to notice the budding talents of the socially and politically undesirable. Their last concerted action, as an organized gang, was the spit on the grave of D. H. Lawrence, almost before his body was cold. As they have now faded into obscurity, and the books they praised are as dead as the books they wrote, no purpose would be served by resurrecting their pronouncements.

CHAPTER SEVEN

The Pub and the Club

I

No one who has seen something of life at all income levels, both before and after 1914, can pretend that the poverty and insecurity which are the allotted portion of such of the *intelligentsia* as choose to maintain their integrity during a revolutionary epoch do not result in a good deal of squalor and are not the breeding-ground of what are called "neuroses". As regards the latter,

Arthur Koestler has, I believe, pointed out the truth. " Those who attack the *intelligentsia* for its neurotic dispositions," he observes, " might as well attack the miners for their susceptibility to T.B. It is a professional disease and should be recognized as such without scorn or shame." It is the aim of British public schools and the older universities to control the tendency to neurosis in the most able men they produce by standardizing intellectual processes and cultivating character, good form and the social graces as a corrective to cerebral excess. Two generations of Eton and Oxford suffice for the production of what in England is recognized as an aristocrat while one suffices to produce, from the class standpoint, a "gentleman". Eton, whatever may be its faults, remains one of the most remarkable educational institutions which any country has ever evolved. No matter what may be the raw material it has to work on—Yiddish, Scotch, Irish, Hottentot, German or English profiteer—the boy inserted at one end of the Eton machine, with a cheque for about £4,000 in his pocket, will be turned out at the other a recognizable and, on the whole, agreeable and civilized social type. Only in the case of such ineradicable neuroses as those of a Shelley or a Swinburne, does the machine fail. Or does it fail ? Does it not rather smoothly and painlessly eject what it cannot assimilate ?

For those who have the brains to take advantage of it, and whose parents have, no matter how, acquired enough money to give them the opportunity of doing so, the education provided by our public schools and by Oxford and Cambridge, undoubtedly makes for a full, happy and contented life, a life in which critical appreciation of wine and literature, fine art and good cooking can be cultivated and indulged. It inculcates many virtues, maintains a standard of superficial good manners, and promotes the growth of warm and often disinterested friendships. In a word, it produces a kind of culture which, however faintly, is still flavoured by its Hellenic origin. The only spiritual price exacted for the privileges it confers is conformity, and that is precisely what the artists and those who " aspire to independent thinking " are unable to pay. Particularly were they unable to pay it in that decade of neuroses and creative energy which began in 1919. Some, who had enjoyed the conformist pleasures of pre-war Oxford, hovered uneasily between the Savile, the Reform and the Athenaeum and the Bohemian taverns of Bloomsbury, between Montparnasse and Mayfair. Pubs and Clubs pulled in opposite directions and it was not always the possession of money, or the desire to make it, which decided which of them had the stronger attraction. As usual, a few fortunate souls contrived to make the best of both worlds.

As writers and painters are, for the most part, humanists and democrats it was natural enough that they should gravitate towards almost the only democratic institution which had emerged more or less unscathed from the war. The enemies of freedom, it is true, did their best to kill the public-house. Three years after the Armistice, pubs were only open six and a half hours out of the twenty-four as opposed to nineteen and a half hours in 1914. The penal taxation of alcoholic liquors was, moreover, continued by the Conservative profiteers in pursuit of a deliberate policy to reserve as many as possible of the pleasures of life for the exclusive enjoyment of the privileged. During the Armistice years, London was one of the most expensive capitals in the world for the hard-working young man who wanted to take his girl out for the evening. The amusements of dining and dancing which would cost him five shillings in Paris " set him back " five pounds in London. So mean was the attitude of the governing class that George Lansbury had to fight tooth and nail against Tory obstruction to obtain for Londoners the right to bathe in their own Serpentine in their own park and to drink a glass of beer in its public refreshment rooms.

Not only did the pubs survive, in spite of high prices and restricted hours, but they broadened their clientèle to include a large proportion of the *intelligentsia* of both sexes and soon became the recognised meeting places of figures too well known in the world of literature and art to be ignored. At the same time, the public-house provided—far more so than the "West-End Club" — an exacting test of manners and deportment. Whereas the Etonian " aristocrat", to do him justice, was usually as much at ease in his inn as the artist or "worker", the " bourgeois " found himself exquisitely uncomfortable in a place where every customer is on equal terms with every other, where the rich rub shoulders with the poor, the boss with the hired man, the ignorant with the learned, the good with the bad, the respectable with the outcast. In the pub, the newly acquired " old school-tie", the newly cultivated " Oxford" accent and the hauteur which too often accompanies them, aroused not respect but its opposite. Thus those who worshipped the British fetish of exclusiveness found themselves, paradoxically, excluded from a social milieu which had international ramifications and a freemasonry of its own.   The Victorians often posed the question of what would happen "if Christ came to London", and the free spirits in that, and every other age, had biblical authority for their assertion that He would, once again, consort with " publicans and sinners."

The existence of the free world of the tavern was a challenge, a menace and an affront to the reactionary anti-democratic Conservatives who feared independence of thought and hated " Bolshevism " as the Devil hates holy water.   To the bureaucrat, marching daily to Whitehall in his class uniform consisting of striped trousers, round black coat, Anthony Eden hat, rolled umbrella and old school tie—an outfit to which the present war added the official gas-mask in its neat case—Bohemia was an exasperation because it attracted no less than it repelled.   Every bureaucrat in the 'twenties liked to patronize the arts, to be judged a connoisseur of music, literature and painting, but equally shuddered at the thought of having any personal contact with a possibly dirty, possibly rude and drunken, probably hard-up composer, painter or poet.   On the other hand, occasional association with such people, sufficient to justify a claim to " know " them should they chance to become famous, conferred a certain distinction.

Although gossip about Bohemia never fails to enchant the bourgeois reader, tied to his safe job and regular mode of living, it has to be kept for thirty years or more before he can enjoy it without embarrassment.   The Bohemia of Bloomsbury and Montparnasse in the 'twenties is still too much with us, too near at hand, to escape the obloquy of the respectable—some of whom have tried to forget that they once, themselves, belonged to it— but after a decent interval professors of literature, curators of galleries, bureaucrats and other official personages will be securing knighthoods for writing learned books about its leading figures.   We have lately seen the process at work in regard to the pre-Raphaelite Bohemia of the mid-Victorian period. Rossetti, said the dying Whistler, "was a king".   All the same, while he lived, he wasn't everybody's cup of tea.

II

Between the two wars the more honest of the *intelligentsia* grew progressively poorer and from the Conservative bourgeois' standpoint more and more déclassés.   They identified themselves more and more with the " workers " at whose income level, or below it, they precariously existed without, however, finding it possible to put confidence either in the competence or honesty of most of the workers' leaders. When, after the defection of MacDonald and the formation of the "National Government", the Tory oligarchy dropped the mask and embarked openly on policies which could only lead the nation to disaster, many intellectuals discovered that love of and faith in humanity, like charity, begins at home. Thus the arch-debunkers of the false patriotism which, behind such slogans as "King and Country", seeks to delude the people into backing the policies of international finance, became the chief exponents of the real, deep-seated patriotism of the common people. Those who were politically minded, however, found it increasingly difficult to get a hearing in the press, even in the correspondence columns, while the B.B.C., which from its birth had been under the strict control of the Money Power, continued to bar the air to alarmed democrats. Under the pretext of avoiding "controversy", even the most temperate criticism of Conservative policy was excluded.

Apart from one or two papers of the extreme Left, which had small circulations and little influence, the honour of maintaining the Englishman's right of free speech, in a period when the whole future not only of our own country but of European civilization was being recklessly endangered, belongs to the publishing trade. Even among publishers, however, during the years of crisis preceding the outbreak of the present struggle, a certain amount of private censorship was exercised over the opinions of authors, by firms which had been subjected to Fascist or Roman Catholic infiltration. This tendency, the consequences of which must be fatal to literature, appears to be slightly on the increase. During the " Spanish curtain-raiser " several books by established authors, which publishers were under contract to produce, were suppressed altogether, out of sympathy with the Axis powers, and others were emasculated of everything which might offend the susceptibilities of the Pope's protégé, General Franco. In spite of these attempts at suppression on the part of the few, the regard for the high tradition of their calling on the part of the majority of publishers allowed the truth to emerge. In the 'thirties many of the younger writers, of outstanding talent, laid aside their normal creative activity, for the dangerous work of finding out the facts as foreign correspondents working for the daily press. These men risked not only their lives but their salaries to enlighten their compatriots and warn them of the dangers ahead. Editors cut their messages or distorted them, but the publishers stepped into the breech by giving the public their uncensored accounts of what they had seen and discovered in a succession of brilliant volumes of *reportage*. *Reportage* has thus become the distinctive literary art of the 'thirties and 'forties because it is the most effective means by which writers of first-rate accomplishment can deliver themselves of the truth that is in them.

After the death of D. H. Lawrence, and the organized defiling of his memory which followed it, independent novelists of what may be termed the " sub-Lawrence school " became the victims of a species of class-war by author-critics who, without any unjust reflections on Lawrence's friend and admirer, Aldous Huxley, can best be described as "sub", or " post " Huxleys. Oxford, Cambridge and the larger public schools today turn out numbers of rather arrogant young *herrenvolk* capable of writing novels and literary criticism which, though they have neither the wit, the erudition, nor the outstanding talent and inner sincerity of Huxley's works, are nevertheless highly polished, superficially clever and rather gutlessly intelligent. They are characteristic of the " managerial era " with which we are threatened, for their authors, regimented by their class education and social connections, are born bureaucrats and may be fittingly termed " Nature's First-Class Clerks."

In the *New Statesman and Nation* for September 25th, 1943, there was a review of a novel called " Saturnine " by Rayner Heppenstall, which provides an apt illustration of the class-war, directed against independent writers, to which I have referred. The scene of this unusual story is laid in Kent and St. John's Wood and the dominating element in it may be described as " Yogi-bogey "—astrology, clairvoyance, a Rudolf Steiner group, a view of the after world. Loss of memory and the sensation of rebirth are handled with uncanny perception. A number of Mr. Heppenstall's characters belong to the harassed, hard-up section of the *intelligentsia* who suffer from the " neurotic dispositions " which Mr. Koestler rightly defines as a " professional disease ". I thought I recognized in one of them a projection of perhaps one of the most distinguished women poets of the 'twenties. They are curious, unregimented people, with no clearly defined class background. No doubt they drink beer in pubs rather than double whiskies in smart " American " bars, possibly their sex morals are not much stricter than those prevalent in Mayfair, but they are original, not common, and their milieu is one in which poets and creative artists find it possible to exist and breathe freely. Such at least was my impression of this book when I read it. *The New Statesman and Nation* review, signed Philip Toynbee, corrects me.

"I doubt whether there is any category in the world", Mr. Toynbee says, "more difficult to describe than the déclassés drunks and fornicators of Bloomsbury's less engaging streets. As a category they are bogus, self-conscious and unintelligent, their lives nasty and brutish. It would be easy to satirise them, but almost impossible to examine them with that detachment which all human beings deserve at a novelist's hands. Mr. Heppenstall is in great danger of writing as bogusly as his characters talk ; for it is evident that he admires them and that he has dramatised their lives (the only possible way) in terms of Baudelaire and Verlaine. The book is a succession of irritations. The exaltation of squalor, the apotheosis of the tapeworm and human excrement, revolts far more by its pathetic self-consciousness than by any simpler impropriety."

Shortly after reading Mr. Toynbee's review of "Saturnine", I observed in the highbrow weeklies long and flattering notices of a novel, by himself, called " The Barricades ". Filled with curiosity to see whether he avoided the faults he castigated in Mr. Heppenstall, I got it from the library and studied it with some care. The period is roughly 1937, shortly after the outbreak of the Franco Rebellion. The principal character is a school-master named Rawlins, a man in the late thirties, who has been sacked, partly for drunkenness and partly for expressing sympathy with the Spanish Republic. He is not, however, "déclassé", far from it, and shows more evidence of repressed homosexuality than tendency to fornication. Proof that we are mixing only with the best people—that is to say, the rich and those who cadge from them—is provided by the fact that Rawlins, after his dismissal, comes to London and drives at once to the Ritz. After changing for dinner he goes in search of a drink. In the brightly-lit underground bar he sits down on a high stool and orders rye whiskey and ginger ale. A group of young people come in—a Mayfair lovely, a White Russian choreographer named Igor, and a shiny profiteer—and start singing the praises of General Franco. Rawlins contrives to butt into their conversation, by pretending acquaintance with a man whose name is mentioned, and eventually gets himself accepted by Lady Rose Palliser and Igor, in spite of the fact that his fraud is discovered.

F

Many whiskies soften his vision, but when he goes out with his new friends he is comforted to see " signs of wealth everywhere : silent cars, many taxis, and even tall people on the pavement in black hats and evening dresses". Before he has spent quite all his money one of his former pupils turns up, a boy of eighteen called David Markham, who has run away from school with the object of joining the International Brigade. Rawlins, mindful no doubt of the fact that Markham's father is a rich man, endeavours to dissuade him from going to Spain on the ground that the Republicans were defeated anyway, so what was the use of his risking his life in a lost cause. I should hesitate to call this character, Rawlins, a "tapeworm", but men like him undoubtedly helped to spread dry rot among the English Left at the very moment when boldness and vigour were essential. As a matter of historical fact, the Spanish Republic need not have been defeated had the Opposition leaders in the House of Commons been less cowardly and incompetent. The sinking of British ships trading legitimately in Spanish waters, by German and Italian bombers, should have been made a national issue by the Labour Party. Had Mr. Attlee courageously appealed to the pride and patriotism of the British people, the Chamberlain Government must have fallen and the fraud of " Non-Intervention " would have collapsed with it. Unfortunately, the Left—and its press—was permeated by pink defeatists of the Rawlins type, and Mr. Attlee, instead of opposing, appeased. Defeatist arguments made no impression on young Markham, but Rawlins introduced him to his new Ritz-bar acquaintances and Lady Rose's sex appeal succeeded where reason failed. Rawlins consoles himself by borrowing £50 from the youth. Had he been déclassé—and squalid—he would have contented himself with a fiver. At a later stage in David's seduction the party hire a car and drive out to a well-known and very expensive riverside restaurant where they all get disgustingly drunk. Lady Rose, in addition to being a Franco fan, is a nymphomaniac who gets a kick out of male virginity. She therefore carries off her romantic schoolboy to the country house of one of her opulent friends and, until she gets bored and wants a change, amuses herself by teaching him the facts of life. As she is off the " top shelf " she is not, according to Mr. Toynbee's standard of values, a "fornicator."

The ex-schoolmaster, before proceeding to Paris on young Markham's money, enters a common " boozer " to quench his inordinate thirst for hard liquor. " He went into a public-house

and ordered whisky. A mechanical piano was playing and three
sailors were conducting as they sang. Everyone was singing and
the sound of their voices beat unpleasantly on Rawlins' ears.
Two drunk women with cropped hair were leaning against a
table, flapping their hands. They were both very ugly. The
sailors swaggered up and down the floor, sometimes scraping
their feet into a pansy dance step. Rawlins drank his whisky
and stared morosely round him. He felt a shiver of nausea, as
cold as a draught ; Igor's malice, Markham's folly and his own
weakness were all swallowed up in the obscenity of this public-
house". Why blame the public-house ? The sailors had, quite
possibly, earned their fun by risking their lives in British ships
trading with Spain and the cropped-haired women had probably
done a day's work in a studio or newspaper office, and could
hardly have been any drunker than was Lady Rose Palliser in
the restaurant at Bray.

It is perhaps unnecessary to follow Rawlins to France where
he is picked up by a millionaire peer, whose father was ennobled
by Lloyd George for making munitions, and carried off as a
kept " companion " to a villa in Cannes. Nasty ? Brutish ? It
depends, of course, on the point of view.

I am not concerned with the respective literary merits of Mr.
Heppenstall's " Saturnine " and Mr. Philip Toynbee's " The
Barricades", but rather with their social and political implications
and their value as documents to the contemporary historian.
The two books make an almost perfect contrast and well illustrate
the cleavage which developed in the *intelligentsia* of the 'twenties
between members of clubs and frequenters of pubs. Mr. Toynbee
can hardly complain if his readers gather that everything which
really matters is wealth, the social distinction which wealth—no
matter how gained—continues to confer, and the refined pleasures
and amenities which money buys. Although the ex-schoolmaster
has to borrow from his pupil, it is clear that he has received the
sort of expensive class education which, if skilfully exploited,
can enable him to be taken up by the rich and titled friends of
General Franco. The title of the book, " The Barricades", is
significant. Rawlins is intelligent enough to adhere, intellectually,
to his country's cause. But he is so conditioned by his education
that, when it really comes to the question of barricades, he sides
automatically with those who have the money and who both
make and control the big guns. Mr. Heppenstall's principal
character, on the other hand, with his interest in astrology and

occult religions and his pacifist tendencies, finds the rich so
intolerable that, in a neurotic moment, he clumps a rich friend
over the head. Finally, when the present war breaks out, he
joins the Army in order to defend the bad against the worse. It
is precisely such men who, when given the chance, have borne
the brunt of what the profiteers dismiss rather contemptuously
as the "actual fighting". In terms of achievement, it is the
England of the pub-frequenters which has insisted on survival,
borne the burden and heat of battle, toiled in mines and work-
shops, kept the arts alive, put traitors to shame, kept a precarious
hold on democratic principles, maintained the human decencies
and upheld a moral code which is sounder and less hypocritical
than the Victorianism it displaced. If the centres of community
life are squalid and obscene, as they sometimes are, it is the
brewers who own them and the misgovernment which has
delayed their improvement, not the people who use them, who
deserve the blame.

From the Ritz-Carlton-West-End-Club world which Mr.
Toynbee describes with so much complacency, little emerged
during the 'twenties and 'thirties of which as a nation we have
any reason to be proud, though it was not quite so vicious and
self-indulgent as Mr. Toynbee suggests.

What, for convenience, may be called the "old school ties"
have produced a charming minor art, and not a few minor
masterpieces. In the 'twenties, apart from Aldous Huxley,
Virginia Woolf and Lytton Strachey expressed the spirit of their
age ; Evelyn Waugh, at the close of the decade, satirized it
brilliantly in "Decline and Fall" and "Vile Bodies", and even
the frustrated 'thirties were enlivened by the engaging humour
and versatile gifts of John Betjeman, Osbert Lancaster and Rex
Whistler. But, generally speaking, the intelligent young of the
propertied classes, like the intelligent old, found themselves
forced by the pressure of events to obey the promptings of
conscience and desert to the popular side. The fact that the
"swing to the Left", so clearly discernible today, has begun to
permeate the middle and upper classes, is due in large measure
to the "new morality" preached and promulgated by the
intelligensia of the 'twenties.

III

"Goodness", if the genuine article, is irresistibly attractive,
especially to backsliders. Most people like to "do the decent

thing " when their muddleheads permit them to grasp what it is.

For the simple and the sophisticated alike, the emergence of " a really good man " who is lovable and filled with loving-kindness, who sets an example by his modest and upright life, is an invaluable aid to the clarification of mental processes. In the 'twenties, the presence among us of St. George of Bow and Bromley probably had more effect than we consciously realised. I must confess to being temperamentally allergic to preachers, but on the few occasions when I heard George Lansbury address an audience, and on the even rarer occasions when I met and talked to him in person, I was deeply moved. I suppose, in the course of his long life, he must have had a similar effect on hundreds of thousands of others. He was, take him all round, one of the best men I have ever come across, or even heard of, in my lifetime. Between the wars, he was almost the only Cabinet Minister who ever made himself beloved by the masses or did anything to deserve their trust and affection. He brought to politics a totally new conception of the duty of an elected representative of the people. He strove with all his heart to increase the sum total of human happiness by such simple, practical means as facilitating mixed bathing in the parks, breaking down the opposition of " the trade " to the licensing of refreshment rooms in public gardens, and encouraging all legitimate pleasures and healthy recreations. In these activities he showed himself both a devout Christian and a good Socialist. His reforms, although they cost nothing in the way of public expenditure, were nevertheless carried out in the teeth of Tory opposition. He showed up the Conservative attitude of perpetual negation of the wishes of the people, of automatic frustration of their desire for the simplest improvements and reforms, as it had never been shown up before. (In sharp contrast to the wisdom and humanity of " dear old George " was the campaign carried on by the Lord's Day Observance Society, of which Sir Thomas Inskip, now Viscount Caldecote, was President. Inskip, who sponsored the Sedition Act and subsequently achieved notoriety as the " co-ordinator " of our defences, revealed his state of mind at a Church Congress at which he stated that " the trouble with the English is that they have too much liberty." Certainly no Conservative ever did more to curtail it in the interests of a minority whose views are repudiated by the main body of Catholics, both Anglo and Roman.)

Lansbury's importance in the 'twenties was less due to what

he was able to accomplish during his short term of office than to
his personal character and the things he stood for. He was a
genuine patriot and though his pacifism was too far ahead of
his age, and proved impractical and unrealistic in face of human
stupidity and wickedness, it was firmly based upon economic
theories which mankind must either accept and act upon or
perish. It is in defence of these theories, however dimly they
may be apprehended, that, by one of those queer paradoxes of
which history affords so many examples, anti-Fascists are now
fighting, under the inspiring world leadership of such men as
Marshals Stalin and Tito. Both as editor of the *Daily Herald*
in its heroic days, and throughout his career as a politician,
Lansbury was an exponent of the kind of Humanism on which
"the new morality", rising from the disorder and mental ferment
of the 'twenties, was based. Generally speaking, anyone who
expressed any desire to improve the lot of the exploited and
injured, or proposed any remedy for the mortal sickness of
acquisitive society, was regarded by the Conservative class as
the vilest of criminals, an untouchable, an outcast, in short—a
" Bolshevik."   George, himself, had been imprisoned by the
Tories in the days when he was a Poplar Guardian, and was
therefore, like so many heroes of the class struggle, a "gaol-bird."
The House of Commons, however, even at its worst, is a fairly
shrewd judge of character and its members are usually capable,
on personal grounds, of feeling respect, even affection, for
opponents. With Lansbury, his personal popularity was due to
what I have called " the irresistible attraction of goodness." No
one, as they say, " could help liking him." The fact that he was
without any trace of snobbery or personal ambition increased
his prestige with those of the ruling class who were accustomed
to win over Labour leaders by social blandishments and flattery.
The mere existence of Lansbury helped, therefore, to undermine
the prejudices of the rich both against Socialists and their theories.
When property became tougher, as it did in Italy, Germany,
India and outlying parts of the British Empire, the danger inherent
in " goodness " was quickly realised, and men like Lansbury were
the first to be hurried off to the gallows and the concentration
camps. In Great Britain, morality of one kind or another, and
religion of a sort, were still too instinctive and widely diffused,
even after the corrupting influence of war-time profit-seeking, to
make any such action against Lansbury tolerable. Punitive
measures against political opinion were reserved for the poorest,

the most obscure and defenceless of the Left, and, where writers were concerned, the weapons of ostracism, insult, or press boycott were chiefly used against those whose publicity value was insufficient to enable them to retaliate. When Mosley started his activities, although he appeared to enjoy considerable favour with the Home Office and the London police, and was boosted by the Rothermere press, he was too late.

In contrast to the simple integrity of Lansbury were the methods employed by Ramsay MacDonald and his successors in the Labour leadership. These were based on what schoolboys call " sucking-up " and consisted in proving that Socialist ministers could wear white ties and tail-coats as impressively as their betters, could acquire the arts of genteel deportment and learn to pick out the right knives and forks just as easily as any profiteer.

The influence which the revolutionary *intelligentsia* of the 'twenties had upon the younger generation of the educated bourgeoisie was no less far-reaching and politically important than its influence on the masses. Ideas, once set going, in however narrow a circle, get into the air which all must breathe, become simplified in the process and finally change the whole atmosphere. Few trouble to trace them back to their sources, nor is any such process necessary, desirable, or even possible. If it is true that the great minds think alike, it is equally true—especially in England—that the good hearts feel alike. Whereas the civilization of France, to which the whole world is indebted, is essentially a civilization of the mind, it can be claimed that the world owes scarcely less to the civilization of England which is essentially a civilization of the heart. If ever two countries should be united for the good of humanity it is surely England and France.

Among the ideas which floated about in England and generated those feelings which enabled us, at what has seemed the thirteenth hour, to save our future, was a revulsion against the " profit motive " both as an incentive to endeavour and as a basis of national policy. Who, when all is said, works for profit? Certainly not the soldier, not the young manhood of a nation in arms. Certainly not the millions of women hospital workers, welfare workers, and other humble auxiliaries in any national effort. Certainly not the school-teacher, the parson, the scientist or the artist of integrity. The fashionable doctor could not look his soul in the face if he did not devote a good deal of his energy

and skill to working for the community without payment. Even
the managerial technician and the despised bureaucrat does not
work for profit. The former would be no worse off if he employed
his brains and talents in the service of the community, rather
than in earning dividends for a group of parasitical directors and
shareholders.

The miners' demand for the nationalization of their industry—a
demand endorsed by the Sankey Commission in 1919—found a
response in the hearts of millions of the humble and inarticulate.
Why should a small group of reactionary coal-owners, whose
title-deeds were granted in one notorious case, five centuries ago,
by a boy of twelve, derive fabulous wealth from the toil and
sweat of men whom they were too mean to pay a living wage?
If the English, like the Russians, owned the natural resources
of their country, the miners could get £10 a week, the dangers
of their work would be removed by modern scientific methods,
and coal might be sold at a reasonable price. Why should not the
people own the land they fought for, the land which a million
young lives had ransomed with their blood? Why should the
millions who had fought, toiled and survived not be housed
at least as well as the horses, dogs, and cattle on a profiteer's
estate? If such ideas were put into words only by the few, they
got sufficiently into the atmosphere to awaken the feelings of
the many. They created a widespread resentment, a sense of
frustration and injustice which grew all the stronger because it
found no means of political expression. In 1940 the Conservative
Party, after provoking the second world conflict, were able to
exploit Churchill's popularity so as to give them the control
and direction of it. The politically minded among the working-
class watched their leaders on the one hand rebuffing the millions
of their black-coated comrades who shared all their aspirations,
and, on the other, tamely collaborating, at the expense of their
principles, with a Party which had no " ideological preferences "
and openly admitted that it was " not fighting an anti-Fascist
war."

In his able book, " So Far . . .", W. J. Brown, M.P., thus
sums up the political situation in the 'twenties. " The supreme
tragedy of British politics in my adult lifetime has lain in two
circumstances : first, that the Labour Party grew big enough
to destroy the Liberal Party without becoming big enough to
take its place ; and second, that it failed to throw up a leadership
capable of achieving an accommodation with the Liberals on

the basis of the Greatest Common Measure of agreement possible to them." But the moral conscience of the people, aroused in the 'twenties, has been steadily quickened, by events and their confused aspirations, though frustrated, have never been suppressed. It is this mass-feeling which, in England, slowly but inevitably, affects political changes.

It is the function of an *intelligentsia* to throw its stones of thought into the pond and this, in the 'twenties, it fulfilled. The result will be visible perhaps one year, perhaps five years, perhaps ten years hence. No effort is wasted. Even the books which are quickly pulped find their destined handful of readers. Ideas are among the few things which even the bombing aeroplane is powerless to destroy. They arise like ghosts from the graves of those who gave them shape.

CHAPTER EIGHT

ART AND LETTERS

I

In his essay on Sickert (in the memorial volume, edited by Miss Lilian Browse), Mr. R. H. Wilenski pays a well-merited tribute to the creative activity in the arts, which characterized the " idealist 'twenties " and died down in the decade of frustration which followed them. It was, he says, " a period of high enthusiasms, exploring energy, creative power and commonsense in all aspects of international endeavour, a period which accomplished so much before the Nazi-Fascist propagandists, for their own ends, launched their wide campaign in the 'thirties to discredit its aims and belittle its achievements." Sickert, though too old to lead new crusades and too individualist to be a " dependable member " of any group or society, was sensitive to the influences surrounding him and developed his style in several exciting directions in sympathy with the spirit of the age. Much of his time was spent in Dieppe, but he flitted in and out of the London Group and, at the end of the decade, was received into the ranks of the Royal Academicians with whom, however, he quickly quarrelled. To the 'twenties belong his theatrical portraits, such as " Sir Nigel Playfair in ' She Stoops to Conquer,' " his " echoes " of the early Victorian illustrator, Sir John Gilbert, and his large mural painting, " The Raising of Lazarus." With the sculptor, Jacob Epstein, he was one of the dominating figures in British art throughout the decade, though neither started a " movement " of his own or was intimately associated with any of those in vogue. Sickert's influence, however, on many of the younger painters, was marked and is still apparent in their work.

Of the avant-gardist groups which had flourished before the war the only important survivor was the London Group which, under the influence of Roger Fry, rapidly consolidated its position. All the leading artists of the time, including Sickert and Epstein, showed their work, either regularly or intermittently, at its crowded exhibitions, which became the focal point of post-war artistic exuberance. The Group had lost several of its most able and distinguished members during the war years, but a sufficient stiffening of the original members remained to carry on its traditions and attract new blood. Spencer Gore, described by Rutter as "the Schubert of English impressionists", had died in 1915, and Harold Gilman, who was President in 1918, succumbed in the following year to the influenza epidemic. Among the pre-war members who survived were R. P. Bevan, Charles Ginner and Wyndham Lewis, though Bevan died in 1925 and Lewis " whose semi-cubist, metallic-coloured portrait of Ezra Pound " had, as Rutter expresses it, " the smashing strength of iron among potsherds " soon seceded and for the rest of the decade devoted himself mostly to pamphleteering and the writing of his masterly satire, " The Apes of God." His place as an expounder of doctrine was taken by Roger Fry, and W. Bernard Adeney, described by Rutter as " a blameless echoer in biscuit and pale-green tints of Cézanne's less successful nudes and landscapes", followed Gilman as the Group's President.

The critical text-books on the new trends in the plastic and applied arts most in vogue were Roger Fry's *Vision and Design*, Clive Bell's *Since Cézanne*, which appeared in 1922, and R. H. Wilenski's *Modern Art*, which came out five years later. Clive Bell had coined the phrase " significant form " to describe those early sub-fusc paintings by Cézanne which the dealers had foisted on London collectors before most of them realised that Cézanne had applied himself to the problem of colour with triumphant success. In the early 'twenties there was a wide-spread cult of " significant form " but before the end of the decade, when Cézanne's mastery of colour had been fully appreciated, this faded away, to give place to the lobster-tinted nudes of Mark Gertler and the " strawberry jam " flower-pieces of

Matthew Smith. Matthew Smith, who today, comes second in critical esteem only to Augustus John among living English painters, was perhaps the most important of the London Group men whose work first attracted attention in the 'twenties. William Roberts, originally a disciple of Lewis, remained faithful to his Vorticist manner but established himself as the solid " meaty " painter he still remains. The Nash brothers, Duncan Grant, Vanessa Bell, Edward Wadsworth, the poster-designer Edward McKnight Kauffer, and many others struck out in what, at that time, seemed excitingly new directions, while the Spencer brothers, Gilbert and Stanley, laid the foundations of their present popularity.

Paul Nash and C. R. W. Nevinson, whose war pictures had expressed the anguish and agony of the battlefield with an honesty of feeling which even the philistine could appreciate, now developed their brilliant talents in the exploration of fresh fields. John Nash, Paul's retiring and diffident brother, brought an original eye to bear on the landscapes of the Thames Valley, which he painted with quiet integrity and a charm not less captivating for being slightly morose. Of the younger sculptors of the Group, Frank Dobson, now an A.R.A. (such are Time's revenges) was easily the most outstanding, though the influence of Maillol on his work offended academic taste.

The War memorials which appeared all over Europe and soon became a feature of English towns and villages, supplied sculptors in the Royal Academy tradition with profitable commissions, but the official mind, though tolerant of foreigners like Mestrovic, fought shy even of Eric Gill, whose *Stations of the Cross* in Westminster Cathedral had brought him fame, especially among his co-religionists. Still more did it fight shy of the disturbing and strongly racial art of the American Jew, Jacob Epstein. Epstein received no commission for a public monument between 1912, when his Oscar Wilde memorial was set up in the cemetery of Père Lachaise, and 1925, when his memorial to W. H. Hudson, the lovely *Rima*, was unveiled in Hyde Park and attracted indignant crowds. In 1929, however, the progressive spirits in the London Underground Railway, whose intelligent patronage of young painters did so much to revive the art of the poster, commissioned his *Night*, which was set up over the entrance to their head offices, in Broadway, Westminster. Again, the amateur art critics in plus-fours who had thrown paint over *Rima* attempted to hurl pots of tar at Epstein's new masterpiece, but were fortunately restrained by the police. (This may be regarded as a significant foretaste of the Fascist frenzy which, in 1943, disfigured Lenin's bust in Holford Square. On the latter occasion the police looked the other way and Mr. Herbert Morrison declined to "intervene.")

Among the artists whose reputations were established before the war, Augustus John added to his laurels in the 'twenties by his flamboyant portrait of the Portuguese 'cellist *Mme. Suggia* (1925), which remains one of the masterpieces of his "big bow-wow" style. Orpen, after finishing his official job of painting the political stuffed-shirts at the Versailles Peace Conference, had a few more years of creative energy before his death. He signalized his release from the Army by painting his masterly *The Chef of the Hotel Chatham*, and in 1923 produced one of his last and best pictures, *To the Unknown Soldier*. Ambrose McEvoy, Sir William Nicholson and Wilson Steer all maintained or increased their prestige. Nicholson's *Girl with the Tattered Glove*, in the Fitzwilliam Museum at Cambridge, and Steer's *Mrs. Raynes* (1922) are two of the outstanding portraits of the decade. Among the younger men, Henry Lamb achieved a striking success with his *Portrait of Lytton Strachey*, now in the Tate Gallery.

In Paris, the traditional birthplace of new movements, Cubism and Futurism in painting were succeeded, in turn, by Dadaism, Surrealism and Expressionism and, in architecture, by Purism, Functionalism and *le style mechanique*, launched by Ozenfant and Jeanneret (Le Corbusier). The outstanding figures of the *Ecole de Paris* were still Picasso, Braque and perhaps to a less degree Matisse. The flat geometrical abstractions of Fernand Leger, who in pre-war days had taught in the Academy which Mme. Vassilieff had established in a large workshop in the Avenue du Maine, acquired a considerable vogue and influenced English avant-gardists, particularly Mr. Ben Nicholson. This kind of "escapist" painting reflected post-war nihilism in its most acute form and satisfactorily expressed a mood which the impact of world events has made recurrent.

The Polish poet-dealer Zborowski's stable of avant-garde geniuses, whose work no other dealers would look at while Modigliani, the leader of them, was alive, suddenly became the rage after his death. With the help and encouragement of the Sitwell brothers, T. W. Earp and Nina Hamnett, a show of Zborowski's protégés had been held in London in 1918, but had failed to attract much attention. Few of the leading critics troubled to visit it, although it was London's first opportunity to appreciate the work of Modigliani, Soutine, Kisling, Derain, Pascin and others of lesser fame. The response was almost nil. A basketful of Modigliani's drawings were offered at five shillings each, but even at this price hardly any were sold. One of Modigliani's most famous nudes was nearly bought by a wealthy young collector for £50, but an English painter, who claimed to be a friend of Modigliani, dissuaded him from the rash act. A few years later the drawings which could have been bought for five shillings in 1918 could have been sold in the United States for fifty pounds, while the nude which failed to find a purchaser at £50 changed hands for prodigious sums.

Apart from the painters who gained the attention of the critics and connoisseurs during the 'twenties, there were several men of talent who were still painfully and penuriously struggling for recognition and only achieved the success they deserved in the 'thirties. One of these was John Armstrong who, like so many other of the more promising talents, received his first substantial encouragement from the good taste and enterprise of the publicity department of the London Underground Railways.

Even the briefest survey of art in the 'twenties should not close without a reference to the paintings, water colours and drawings of that most original, authentic and least commercial of artists, Nina Hamnett. Of the English " Montparnos ", who worked in Paris until the slump drove them back to London, Nina was the best known, although owing to her Bohemian habits, personal popularity, and enormous acquaintance among the Anglo-American good-timers, she was, paradoxically, one of the least appreciated.

II

The vitality of English art during the 'twenties, the creative activity and exploring zeal of the younger men who had escaped from the bondage of the war years and now rejoiced in their freedom met with a cold response, if not active, even violent hostility, from the art-hating British public and the more philistine of the " national " newspapers. This had an effect on the psychology of painters, particularly in their relations with writers, which, so far as I am aware, is unknown in France.

In the first place it tended to breed in them an affected arrogance, which is an inevitable result of real or imagined " persecution." Secondly, it made them intensely suspicious and perpetually on the look-out for slights and insults. The camaraderie which exists in France between brothers of the pen and brush was the exception rather than the rule in London. Painters and sculptors tended to look on writers as natural enemies, like the dirty philistine bourgeoisie, exceptions being made in the case of potential patrons and dispensers of publicity. In other words, they were tolerated if they were " useful " and looked down upon if they were not. As a result the most fantastic concepts of painters as individuals and artists as a class, were foisted on the reading public by journalists and popular novelists. The neuroses of a Modigliani, which led to exhibitions of intoxication in crowded cafés, were taken at their surface value and romanticized for purposes of fiction. Few realized that, apart from these ebullitions, Modigliani was just a diffident, rather shy, sensitive, and well-educated " bourgeois " Jew. It became the fashion to represent painters as over-sexed alcoholics, brilliant, immoral, and full of a dangerous fascination. To anyone whose circumstances had brought him into close contact with painters throughout a life-time, these fancy pictures were ludicrous in the extreme.

Among those whose lives are mainly devoted to the plastic arts there are unquestionably a number of men of outstanding intellectual eminence who would be notable figures in contemporary life, regardless of the medium through which their personalities found expression. In this connection it would be appropriate to mention Augustus John, Sickert, and Percy Wyndham Lewis, all of whom must be regarded as leaders of the *intelligentsia* of the 'twenties, apart from their painting. The general run of artists, however, in England—as in France— are men with one-track minds who, whether they are endowed with genius or are no more than honest and talented craftsmen, are concentrated on their work, to which everything else, including personal relationships, takes second place. Artists of this kind, and they form the majority, are usually exceptionally happy men and women, and frequently live to a great age. The community is enriched by the beauty they create and often only poorly rewards them for the fruits of their quasi-monastic detachment. From the novelist's standpoint, however, such figures are unpromising material. The bearded, pipe-smoking landscape painter, with his bread and cheese, his " can of ale " in country pubs, and his incessant shop-talk when he meets his confrères, cannot be faithfully represented to the outside public as anything but a crashing bore. Thus an imaginary artist-type had to be created with the face—in the 'twenties—of a Rudolf Valentino, the morals of a Casanova, and the alcoholic habits of a Modigliani.

As if conscious of their social deficiencies and determined, through the realization of them, to present a united front to the philistine enemy, little colonies and groups used to assemble in remote villages in Cornwall, Brittany or the Channel Islands, where they developed a collective arrogance, based on mutual admiration. When they appeared on the battlefield of London they kept together, for defensive purposes, and developed a haughty exclusiveness for fear of being excluded. The intimates of Newquay or Lamorna, of Sark or Sennen, of Concarneau or Cagnes, "belonged", while the rest were mere "outsiders." These peculiar social antics on the part of worthy but tedious painters amused or irritated the writing fraternity, according to their temperaments. In the Café Royal a friend and I, both of whom had known a certain rather prominent painter for a good many years, used to watch his behaviour on making his entries, with the liveliest interest. His eye would search the assembled drinkers first of all to pick out potential patrons, then, failing them, to discover some publicized figure whom it might be worth his while to be "seen with." If he found one, our existence, even if we were sitting at the next table, was ignored. If, on the other hand, he drew a blank, if there was absolutely nobody in the café who could be useful to him, he came over and planted himself on us for the rest of the evening. When he was "natural", he was quite a good chap, though inclined to monopolize the conversation by discoursing on his work to the exclusion of other topics. After some years of this kind of thing I felt inclined to say to him, as to other painters of my acquaintance, "Look here ! Can't you save trouble by making up your mind whether we know each other or whether we don't ?" I put off doing so until I joined the staff of an art magazine, started "doing the shows", and thus became, if not a "critic", at least a dispenser of publicity. After that there was no uncertainty. All the painters I had so much as shaken hands with during the past thirty years developed the liveliest and most agreeable recollections of our casual contacts.

III

If the associations between the main body of painters and the literary fraternity were not always as cordial as they might have been in the 'twenties, there was at least one painter who leapt the barricades and practised both arts with equal distinction. Wyndham Lewis, the painter in question, can hardly be said to have acted as a harmonizing influence. The butterfly impishness of Whistler was the gentlest fun compared with the vein of mordant satire developed by this new exponent of the art of making enemies. Apart from Lewis, who as a writer was a professional among professionals, Augustus John and Sickert, when they chose to use the pen, expressed themselves with an ease and confidence which disconcerted those of us who had to do it for a living, while musicians like Philip Heseltine, and mathematicians like J. M. N. Sullivan—a genial figure with curly black hair, very thick glasses, a disarming smile and a perfect understanding of Einstein's theory of Relativity—were scarcely less proficient in a medium not normally their own.

The struggle for life, in a *métier* which at one time yielded reasonable rewards, became fierce indeed when a swarm of talented amateurs, using any chance advantages of birth, money or social connexions, invaded the market with their wares. The cut-throat competition led to the formation of gangs and rackets, and even poets developed " tough " methods of getting their share of the limelight, which showed that Oxford (and all that) was no less enterprising than Chicago.

The decade which accepted El Greco, whose *Agony* had been bought by the National Gallery in 1919, as its most inspiring " Old Master ", which hailed among its greatest modern masters Cézanne, Rouault, the *douanier* Rousseau, Braque, Matisse and Modigliani, which delighted in all the most daring developments of Diaghilev's Russian Ballet, was clearly prepared for similar excitements in the field of poetry and fiction. Apart from the reverberating explosion of James Joyce's *Ulysses* and the later verbal experiments of Joyce and Gertrude Stein, these chiefly took the form of satire, " debunking ", idealistic protest, and surrealist " escapism " which expressed itself in fantasy and nonsense. Generally speaking, since writers deal principally in ideas, they were more immediately sensitive to current events, to post-war problems, social conditions and the confused aspirations and bewilderments of youth, than those who practised the plastic arts. A successful effort, however, was made by Virginia Woolf to rise above the battle into forms of pure creation which gave her exquisite sensibility full scope. Her *Jacob's Room* appeared in 1922 and *Mrs. Dalloway*, regarded by E. M. Forster as one of her masterpieces, three years later. The originality of her style entranced a small circle of appreciative contemporaries and may, for all we know, confer on her a place among the " classics " similar to Jane Austen's.

Writing of *Jacob's Room*, Forster remarks that " the blobs of colour continue to drift past ; but in their midst, interrupting their course like a closely sealed jar, rises the solid figure of a young man. The coherence of the book is even more amazing than its beauty. In the stream of glittering similes, unfinished sentences, hectic catalogues, unanchored proper names, we seem to be going nowhere. Yet the goal comes, the method and the manner prove to have been one, and looking back from the pathos of the closing scene we see for a moment the airy drifting forms piled into a colonnade."

" Escapism " of a different order was supplied by Ronald Firbank, whose once familiar figure was still occasionally observed standing, with his hat on the side of his head, at the entrance to the Café Royal. He spent most of his remaining years abroad and died in Rome, in circumstances which have been described by Sir Osbert Sitwell. Firbank belonged, in the quality of his wit, more to the 'nineties than the 'twenties. At times, we are reminded faintly of Max Beerbohm, at times of H. H. Munro (" Saki "). He was both in the English tradition of Surrealist nonsense and in the equally English tradition of Catholic humour, both " Anglo " and " Roman ", which survives in Sandys Wason, Evelyn Waugh and John Betjeman. He was a sensitive, consciously rather absurd but always disarming figure. His excessive shyness required the fortification of a great deal of champagne which, fortunately, he was rich enough to afford. Like Charlie Mouth, the happy black boy in *Prancing Nigger*, who, as Forster says, " passed through the customs at Cuna-Cuna with a butterfly net and nothing to declare," he was entirely purposeless, frivolous and inconsequent. But what fascinating, irridescent, brightly coloured butterflies his net contained !

A vein of fantasy of a very different order from Firbank's was successfully exploited by David Garnett, whose " Lady into Fox " and " Man in the Zoo "—heavy, post-graduate trifles, in a prose style imitated from Defoe—were hailed as masterpieces by all the mandarins of criticism. Dons chuckled over them ; even bishops tee-heed discreetly over the choice of a public school for semi-vulpine children. The enormous sales achieved by these " carved coconuts ", as someone irreverently called them, are interesting, in retrospect, as showing the importance, in the 'twenties, of belonging to a literary " dynasty." Firbank had no such advantages. His public has always been restricted, yet the black boy with his butterfly net has managed to survive all the changes in literary fashion.

Aldous Huxley, like David Garnett, came of an intellectual dynasty which, besides the great Thomas Henry Huxley, included such figures as Matthew Arnold and Mrs. Humphrey Ward. He was at Eton and returned there as a master during the war years. Although there is a legend that philistine pupils once locked him into a cupboard, there is evidence, in the exceptionally large number of Etonians who " took up " literary journalism and practised, or at least criticized, the arts, after his departure, that he had considerable influence in popularizing culture, in its widest sense, at that ancient seat of learning. A favourite subject for discussion in the 'twenties was what would have been the result if Huxley had been born in a miner's cottage and D. H. Lawrence had been brought up at Eton and Oxford. Similarly, one of the most rasping personalities of the 'twenties used to ask us to imagine Osbert, Edith and Sacheverell Sitwell as the children of a small tobacconist in the Kings Road, Chelsea, who made their contacts with artists only by selling them packets of cigarettes. " We should all of us have said that Sachy was a nice intelligent young fellow," the critic boomed, " but where would he be *now* ? " We deduced from this unanswerable query that what the speaker intended us to realize was that he himself belonged to that order of genius that, whether born in a palace or on a dung-heap, cannot be suppressed. We left it at that. Huxley's early novels, " Crome Yellow ", " Antic Hay " and " Point-Counter-Point ", amused, stimulated and charmed those who belonged to the circles from which his characters were drawn, shocked and disgusted pious old Ulster journalists, like James Douglas, and have since made the 'twenties glamorous for several generations of intelligent young people in London and the provinces. No such blend of talent, wit, refined smut and erudition had been seen before, except in Norman Douglas's " South Wind ", to which novel, as some observed, the touch of genius, the one thing missing in Huxley's books, was added. Of the latter "indefinable something", discernible in the best of Firbank, as also in two books by his disciple Evelyn Waugh— " Decline and Fall " and " Vile Bodies "—Huxley's brilliant novels showed no authentic sign. In place of it there was a trace of the minor prophet's melancholy, a deep-seated disgust, a vein of mysticism and a critical faculty so detached and so honest that he was able to recognize and admire in D. H. Lawrence the divine fire which he himself lacked. For if Lawrence was not a " genius " the word has no meaning.

As I write, I can call to mind quite clearly the appearance of those outstanding literary personalities of the 'twenties with whom I had any personal contact ; I can hear their voices, remember how they talked, looked and behaved, and the impression they made on their contemporaries. With some I had only a brief or limited acquaintance, others I knew intimately and have some right to regard as personal friends. Now, as I sit in my study, in my lonely and remote cottage, they file past the eye of memory—D. H. Lawrence, Norman Douglas, Aldous Huxley, Osbert, Edith and Sacheverell Sitwell, Harold Monro, Mary Butts, Theodore and Llewellyn Powys, Philip Heseltine, Evelyn Waugh, Siegfried Sassoon, Percy Wyndham Lewis, Richard Aldington, Ford Madox Ford, Violet Hunt, H. D., A. E. Houseman, Ethel Colburn Mayne, T. W. Earp, T. S. Eliot, Ezra Pound, H. G. Wells, W. H. Davies, Rose Macaulay, Anna Wickham, and a whole galaxy of Irish stars, like " A.E.," W. B. Yeats, James Stephens, and James Joyce. In this cavalcade of human beings, all of whom left their mark on the decade, one figure stands out as being indubitably in the " Shelley " class—it is the figure of D. H. Lawrence. A number of tedious, pseudo-scientific works have been written, since Lawrence's death, about his "message", his complexes, and his " sex-life " (if any). No doubt, as even his schoolfellows were aware, he was in love with his mother. Quite possibly, it was the feminine side of his nature, a streak of latent homo-sexuality, which made him dwell so much on muscles, loins, the dark mysteries of primal instinct, plumed serpents and what not. I shall not risk betraying my ignorance by following learned " Bloomsburies " of both sexes into these unedifying bypaths. I prefer to take Lawrence as I found him. Like all writers of genius, his work is uneven, indeed some of it seems to me the purest tosh. At his best, as Richard Aldington's admirable

anthology establishes, he was a master of descriptive prose, one
of the greatest in our language.   His poems, novels and short
stories are exciting, not only on account of their psychological
perception but also because of the capacity for observation revealed
in them.   Lawrence had " eyes " where most of us have " no
eyes."   Nothing in nature escaped his appreciative notice, from
the smallest insect, bird or wild flower in an English wood to
the   composition   of   an   alien   landscape.   His   sensorium
registered the most delicate vibrations of colour, sound and
feeling and recorded the anguish of a trapped rabbit no less
poignantly than the secret emotions of a frustrated school-
mistress.   He was more sophisticated, more of a mystic, less
child-like than W. H. Davies, another man of genius, but shared
with Davies the quality of being, *sui generis*, first-rate.   In
personal relations Lawrence was quite capable of outbursts of
violence, particularly of impatience with snobs, bores and
" stuffed shirts."   He was on many recorded occasions even
more savage towards his friends and admirers than towards
those who disliked him or whom he actively detested.   This
tendency to tantrums seems to me to have obscured the fact that
in his ordinary dealings with people of all grades and conditions,
of all races and colours, with whom he came into casual contact,
his natural courtesy was almost Christ-like.   To Lawrence all
God's children were primarily human beings, with equal human
rights *qua* their humanity, regardless of whether, in their
secondary aspects, they were peeresses, working-men, publishers,
millionaires or paupers.   This fact is evident in his published
letters, the tone of which is predominantly genial, chirpy and
completely natural and unaffected.   Even his petulance, his
occasional venom, is spontaneous and unaffected, never arrogant.
A story is told of Lawrence that, when travelling in Mexico, he
heard that a distinguished (and wealthy) English author happened
to be in the same town and wrote politely to suggest that they
should meet.   In reply he received a letter of regret from the
wealthy (and distinguished) colleague's secretary.   I suppress the
distinguished colleague's name because from what I know of him
the story does not seem to be in character and is, therefore, quite
possibly apocryphal.   But it is the sort of thing which might
quite easily have happened to Lawrence and it illustrates the
difference between the manners of the " first-rate " and those of
the second-rate.   The miner's son, like the carpenter's son, had
the sort of manners which we are still apt. fancifully, to refer to

as "aristocratic". It would be safer to say they are the manners of the "best" people, using the word in its stricter sense. Of the élite.

W. H. Davies, unlike the horde of bogus Celtic literary-gangster "tramps", who at one time infested Fleet Street, had a similar simplicity and directness. Even the seagulls recognised it and responded. I visited Davies once or twice when he was living in a dingy back-room in York Buildings, Adelphi. Following his usual practice, he regularly put pieces of bread out for the birds, in this case hungry Thames gulls. They flocked in such numbers round his windows and left so many visiting cards that they created a nuisance and he told me, ruefully, that he had been asked to leave in consequence. Anything wounded, hurt or hungry, human or animal, appealed to this little wooden-legged St. Francis, whose simplicity made him as much at ease in a Mayfair drawing-room as in a doss-house. In the war years when poets were assembled by some great lady to recite their verses in aid of charity, Davies stumped up to the platform, said his poems without diffidence or affectation and scored the one success of the occasion.

A "genius" of a different order was Philip Heseltine, better known as "Peter Warlock". I am not competent to express an opinion on his work as I am not a musician, but judging from the tributes paid to him after his death by such friends and contemporaries as Cecil Gray, Constant Lambert and Bernard Van Dieren, the word "genius" would seem not inapplicable. I use it, in inverted commas, to indicate the effect of his personality on those who knew him. The effortless superiority of his cultural equipment as with so many old Etonians, Aldous Huxley included, was rather overwhelming at first to minds less opulently furnished. Fortunately for most of his friends, he had an inordinate appreciation of "livelier liquor than the muse", an appreciation which we were able to share on equal terms. I look back on many evenings passed at the Café Royal, at the Café du Dome, or at the now famous "Antelope"—where the beer he most approved of was dispensed—when I had opportunities of watching the mild and gentle Philip slowly developing, by stages, into Peter Warlock, and, finally, into "the old bold mate of Henry Morgan". Tall, pasty-faced, with a wisp of beard, it was his deep-set eyes and demoniac smile—a smile which became more lewdly devilish as the evening proceeded and his blasphemies became more daring—which gave the *clou* to his enigmatic character. The fashionable theory of " schizophrenia " which I once used to describe the discrepancy between Heseltine and Warlock has been rejected by a friend, who asserts that the only real difference between them was that between " Philip drunk and Philip sober ". I prefer the more romantic explanation when I recall a Ouija-board séance I attended in Dublin, at which the " control " ordered him out of the room because he was pursued by " evil influences." Like D. H. Lawrence, his close friendship with whom ended in a violent quarrel, and so many other people in the 'twenties, he was a student of all forms of occultism and black magic, and it is not beyond the bounds of possibility to believe that he was at times " possessed ". Whatever the explanation, the world has been enriched by his music and his strangely beautiful and disturbing songs. Perhaps, therefore, the possession was nothing more sinister than the divine afflatus we call inspiration. When he believed it had deserted him, he sent his girl-friend out to a dance, put the cat outside, and gassed himself in his Chelsea flat in December 1930. I attended his semi-secret funeral at Godalming, which I have described elsewhere.

Of the poets of the 'twenties, the dominating, or at least the most fashionable, figure was T. S. Eliot, whose " The Waste Land " had a powerful but, as I heretically believe, pernicious influence on his younger contemporaries. It is unfortunate, for Europe—perhaps also for the United States—that cultured Americans who make the return journey to the " old " countries are nearly always heavily burdened with a sense of the past. They are therefore sentimental reactionaries, either social snobs like the amazingly gifted but deplorable Henry James, or culture-hounds like the tragic-comedian Ezra Pound, or dons-with-a-difference like the religious-materialist Eliot, whose intellectual climate seems to me about half a century behind our times. The importance to the world of those old trees, France and England, is that their roots are so deep they are constantly able to put forth new shoots. Branches may wither, decay and fall down into the waste land, but when Spring comes—look, the new leaves and blossoms have come through ! It is not the age of Europe, but its perennial youth, its restless, progressive exuberance of life, its perpetual modernity and its capacity to throw off " Main Street " provincialism and rise above material concepts which ought to inspire deracinated transatlantic pilgrims. As a "cradle" Anglo-Catholic, who has watched the changes which have taken place in religious thought and feeling over a period of half a century, I cannot take kindly to the now faded and outmoded brand of Anglo-Catholicism of which Eliot seems to be our chief exponent. Much as I appreciate his practical cats, and his amusing early verse, in French and English, and greatly as I respect his critical erudition, the influence of that dangerously wrong-headed and soul-destroying visionary, Charles Maurras, seems too apparent in his mental make-up to enable me to swallow his work without digestive qualms. This may be because I am one of those who believe that Christianity without Socialism, or divorced from Socialism, is a contradiction in terms.

Among the other poets of the 'twenties the most widely read and appreciated by the general public was Siegfried Sassoon, whose bitter " Counter-Attack " made a deep impression on everyone capable of generous indignation or imaginative sympathy. Edmund Blunden's pastoral poems, the poetry of Harold Monro and the adroit and witty verses of Humbert Wolfe had a considerable vogue among those who did not wish to be disturbed by strong emotions, and Victoria Sackville-West's long poem "The Land", appealed to a revived sentiment of English racial consciousness. The Sitwell trio announced their arrival on the literary battlefield with a disconcerting but highly successful fanfare of unfamiliar trumpets. Their publicity received no setback from the fact that Noel Coward satirized them in a popular revue as the "Swiss Family Whittlebot", in a sketch in which Maisie Gay surpassed herself. Osbert Sitwell's polemical pamphlet on "the Squirearchy", "Who Killed Cock Robin? Or Jolly old Squire and Shanks's Mare", added to the general feeling of light-hearted gaiety and liberation, while in his mockery of conventional military types, including horse-addicts and other British fetish-worshippers, we can perhaps trace the origin of some of the amusing " pocket-cartoons " of Osbert Lancaster. Apart from the poets who contrived to catch the public ear there were several whose work, though known only to the few, has proved enduring. E. Powys Mathers, Edgell Rickword, T. W. Earp, and certainly Anna Wickham, still await their almost inevitable re-discovery.

Popular fiction, whether of the highbrow or the lowbrow variety, was almost entirely " escapist " in the 'twenties. The public was numbed and apathetic, and it was not until the end of the decade, when Richard Aldington published his " Death of a Hero", that war-scarred writers felt able to look back upon and record their experiences. The political agitations, the pathetic idealism of the educated youth of the lower middle-classes, were treated only as subjects for ridicule by the "circulationists". One brilliant Cambridge wit, though proclaiming her advanced ideas, took a special delight in deriding those of the politically minded young whose parents had been too poor to provide them with a University training. The "Girton titter" became a fashionable literary note. I found echoes of it in an otherwise amusing novel published as recently as 1940, four years after the Fascist invasion of Spain. Nothing seemed funnier in the 'twenties, to clever upper-middle class spinsters, than the spectacle of pimply young clerks and under-paid typists attending Socialist meetings and presuming to be interested in matters they were, of course, too half-baked to understand. Political discussions were regarded as bad form, the few novels of ideas which got into print were sneered at by the reviewers as "propaganda", and any trend of conversation which might lead to controversy was suppressed by the suburban hostess. In this, with conscious and carefully cultivated gentility, she imitated the manners of her Edwardian betters.

Novelists who established what might be termed a "lucrative practice" in the 'twenties among middle-class subscribers to the circulating libraries were Alec Waugh, whose public school story "The Loom of Youth"—"Loomers", to young Oxford—had brought him sudden fame, Gilbert Frankau, son of the able novelist who wrote as "Frank Danby" and satirised pre-war society, G. B. Stern, Sheila Kaye Smith, Michael Arlen, Margaret Kennedy and many others whose names I have forgotten. A notable newcomer was Ethel Mannin, who later in her career developed a social conscience, fortunately without diminishing her sales. Much of the popular fiction market in the 'twenties was captured by the crime novel, of which Edgar Wallace was the chief exponent.

For the benefit of the highbrows, Charles Scott-Moncrieff translated Marcel Proust's gigantic novel, "A la Recherche du Temps Perdu," and followed this up with translations of Stendhal's "La Chartreuse de Parme" and "Le Rouge et Le Noir." Scott-Moncrieff, whom I first met in 1907, soon after he left Winchester, suffered severely in the war and, as a result of his wounds, could only walk with the aid of a heavy surgical boot. When in the vein, he was extraordinarily witty, but he left little original work behind him except a number of lampoons and satirical verses, mostly written to amuse his friends. So far as I am aware they have never been collected. He will be remembered as one of the great translators, a field in which few other Englishmen have achieved enduring fame.

IV

To appreciate what was going on among the small group of avant-gardists who gave the 'twenties that touch of glamour in the eyes of the younger generation which it has now acquired it may be useful to cast a retrospective glance at some of the obscure and ephemeral periodicals, mostly kept going by unpaid contributors, which sprang up and withered during the decade. In opposition to the orange-covered organ of the Establishment—Sir John Squire's *London Mercury*—Harold Monro's monthly *Chapbook* established itself as the chief rallying point for living verse and criticism. In the regular, or "commercial" press, the outstanding critical journals in 1919 were *The Athenaeum*, then edited by J. Middleton Murry with the assistance of Aldous Huxley, and the *Westminster Gazette*, the " sea-green incorruptible" Liberal evening paper of which Miss Naomi Royde-Smith was literary editor. The American *Little Review*, which had maintained its English connexions during the war years through Ezra Pound and John Rodker, still exerted a powerful influence among the advanced and lived up to its claim to be " the magazine that is read by those who write the others". Margaret Anderson was the editor-in-chief, Ezra Pound the London editor, and Jules Romains the French editor. In many respects it was a forerunner of Ford's *Transatlantic Review*, which was started in Paris in December 1923 and survived for a year. Among the contributors to the *Little Review* of January 1919 are W. B. Yeats, " The Dreaming of the Bones", May Sinclair, James Joyce, an instalment of "Ulysses", and John Rodker. In the June number we find the first chapter of Dorothy Richardson's "Interim", another episode from "Ulysses", and an amusing attack on Ezra Pound by John Cournos, called "The Death of Vorticism". (Ah, what fun we had when we were young and had the guts to go for each other !) Other *Little Review* contributors were Mary Butts, A. R. Orage, Ethel Colburn Mayne, T. S. Eliot, Wyndham Lewis and Ford Madox Hueffer (Ford).

Connections with Ireland were necessarily impaired by " the

troubles ". Dublin ceased to be an important literary centre, its writers migrated to London or Paris and such weekly reviews as P. J. Little's *New Ireland*, became almost exclusively political. Just before the Armistice, however, it published a short critical article by " Lucius " on Ford's " On Heaven and Other Poems ", Walter de la Mare's " Motley and Other Poems ", " Look ! We have come through ", by D. H. Lawrence and Bernard Gilbert's " Rebel Verses ". What reviewer of today could hope to collect such a bag for one notice ? No sooner do I ask this rhetorical question than the disturbing thought assails me that I am growing old. Can it be that my failure to recognize, among the young poets whose works I read in the highbrow magazines, the Lawrences, Fords and De la Mares of today, is merely due to the dimmed eyesight of old age ? I hope that this, indeed, is the true explanation ; not the insidious, blighting spread of Fascism, which destroys all beauty and all the hopes which can inspire a lyric rapture. In Dylan Thomas, who treats me when we meet with a kindly indulgence, for which I am grateful, I recognize some of the qualities and characteristics which have marked the great poets I have known, but his verse, which I have read attentively, leaves me bewildered. Obviously there is a bardic quality, a strange kind of music . . . but why does my heart not haste ? I am not initiated, therefore it would be presumptuous of me to comment on what I do not understand.

Returning to Lucius, I find from a torn press-cutting that he describes D. H. Lawrence as " easily the most interesting literary figure in England at the present time " (June 1918). Two stanzas are quoted from an early poem which Lawrence himself disliked and discarded from his collected verse.

> " They dwelt in a huge hoarse sea-cave
> And looked far down the dark
> Where an archway torn and glistening
> Shone like a huge sea-spark.
>
> " He said : ' Do you see the spirits
> Crowding the bright doorway ? '
> He said : ' Do you hear them whispering ? '
> He said : ' Do you catch what they say ? '

The concluding notice, which deals severely with a blameless little book by the late Bernard Gilbert, has a strangely familiar ring. Can it be that I have accidentally preserved this scrap of newsprint because I myself was Lucius ?

To a short-lived literary review called *Art and Letters*, edited by Osbert Sitwell and Herbert Read, which appeared in 1919, I contributed a more elaborate panegyric on D. H. Lawrence, which was later reprinted in a volume of critical essays called " Reputations."

One of the liveliest avant-garde publications of the early twenties was *Coterie*, edited by an Oxonian Indian named Chaman Lall, and published from Frank (" Bomb ") Henderson's famous Left Wing bookshop in the Charing Cross Road. The English " editorial committee " consisted of T. S. Eliot, T. W. Earp, Richard Aldington, Aldous Huxley, Nina Hamnett and Russell Green. I have preserved a copy of the fourth issue, possibly because it contains some verses by myself. Among the more eminent contributors to this number, which, apart from Huxley's one-act play, is almost wholly devoted to verse, were Aldous Huxley (" Permutations among the Nightingales "), Richard Aldington, Royston Dunnachie (Roy) Campbell, Frederick Manning, H. D., Paul Selver, Amy Lowell, Iris Tree, L. A. G. Strong, Russell Green and C. B. Kitchin.The illustrations were drawings by Nina Hamnett, Henri Gaudier-Brzeska, Zadkine, C. M. O'R. Dickey, and André Derain.

The original *Coterie* came to an early grave but was revived in November 1925, under the editorship of Paul Selver and others of the original "English editorial committee". *The New Coterie* had a cover design by William Roberts, and this time contained more prose than verse. The contributors included Martin Armstrong, Clifford Bax, Karel Capek, T. W. Earp, Louis Golding, Douglas Goldring (a longish short story called " You Don't Know Molly "), Robert McAlmon, Liam O'Flaherty, T. F. Powys and Paul Selver. Augustus John, William Rothenstein, Jean de Bosschère (a Belgian imitator of Beardsley), Pearl Binder, Jacob Kramer and Capek supplied the illustrations.

A circular letter had been sent out, before the first number of *The New Coterie* appeared, inviting contributions, which met with the response indicated above. Only one of the writers approached, an eminent poetess, took offence at the modesty of the payment offered. No periodical devoted entirely to literature and art could hope to show a profit in 1925 and the fact that the editors sent token cheques to their contributors was evidence of generosity on their part, since the cheques did not come out of the public's pocket but out of their own.

In the second issue there was again a story by T. F. Powys and contributions in prose and verse by such writers as Robert Nichols, Rhys Davies and Nancy Cunard.

While *The New Coterie* was struggling to find a public for a group of authors, most of whom have since made their mark, the commercial gangsters of the literary world were engaged in cornering markets, log-rolling each other in the columns of the periodicals in which they had managed to establish themselves and either ignoring or insulting the independents. From some secret fastness in Bayswater, the whereabouts of which was kept as closely guarded as the headquarters of Marshal Tito, Wyndham Lewis observed these manifestations of corruption with a savage and piercing eye. Occasionally he sent out spies to attend cocktail parties, studio binges and critics' confabulations, charged with the duty of reporting what they saw and heard. From time to time provocative and stimulating works, among them " The Art of being Ruled," and " Time and Western Man " erupted from the stronghold of the Enemy, which gave a foretaste of the final onslaught, the huge satirical novel called " The Apes of God."

As I no longer possess a copy of this sinister but enduring masterpiece I will quote from two contemporary reviews which gave what seems to me a fair description of it. " First known to the public as an artist of the abstract and intellectual school," wrote Naomi Mitchison, " Mr. Wyndham Lewis has recently developed into a species of literary searchlight, throwing dazzling and scorching beams into every cranny of the social system . . . He remorselessly pierces our insular fogs of sentiment and illusion, and throws up into sharp relief the underlying currents of society. The subject matter of his new novel, 'The Apes of God', is the rich Bohemia of London, the coterie-world of the ' gossip-column class ' in the year 1926, just before the General Strike. . . . Like a series of exhibits mounted upon slides, the *poseurs* of this decaying world of sham and irresponsibility are seen under the high-power microscope of Mr. Lewis's mercilessly analytical mind. With the aid of a whole gallery of meticulously drawn portraits (the detail is incredibly finely elaborated) we are shown the workings of a society in intellectual and moral dissolution."

Richard Aldington, in *The Referee*, wrote that " it is always one of the thrills of the year to find out what Wyndham Lewis is up to now ; he hates more thoroughly and efficiently than any writer living, and is probably effective in destroying what he hates. I can't imagine what or whom he likes, but at the moment he specially dislikes homosexuals of both kinds, the war generation still pretending to be young, messy-minded people such as Jews and Irish, artists and writers who happen to have private means, and the Sitwell family—also probably a good many others of his contemporaries whom I am not gossip-column-ape enough to recognise. . . . It is exceedingly well-written, sometimes brilliantly funny, making one think hard, keeping one's mind bright and responsive the whole time—as a cold bath."

Almost all the leading independent writers of the time hailed " The Apes of God " with acclamation, though some, like W. B. Yeats, took exception to the attack on the Sitwells on the justifiable ground that their distinction as poets, particularly Edith's, ought to have preserved them from Lewis's derision. Others who had suffered in the past from their own barbed shafts were glad, vicariously, to get their own back. As, when we were all young together, the Sitwells had gone out of their way to be amiable to me and I knew nothing about their quarrels, I agreed with Yeats.

Clifford Sharp, then editor of the *New Statesman*, commissioned Roy Campbell, the poet, who had been reviewing for the paper for the past six years, to write the notice of "The Apes of God". Sharp, whatever may have been his shortcomings, was a man of courage. He was not the kind of editor who sits in his office on press-day, sweating with funk, and telephones to persons of importance to ask their advice on " what line " his paper should take. He used his own judgement on politics, picked his reviewers with care and gave them a free hand. He was, however, away on leave when Roy Campbell's review was delivered and a Mr. R. Ellis Roberts, who had joined the staff, had become responsible for the literary part of the paper. Mr. Roberts rejected the review, with an accompanying letter, subsequently printed in facsimile by Lewis in " Enemy Pamphlets, Number One", in which he said : "I am afraid I cannot publish your review as it stands, even over your signature. I find you take a far more serious view of its merits than I can, and indeed take Mr. Lewis altogether more seriously than I think is justifiable. . . . My serious complaint against the notice, in so far as it concerns Wyndham Lewis, is that you ignore what seems to me his obvious lack of composition—he can only *write* in sentences, or occasionally in paragraphs. Would you have any objection to my publishing the review—unsigned, of course—with such modifications as I think good?"

The author of "The Flaming Terrapin" was not the man to put up with this kind of thing and promptly told Mr. Roberts "to go to hell." A terrific row blew up, which kept literary London entertained for weeks, and the unfortunate Mr. Roberts soon found himself immortalized as the king of ape-critics. It was a head-on collision between two acknowledged leaders of the literary avant-garde and the powerful forces of what Ford Madox Ford used to call the Establishment. On the whole, without unfairness to Mr. Roberts, I think it can be said that Wyndham Lewis and Roy Campbell had the best of it.

V

As a footnote to these necessarily rather disjointed comments on the literature of the 'twenties it is interesting to see what happened to some of the writers of the period when the Fascist onslaught on civilization spread to Spain. In a revealing pamphlet called "Authors Take Sides", the results of a question-naire put to a number of British writers and poets, were printed without comment.

The statement of the international committee which initiated this investigation—it included, among others, Louis Aragon, W. H. Auden, Nancy Cunard, Brian Howard, Heinrich Mann, Ramon Sender, Stephen Spender and Tristan Tzara—runs as follows :

"It is clear to many of us throughout the whole world that now, as certainly never before, we are determined or compelled to take sides. The equivocal attitude, the Ivory Tower, the paradoxical, the ironic detachment, will no longer do.

"We have seen murder and destruction by Fascism in Italy, in Germany—the organization there of social injustice and cultural death—and revived, imperial Rome, abetted by international treachery, has conquered her place in the Abyssinian war. The dark millions in the colonies are un-avenged.

"Today the struggle is in Spain. Tomorrow it may be in other countries—our own. But there are some who, despite the martyrdom of Durango and Guernica, the enduring agony of Madrid and of Bilbao, and Germany's shelling of Almeria,

are still in doubt, or who aver that it is possible that Fascism
may be what it proclaims it is : ' the saviour of civilization.'

"This is the question we are asking you : Are you for, or
against, the legal Government and the people of Republican
Spain ?

"Are you for, or against, Franco and Fascism ? "

How did the literary figures of the 'twenties, rising or established, respond in 1937 to this searching enquiry ? The greater
number of them, including some of the most eminent, either
never received it or forbore to commit themselves. But of those
who answered, the majority were uncompromisingly opposed
both to Fascism and Franco. Even Rose Macaulay, who during
the Irish " troubles " seemed to me inclined to sit on the fence,
came now definitely off it. "Against Franco", she tersely
wrote or wired. Others equally uncompromising were Lascelles
Abercrombie, Martin Armstrong, J. D. Beresford, Gerald Bullett,
Thomas Burke, Arthur Calder-Marshall, A. E. Coppard, Norman
Collins, Cyril Connolly, C. Day Lewis, Havelock Ellis, Liam
O'Flaherty, Ford Madox Ford, Louis Golding, Douglas Goldring,
James Hanley, J. L. Hodson, Laurence Housman, Aldous
Huxley (qualified with pacifism), Storm Jameson, Rosamund
Lehmann, Jack Lindsay, Eric Linklater, F. L. Lucas, A. G.
Macdonell, Ethel Mannin, Naomi Mitchison, Eleanor Mordaunt,
Robert Nichols, Sean O'Casey, J. Middleton Murry, Raymond
Mortimer, Herbert Palmer, Lewellyn Powys, V. S. Pritchett,
Edgell Rickword, Edward Sackville-West, James Stephens,
Thomas Sturge Moore, Naomi Royde Smith, Rebecca West,
Clough and Annabel Williams-Ellis, H. R. Tomlinson, Sylvia
Townsend Warner, Helen Waddell, Rex Warner.

Among the " neutrals " were Vera Brittain and that extremely
competent and highly paid purveyor of clean " lurve " for
working girls, Miss Ruby M. Ayres. " Uninformed interference
in international politics is more to be dreaded," the latter wrote,
" than any anticipated danger resulting from the conflict in
Spain. As a professional writer I dread amateurs."

T. S. Eliot replied : " While I am naturally sympathetic, I
still feel convinced that it is best that at least a few men of letters
should remain isolated, and take no part in these collective
activities."   Charles Morgan is less comprehensible, though
equally bloodless, and shirks the moral issue by making no
distinction between the legally elected Government and the

Fascist invader. "In politics, I care chiefly that a man's thought be not regimented or his art censored, and that he may live as he pleases so long as, within a rule of law he has shared in making, he offers no violence to the health or integrity of others." Other "neutrals", were H. G. Wells, Alec Waugh, Vita Sackville-West, Malachi Whitaker, W. J. Turner, and Ezra Pound.

Franco's avowed supporters were Edmund Blunden, Arthur Machen, Geoffrey Moss, Lady Eleanor Smith, who writes "naturally, I am a warm adherent of General Franco's, *being, like all of us, a humanitarian*", and Evelyn Waugh.

The actual figures for the different classes are 127 against Fascism and Franco, 17 neutral, and 5 Franco-fans. In the minority groups, however, are some of the best known, or at least what Americans call "socially prominent" names. Should the present war result in the kind of "corporate state" which appears at this writing (1944) to be the dream of many influential reactionaries, high positions in the Writers' Guild—on the form shown above—should be accorded to the neutrals and "collaborators." For the anti-Fascist majority, presumably the alternatives will be either conformity or expulsion.

PART II
SOME PERSONAL MEMORIES

CHAPTER ONE

IRISH INFLUENCES

I

The window from which my Irish wife and I first looked out upon London in January 1919 was delicately dimmed by the Celtic twilight which filled the book-lined and ghost-haunted room behind it. It was a room in which a great poet, perhaps the greatest lyric poet of our age, had written many of his immortal lines. The influence of his over-powering and, perhaps, slightly sinister personality still brooded over his belongings. It affected me so strongly that I came to feel that the house was haunted by its absent owner. It occurred to me, too, that some of the disembodied spirits whom Yeats was in the habit of summoning for consultation, may have been unable to find their way back to their astral home. Colour was lent to this view by my discovery, one morning, of strange chalk marks, in the shape of a turkey's claw, on the top of the poet's writing-desk. Betty, though cynical about the ghosts, fairies and leprechauns with which, throughout her youth, she had been familiarized by the conversation of the Dublin mystics who frequented her mother's *salon*, confessed to feeling strange qualms in certain dark passages and corners. The kitchen, for example, in which stood the bookcase containing Yeats's occult library, always scared her. I have heard since that the magical treatise of Abramelin, translated by Macgregor Mathers, has qualities calculated to have an adverse effect on fried bacon and poached eggs. A friend, who once possessed a copy, was moved by the mishaps it caused him to drop it discreetly into the Thames. Another disturbing patch of ghostliness was the stretch of hall between the bottom of the stairs and the front door. When we went out at night I used to go first and open the door so that Betty could dash across it to the safety of the paving stones outside. At the end of our six months' tenancy, when Yeats's lease expired and he removed his furniture, the three-floored maisonette was taken over by Franklin Dyall and Mary Merrall. They had the place, which badly needed it, re-decorated. Apparently the ghosts were removed with Yeats's furniture, blue-green curtains, Tarot cards and magical books, for I never heard them complain either of queer " feelings " or mysterious chalk marks while they lived there.

Though I yield to no one in my admiration of W. B. Yeats as a poet—and was sincerely grateful to him for letting us his rooms at 18 Woburn Buildings, while we were looking about for a more permanent home—there were aspects of his personality as a man which made him less lovable to groundlings than the rival Dublin seer, George Russell (A.E.). A.E. had the usual Irish facility in expressing himself and was equally prolific as poet, painter and pamphleteer. As a pamphleteer he was first-rate. His painting, however, like his poetry, seemed to me facile, rather woolly, though suffused with the charm of other-worldliness. Possibly he was a much better poet than I gave him credit for. When James Stephens used to say some of his poems to me, in his rich and sonorous baritone, I was always stirred. But how much of the effect was due to A.E., and how much to Stephens's superb rendering of his verses, I was never able clearly to decide. In any case, as a personality A. E. always seemed to me to be far greater than his productions. In the domain of mysticism, " esoteric Buddhism " and what not, I had no opportunities of sitting at his feet among his numerous disciples, but I am certain that his teaching, his Message, was in the highest degree noble and uplifting. Although famous as a mystic, A.E. was also a practical economist and agricultural expert. As a fellow-worker with Sir Horace Plunkett in the field of Irish agricultural co-operation, as editor of the *Irish Homestead* and later of the *Irish Statesman*, his devoted efforts were of lasting benefit to his country. He had a fair share of humour, immense generosity and loving-kindness, breadth of vision and all the moral virtues of a lay priest. Ireland has been rich in such figures, which seem a natural product of the Irish soil, but A.E. surpassed all rivals. He was so outstandingly "good", so universally respected by his compatriots of all classes that, in retrospect, it seems surprising that the British Government did not " frame " him and bump him off. In the case of the unfortunate Sheehy-Skeffington, an admirable crank, vegetarian and pacifist, they shot him first and, as his widow told me with mingled laughter and tears, tried to " frame " him afterwards. Shortly after he was killed in

Portobello barracks, detectives arrived at her house with brown paper parcels containing " seditious literature " which they then solemnly and in the approved manner proceeded to "discover." As the literature was so wildly unlike anything with which the poor fellow had ever been associated ; was, indeed, of a kind which he had spent most of his innocent life denouncing, this official attempt to justify his murder proved a fiasco. Asquith was profoundly moved and shocked, his widow told me, when she called on him in London and gave him the details of what had happened.

Between A.E. and Yeats, though they were contemporaries and life-long intimates, there was a certain divergence of temperament. Yeats had done more than dabble in black magic, in association with a well-known English mage, and traces of these somewhat sinister leanings coloured his whole "aura". A.E.'s magic, on the other hand, was of a snowy whiteness, crystalline in its purity. When, as established pontiffs, they met at social gatherings, I noted, with some amusement, that each lion was inhibited from roaring in the other's hearing. Separately, in the presence of a respectful audience, each could produce a stream of *obiter dicta* calculated to make the fortune of memoir writers. No doubt many of their aphorisms were polished by frequent use. I remember Yeats once saying to me : " the difference between an Irishman and an Englishman is that the Irishman tells the truth to himself and lies to others, while the Englishman lies to himself and tells the truth to everybody else." Another of his favourite pronouncements was : " there is no crime a nation will not commit if only its newspapers are wicked enough." A.E. could equally be relied upon to fire off a succession of quotable sayings for the benefit of any respectful caller at the Plunkett House in Merrion Square.

In contrast to Yeats, who enjoyed " high society " and fancied himself to be descended from a line of aristocrats, A.E. was the complete " democrat "—homely, bearded, unpretentious, and rather sloppily dressed in dark tweeds. Speaking of Yeats on one occasion, not without a hint of malice, he remarked that " Yeats and I "—he pronounced the name Yeets—" were both sprung from the lower middle class." What precisely A.E. meant by this (since Yeats's ancestry was well known)—beyond the fact that both of them, when students together at the Metro-politian School of Art, were extremely poor—puzzled me for many years. Light was shed on it by a passage in Joseph Hone's

"W. B. Yeats", which I came on recently, referring to the quarrel between Yeats and George Moore. In "Vale", Moore mocks Yeats for " thundering like Ben Tillett himself against the middle-classes", and adds : " We asked ourselves why Willie Yeats should feel himself called upon to denounce a class to which he himself belonged essentially . . . with so admirable a parentage it did not seem necessary that a man should look back for an ancestor, and we had both laughed at the story . . . that on one occasion when Yeats was crooning over A.E.'s fire he had said that if he had his rights he would be Duke of Ormonde, and that A.E. had answered, ' in any case, Willie, you are over-looking your father.' "

Although A.E. could not be described as feline in his comments on Yeats, there was a hint that he regarded Yeats's weakness for playing up to social figures as indicating a streak of the charlatan and poseur. As Irish literary men, like members of a large family, understand each other with a devastating clarity, he was probably right.

In this connection, I recall that one of the books in Yeats's kitchen was a treatise on the mystical significance of the phases of the moon, which had been published in America. I read a good deal of it, enough to memorize certain words and key sentences. Some months later, while on a visit to Dublin, my mother-in-law, Ellie Duncan—a life-long friend of Yeats—gave a party at 16 Ely Place to enable the poet to deliver an informal lecture to such of the *intelligentsia* as cared to attend. The subject, to my surprise, was the influence on character of the phases of the moon. I listened spellbound while Yeats explained to his audience that the teaching he was about to expound to them had been revealed to him " in a dream" by a Moorish initiate with whom he had made contact on the astral plane. His listeners, mostly elderly women, stared at him goggle-eyed when he made this rather startling opening statement. As a device for riveting the attention of an audience he was anxious to impress, it struck me afterwards as legitimate enough. At the moment, however—not for the first time in Yeats's presence—I had some difficulty in restraining my irreverent giggles.

II

A retrospective glance at Betty's Dublin home and her remark-able parents, is perhaps permissible at this stage, since they greatly influenced my whole outlook during the 'twenties and accounted for the detachment with which I viewed post-war London.

I suppose that few writers who have now reached the age of fifty, if endowed with the qualities of imagination and sensibility, can look back on a life of settled contentment or conventional happiness. The convulsions of war, economic upheavals and violent revolutionary changes have sooner or later disturbed the equanimity of all but the most phlegmatic. Those of us who were doomed from childhood to a storm-tossed existence have in many cases developed the buoyancy of corks and managed to float successfully, at least for brief periods, into quiet backwaters. Others, who contrived to retain their property, their social position and their privileged status into middle age, found themselves plunged into paroxysms of terror by the march of events. What, they cried, can the world be coming to? Shall I—even I—be reduced to poverty through this dreaded Bolshevism, lose my job, my knighthood and my pension? Instead of mellowing into a contented old age, panic drove them into desperate courses and sent them crowding to fawn at the feet of the Hitlers, Mussolinis and Francos, who promised to save them from what conscience told them might be the wrath to come. The famous lines of the fourth Duke of Rutland, if we substitute " bureaucracy " for "nobility", accurately sums up their attitude :

> " Let virtue, wisdom, art and honour die—
> But leave us still our old bureaucracy."

The position of those who were born at odds with their environment, never climbed on to a branch which looked secure without its cracking behind them, never made any money without promptly losing it through wars or depressions, never climbed a rung or two up the ladder without being pushed off it by events over which they had no control, is, provided they can develop a philosophical habit of mind and retain an enquiring outlook, infinitely stronger than that of established persons who approach old age in terror lest the system which has supported them so long will at last collapse and ignominiously let them down. If we should call no man happy until he is dead, we should also reserve our pity for the despised and injured, the failures and the financially harassed, until we can be certain that they have not gained much that we ourselves have missed. Particularly does this apply in periods of cosmic upheaval and world revolution, when the rich man with much to lose usually finds himself an enemy of the people and therefore liable to be treated as such, while the man who has already reached rock-bottom and arranged his life accordingly, can face what comes to him with equanimity. Both, in the last event, have nothing to lose but their lives : he loses his most cheerfully who does so in a good cause which he cannot reproach himself for having ever betrayed.

When I first made the acquaintance of Betty Duncan and her parents, James and Ellen Duncan, I had already experienced many of the vicissitudes common to Englishmen of my generation. Fond though I was of my father and mother, loyal though I am to the ties of blood and tradition, devoted as I have never ceased to be to the land of my birth, it would be dishonest of me to pretend that the home into which I was born was either happy or congenial. As soon as I possibly could I escaped from it and stood on my own feet.

Both my parents died before 1914 and the publishing firm with which I was connected was wound up soon after the outbreak of war. After the Armistice, like thousands of others, I had no job and no prospects. All the branches on to which I had hopefully climbed had promptly cracked and let me fall. With the resilience of youth, however, I always picked myself up again with the greatest alacrity. It was in one of my temporarily prostrate moments that I fell in love with Betty Duncan who, with complete indifference to my economic situation in what was obviously a crazy and cock-eyed world, reciprocated my ardour. When she produced me at 16 Ely Place I could not but admire her courage. With imperturbable calm my future " in-laws " accepted the addition to their household of an impecunious minor poet with subversive ideas and revolutionary leanings. The type, to be sure, was not uncommon in Dublin : fortunately for me, Ellie Duncan had a strong weakness for it. From the moment of my arrival, I purred with contentment like a stray cat who has at long last discovered for itself the right kind of home. The prevailing atmosphere, indeed, everything about the Duncans' house, from Jim's Chippendale chairs which had been specially made for one of his ancestors, to the grand piano from which Ellie stroked Chopin's nocturnes and Ballades or thundered the Polonaise—charmed and delighted me. In her heyday Ellie had been one of Dublin's best amateur pianists and was specially renowned as an interpreter of Chopin. As I had never before lived in a musical household and my education in the greatest of the arts had been neglected, she seemed a veritable Pachmann. Although music was her principal interest, she took all the arts, so to speak, under her wing and encouraged every cultural activity in Dublin with a relentless and untiring energy. Had she not founded the United Arts Club in Stephen's Green? Was she not the curator of Hugh Lane's National Gallery of Modern Art in Harcourt Street? Lane, a close friend of the family and the beloved " Uncle Hugh " of Betty and her brother, had been drowned when the Lusitania went down, but his influence was still predominating at 16 Ely Place when I first set foot in it. So much so that when Betty and I provided Jim and Ellie with their first grandchild, it was inevitable that we should call him Hugh. When the controversy arose over the Lane bequest, by which, owing to an unwitnessed codicil, England became possessed of the magnificent collection of French pictures intended for Dublin, I was roped in as a member of the Committee formed for their recovery. I well remember the conference, in Ellie's drawing-room, with Yeats and Lady Gregory, Lane's redoubtable "Aunt Augusta", at which the Committee originated.

In spite of Jim's Unionist loyalties—he was a Civil Servant, near retiring age, and head of a minor department in Dublin Castle—most of the Dublin writers, artists, musical amateurs and patrons of the Drama were encountered sooner or later either at 16 Ely Place or at the United Arts Club. Among the more intimate friends of the family were Dermot O'Brien, the P.R.H.A.; Hester Dowden, daughter of Professor Dowden, whose experiments with automatic writing had aroused much interest outside Ireland ; Lennox Robinson ; Joseph Hone; "poor old Percy " French, author of " The Mountains of Mourne " and other world-famous Irish ballads ; Captain Jack White, the Ulster Communist rebel, and Katharine Tynan Hinkson and her daughter Pamela. George Moore, during the ten years he spent in a house almost opposite the Duncans', 4 Upper Ely Place, had been a frequent visitor. Betty told me that, as a child, she used to be forced to sit on his knee and much disliked it. The Duncans' circle of acquaintance was, indeed, enormous, and Ellie rarely allowed eminent visitors to arrive in Ireland without pouncing on them to visit the Arts Club and adorn her parties. The social accomplishments of my new family, though not remarkable in a community where facility in all the arts was the rule rather than the exception, filled me with all the more delight because none of them was taken very seriously. Gaiety and wit, not without a leaven of kindly malice—if " malice " is not too heavy a term for barbs rarely intended to hurt—combined to form the prevailing note of these evenings in Ely Place, under the Terror. Betty, in addition to having been one of Orpen's favourite pupils in her art school days, and a clever caricaturist, was an accomplished singer of Irish folksongs and had been on tour professionally with "poor old Percy". The more solid part of the musical programmes was provided by Ellie, who at the end of the evening was always willing to play dance music if required. Jim obliged with his own compositions, which, like Betty, he sang without accompaniment, while Cruise O'Brien enlivened the proceedings by giving his masterly imitation of " Willie Yeats " pontificating.

If Ellie was the strong man of the Duncan household, and was occasionally mocked by her son and daughter for being more than somewhat of a Leo Huntress, it was Jim who, in the capacity of host, prevented any distinguished strangers whom Ellie had relentlessly lassooed from regretting their capture. Under a slightly artificial grace of manner, that was perhaps too con-sciously *ancien régime*, he had a quality of charm which not even the most fiery Sinn Feiner could resist. A man of the most fastidious personal honour, of the most tenacious loyalty in friendship, of such engrained courtesy that it was incapable of failing, Jim's charm was more that of the Highland Scot than of the native Irish. Like so many Dubliners of the Protestant Ascendancy, I doubt if he possessed a drop of Irish blood. An incurable romantic, events in Scottish medieval history, doughty deeds and famous " scraps " in the long-distant past, were more real to him than any of the contemporary events, of horror and misery, cruelty and heroism, which were taking place within a a few miles of his home. As with so many Celts, his cultural fatherland was France. (Anatole France was, incidentally, his favourite writer.) He spoke French fluently, with the sort of " super-French " accent which prevails in the French Depart-ment of the B.B.C., and being thin, wiry, and light on his feet, was an excellent fencer, fencing being, in his view, a necessary accomplishment for a gentleman. His only concession to current fashions in the Service, as regards exercise, was to play a good game of golf. If Jim, supposing he were called upon, could defend a lady's honour with the épée, he was equally adept at praising her eyebrows in sonnet, rondeau, villanelle or ballade. But Jim's great quality, a quality which excused his unwillingness to disturb himself unnecessarily by taking sides in political arguments, was the fact that you could trust him with your life. He brought out the best in others by always believing in it. He was incapable of letting anyone down.

At a time when I, to a not inconsiderable extent, trusted Jim with my own life, he was in the late fifties. How I wished my new-found home—that oasis of happiness and all *les petits bonheurs* of civilized frugality—in the quiet cul-de-sac off Stephen's Green, could last for ever ! I was glad enough to be back in London, after the ghastly and futile war, but strong ties bound me to Dublin. Half my heart, as one may say, was there. It was a dreadful thought that a handful of London officials and politicians, the governing clique, were bringing fire and slaughter to the Ireland I loved, and arousing bitter hatred throughout the world against the England I loved more deeply still.

Similar emotions were caused me about India, for my principal man friend at this period was Abany Coomar Banerjee, a nephew of Rabindranath Tagore, who was eating his dinners at the Temple after graduating at Oxford. We became, for a time, inseparable and his departure to Calcutta in 1923 was a cruel blow. Our close friendship gave me a permanent interest in the problem of India's liberation from the British Raj.

Why is it, I have often asked myself, almost in a frenzy of bitterness and despair, that Official " England " must so often behave like a grasping, treacherous, brutal " cad ", must so often cringe to and appease our enemies and make enemies of our friends ? I have not only asked myself, but on many occasions when I have strayed into West End Club circles, I have asked such minor bureaucrats as I encountered to explain the inevitability of our backing wrong horses in wrong courses. Most of them were products of Balliol, State-aided Scotch careerists with brilliant third-class minds. Their replies were usually as clear, as closely reasoned and as cogent as leaders in *The Times*. I always emerged from these discussions with " men in close touch " crushed by a dead-weight of seemingly irrefutable arguments which, if propounded by a Judge, would make any jury convict the innocent, and convinced that ability to make the worse appear the better cause is the essential quality for a successful place-man.

I do not know how long the Duncans had occupied 16 Ely

Place before their home was broken up. It may have been ten years, if not longer. Their tenancy coincided with a period in Dublin's social history as brilliant as any which has been recorded since the days of Grattan's Parliament. When I first became one of the family their home had mellowed and one would have supposed it to be as firmly established as anything could be. The financial situation of the family, in view of their tastes and talents, was ideal. Jim, as head of his department, had an ample salary to permit him a life of dignity and comfort, and a substantial pension to look forward to when he retired. Ellie had a salary as curator of the Municipal Gallery and supplemented it by journalism. In Dublin there was no money standard, no extravagance of living. A few pounds a week sufficed for men like A.E. and James Stephens; W. B. Yeats, for the greater part of his life, was content with an extremely modest income. Compared with these eminences Jim was comparatively affluent, and as his personal tastes and habits were extremely frugal, he did not know the meaning of financial cares. It was on the basis of security—a security which in pre-Beveridge days only a fortunate section of the community enjoyed—that he and his wife and family were able to develop a way of living, a standard of civilization, of which a parallel could be found only in France. In England we should have to go back to the days of Dr. Thomas Campion to find anything comparable to it—to find a modest middle-class, neither rich nor poor, but sufficiently well-off to permit the good life, the life enriched by the charms of social intercourse based on the practice and appreciation of the arts. Jim was able to maintain his home and circle as an oasis of neutrality in the midst of a guerilla war which in Dublin and other large towns, Cork particularly, had all the features of a White Terror, because of a philosophical habit of mind and an aristocratic detachment. Like César Capéran, the hero of Louis Codet's charming novel, he was a traditionalist and a humanist. When " the Troubles " produced the Anglo-Irish Treaty and the creation of the Free State, he had reached retiring age. An epoch had ended. He left Dublin, tried for a year to live in Chelsea, gave it up and migrated to his spiritual home—to Paris. There he made for himself a life of modest comfort surrounded by émigré friends, and by elderly French people whose values he shared and who accepted him as one of themselves. The significance of 16 Ely Place seems to me to lie in the fact that the kind of civilization it represented should be possible under any conceivable form of Communist or Socialist economy which events may have in store for us. It was an example of the good life, attainable by all who have the necessary cultivation, so long as they are economically *secure*. Under no economic system need the salary paid for Jim's activities have been appreciably less than the one he received. He snatched the bread from no one's mouth, robbed nobody in the form of profit-seeking, envied no one, harmed no one. Though he attached importance to the station in life in which he was born, he scrupulously observed what he regarded as its obligations. When Jim and Ellie took their daughter to be presented at the Viceregal Lodge in Phœnix Park, the party proceeded in their finery by the Dublin tram, without the least embarrassment or pretentiousness.

As an Englishman I could not refrain from reflecting on the contrast between the Duncans' way of living and that of the English people of the same income group of whom I had any knowledge. Half the things on which the English middle-classes spend the bulk of their incomes would have been considered by Jim mere superfluities. The expensive and mindless " pleasures " of the English made no appeal to him and he was not impressed by the expensive English education for gentility, which turned out boys with no knowledge of any European language or literature, no interest in any of the arts and often no manners except an arrogance based upon stupidity. Qualities of tolerance, geniality, humour and, when required, stubborn courage, the mass of English people possess in abundance, and our history has always been enlivened by eccentrics, originals, rebels and men of genius. But a vulgar press, a vulgar wireless—never more so than when highbrow or refined—vulgar pleasures, a vulgar pervading acquisitiveness and a still more vulgar cult of political ignorance have overlaid the native virtues of our bourgeoisie. A planned economy and the security which goes with it, can only give us the happy life if there is a revival of religious faith accompanied by a substitution of art in daily life for dreary profit-seeking and the dreary bought amusements which are the profit-snatchers' sole reward. What a rich, full and satisfactory life people could have on the pre-1914 purchasing value of £300 a year, if only they had the right education to enable them to live it ! How infinitely preferable was the pre-1914 existence of the cultivated Irishman or Frenchman, at this income level, than that of the comparatively wealthy middle-class Englishman !

CHAPTER TWO

CAME THE DAWN?

JOSEPH KING, who created a job for me at the beginning of 1919 and remained my kindest and most beneficent friend until his death in August 1943, was one of those wealthy eccentrics whom many of us have come to regard as the salt of the English earth. Unlike Aristides he made virtue lovable and robbed the profession of "doing good", which he followed throughout his long life, of its usual irritating and tiresome concomitants. His father had been a Liverpool surgeon and his mother a sister of George MacDonald, the writer of those Scotch fairy tales which delighted the mid-Victorians. Although by religion a Congregationalist, he was at Uppingham under Thring and at the age of eighty-two still remembered his schooldays (and Thring himself) with intense loathing. He took his degree at Oxford (oddly enough he was at Trinity), afterwards studied for the ministry at various theological colleges, and then spent some years as a post-graduate student at the Universities of Giessen and Berlin. On his return, instead of becoming a Nonconformist parson, he was called to the Bar (Inner Temple) and devoted himself to " political, municipal, social and religious work in London". In January 1910 he entered the House of Commons as Liberal Member for North Somerset. During the war years he was one of the pacifist group in Parliament, which included Sir Charles Trevelyan, Arthur Ponsonby, Philip Morrell, and others of outstanding ability. He lost his seat in the Coupon Election, and at the time when I started to work for him he had just joined the Labour Party. In appearance, he bore a striking resemblance to Tenniel's "Mad Hatter", a fact which was seized upon by the *Punch* cartoonist who made him a national figure and provided him with a nickname of which he was secretly rather proud. It symbolized the tolerant affection with which he was always regarded by his political opponents. The fact that the " Mad Hatter " was nearly always right, when events proved the average Conservative hopelessly wrong, did not prevent them from continuing to look on him as a wrong-headed but amiable lunatic.

When I first went down to Witley to spend the week-end with Joe I knew nothing of his background and expected to find myself in the usual arty cottage or dolled-up farmhouse which most of the cranks of my acquaintance then affected. He met me at Witley station with a singular home-made wheelbarrow on which my suitcase was deposited. Together we hauled this contraption up a steep footpath to the top of the hill and then along a road until we came to a large and beautifully designed modern country house. This, much to my surprise, proved to be our destination. It was called "Sandhouse". House-building was one of Joe's hobbies. (After the death of his first wife, Maude Egerton King, he moved to Haslemere and built several other houses of equal architectural merit.) Mrs. King had established a weaving industry, in which a number of local girls were employed. She also edited a paper devoted to peasant arts and crafts, and was a friend and patron of Arnold Dolmetsch and his gifted family. The young Dolmtesches seemed very much at home at " Sandhouse," and were constantly in and out when I was there. The whole place was a hive of industry, of what I took to be a vaguely Tolstoyan type, but fortunately Joe did not turn out to be either a teetotaller, a non-smoker or a vegetarian. He and his wife were charming hosts and I enjoyed every minute of my stay, including the hours I spent in the library with my employer, absorbing political wisdom and doing the work required of me. I cannot, at this distance of time, remember exactly what it was, but I suppose it had to do with the preparation of a pamphlet advocating fair play for the Weimar Republic. Later, through Joe's influence, I became a " paid worker " on Lord Parmoor's "Fight the Famine Council", with which the Buxtons (Charles and Noel) and others were associated, and spent some weeks investigating conditions in Germany on their behalf.

Before going into Germany, I stayed at The Hague as the guest of a group of Germans who were producing a singular paper called *The Word in Three Languages*, dedicated to international reconciliation. Even to my innocent and inexperienced eyes this outfit seemed rather "phoney". In the light of later knowledge, I suspect that they were a bunch of German Secret Service agents, who had been supplied with money for the purpose of establishing contact with Left Wing intellectuals. I disliked all of them intensely except a young Dresden art critic, Doktor Friedrich Markus Huebner, who facilitated my entry into Germany and provided me with a number of introductions to German writers, mostly Communists and Jews, who had opposed the war. At this period my political ignorance was, in some ways, as complete as that of any other young man with a Conservative

upbringing.   My only settled conviction was that the war ought
to have ended in 1917 when Wilson's offer to mediate had been
accepted by the Central Empires,* that it had brought untold
suffering and loss on millions of innocent people, mostly of the
working class, and that it was the product of commercial rivalry
between groups of big industrialists in the various countries
taking part in it.   Contrasted, in every country, was the stubborn
endurance of the common soldier and the corruption and greed
of the commercial classes who robbed the community while
supplying the munitions essential for victory.   From Joe King and
E. D. Morel I had derived some knowledge of pre-war diplomatic
history, which made it clear that neither Great Britain nor France
was as innocent of blame for the outbreak of hostilities as was
officially alleged.   Of the political situation inside Germany
and of the part played by the Allies in suppressing the Spartacist
revolution, of which the murdered Communists, Karl Liebknecht
and Rosa Luxemburg had been leaders, I knew nothing.   I
could not have defined the exact difference between a Socialist,
an Anarchist and a Communist, or explained why the Social
Democrats of the new bourgeois Republic had called in the hated
military caste to suppress "the Reds".   I spoke hardly a word
of German, but though, by a fortunate accident, I had escaped
the trenches, I was as free from civilian Hun-hating as our
soldiers at Cologne.   Most of my school friends had been killed.
Of the men I knew who had survived the years of slaughter,
not one shared the frenzy of the profiteers or the daily rages of
the over-age journalists who wrote for the popular Press.   I
therefore went into Germany with, comparatively speaking,
an open mind, without preconceived ideas, and in complete
ignorance of the secret policies of the men behind the scenes in
my own Government.   My only object was to discover whether
our hunger blockade was really starving the poorer classes and
killing off children and old people.   At the time of my visit
there were hardly any English journalists in Germany.   I could
not have got a visa in London.   I secured it, with Huebner's aid,
from the German Consul at Rotterdam, as the result of my
connection with the Fight the Famine Council.   This was known
to be largely supported by Quakers and the prestige of the Quakers
in Central Europe was already great enough to act like a charm.

* In his book " The Mirror of Europe ", K. Zilliacus says that " a negotiated
peace without victors or vanquished would have been fatal to the old order ".   In a
footnote, he adds : " That is the capital difference between the first and second
world wars.   For in this war a negotiated peace 'without victors or vanquished'
would mean a victory for the Axis, for fascism and for appeasement ".

I found after my return from this adventure that one of the very few English journalists who had got into Germany at the time I was there, had been sending excited messages to his paper representing that he was in almost continual danger of assassination, so strong was the feeling against the English. I am glad I did not read them, as I might have been infected by my colleague's alarm. In my innocence I had no fears for my personal safety and relied—successfully, as it happened— upon pacific intentions and a supply of an English cigarette called " Flags " to see me through. I cannot recall a single occasion when I encountered the least sign of personal hostility due to my being an Englishman. The train in which I crossed the Dutch frontier into Germany contained a number of prisoners of war, who had been released some months later than their relatives had expected. At each little station a group of them alighted and were embraced by their wives and families. The garlands of flowers and green leaves with which the stations had been decorated in honour of their return had long since withered. I was gratified to see that the men looked healthy and as if they had been well fed.

I went first to Stuttgart. The town was very full, but an English-speaking head waiter at the Hotel Marquardt took pity on me and found me a room in a *gasthaus*, not far from the flat he occupied with his English wife. He apologized for the plainness of the accommodation but I was thankful to get a bed at all. Before turning in I spent an hour talking to these good samaritans. The wife, a Cockney, with a pale myopic son wearing large spectacles, gave me a torrential account of her adventures in London before, through the good offices of the Quakers, she had been repatriated to Germany. In England, after her husband was recalled to fight for his country, she had suffered both from poverty and hunger and from the unkindness of her relatives. " Me rich sister, wot lives at Notting 'ill, wouldn't give me so much as a milk pudding," she complained. " She wanted me to chuck my man because 'e was an 'un, but Fritz has always been a good husband and father, and I didn't see why I should. When the Quakers—and they *was* kind, they took no end of trouble— got me sent back with a lot of other wives, I went and caught flu and had to go to hospital. As soon as the German women heard there was an English *frau* in the ward, they couldn't do too much for me. Lent me their 'ot bottles, they did . . ." The war, to these people had just been a calamity, an act of God.

I

They knew nothing of its causes, nothing about the " rights and wrongs " of it, and certainly never desired it.

On the following day I called on Clara Zetkin and had tea with her in the apple orchard outside her villa, overlooking the red roofs of Stuttgart.   At the time I knew little about her record but I can well understand how she came to inspire Louis Aragon's great novel, " The Bells of Basel ".   In my experience men and women who, for one reason or another, can be described as truly " great", are easily recognizable.   Clara Zetkin was clearly in this category.   She was like a prophetess, one who saw far into the future, and could foretell with a certainty which lent her indomitable courage, the ultimate triumph of the cause she stood for.   At the time I met her, she was already growing old.   She was a highly cultivated woman, apparently used to living in easy circumstances.   It is amusing to recall that, like most revolutionary leaders, she was as " middle", or even " upper middle " class as some of the editorial committee of our own *Daily Worker*.

At Frankfurt I called on Dr. Simon, editor of the *Frankfurter Zeitung*, and later went to tea at his luxurious flat where I met a retired General, who was polite but eyed me with disfavour. He was probably the only German I encountered during my journey whom an English diplomat would have considered fit to speak to.   I enjoyed my visit to this attractive old city and had interesting conversations with Dr. Hugo Seckel, who had translated my novel " The Fortune", with Hermynia Zur Muhlen, the translator of my naif revolutionary play, " The Fight for Freedom", which was then appearing in *Die Wiesse Blatter*, one of the numerous Left Wing periodicals which sprouted into existence after the Armistice, with Fritta Brod, a well-known actress, and a number of other people connected with the stage. In all of them I found the same burning faith that " the dawn " was at last breaking and that the triumph of International Socialism would see the beginning of a brave new world.   I am glad to know that at least one of this group managed to escape to England with her husband and thus escaped the concentration camps.

I went on from Frankfurt to Dresden, where I spent some happy hours in the magnificent art gallery and had a long conversation with the Czech artist, Ottokar Kokoschka.   It was interesting to discover that, during the war years, the German authorities had been lavish purchasers of modern art.

At Munich I found myself, as Clara Zetkin had warned me

I should, in an atmosphere of tension not unlike that of Dublin during the guerilla war.   Kurt Eisner, head of the short-lived Bavarian Communist Republic, had recently been murdered by a young reactionary aristocrat, and all the Commissars of the former Red Government were in hiding, and in danger of their lives.   I stayed at the famous Vierjahreszeiten Hotel, where the opulence of the furniture and fittings contrasted with the patched sheets and towels, poor food and ersatz coffee.   The people to whom I had introductions seemed frightened of talking to me, even in English.   I called on a famous Jewish eye specialist and found him in a state of great agitation.   He was expecting to be raided at any moment by the White Terrorists and was overcome with anxiety about the future fate of his wife and young daughter.   When I went to see him again, two days later, deeply concerned by what he had told me, the blow had evidently fallen, for the house was closed and deserted.   I was never able to discover what happened to these unfortunates, but concluded they were murdered like so many of their fellows.

In Berlin I had interviews with Karl Kautsky and several other Socialist leaders, but was too ignorant of German and knew too little of the confused political situation to gain much benefit from them.   This I regret, for they might have opened my eyes to the way in which some of the British authorities were, even then, backing the reactionaries and helping to sabotage the revolution.   I met Georg Kaiser, the dramatist, and Arthur Hollitscher, a pacifist writer of travel books, but failed to see Ernst Toller, who was already in prison.   Years later I met Toller in London, with Ethel Mannin, shortly after one of his plays had been performed.   He was a charming man, with many friends, but the strains to which he had been subjected were too much for his nervous system and he committed suicide.   My chief friend in Berlin was another Jewish dramatist, Ludwig Rubiner, who was then staying in Busoni's sumptuous flat in Wilmersdorf, which had been lent him by the pianist.   He made an appointment for me to call there one afternoon to meet his wife, who had been a Commissar in Munich under the Commune and was, in consequence, " on the run".   I arrived punctually, but when, after half an hour, there was still no sign of Frau Rubiner, Ludwig began to grow increasingly alarmed. At last we heard the front door open.   " There she is," he cried. His relief was premature.   A moment later she entered the great music room, followed by detectives who had seized her outside the flat. The charge was one which, if she were convicted, might entail a sentence of death. The couple were devoted to one another and their parting, under the contemptuous eyes of the detectives, who had evidently kept their jobs under the new régime, was one of the most harrowing I have ever had to witness. After Frau Rubiner had been taken away, her husband and I drove about Berlin searching for the Jewish advocate Haase, to beg him to undertake her defence. We were unsuccessful, and some time later Haase, like Rathenau, was murdered. Frau Rubiner was tried and escaped with the light sentence of thirteen months' imprisonment. Her husband, worn out with the strain of the trial, died before the sentence had been served.

In Berlin, as in the other German cities I visited, I had ample evidence of the effect of the hunger blockade on the professional and working-class population. I called on the English wife of a German violinist, whose family I had known in former days. She was a brilliant pianist and she and her husband made their living by giving music lessons. Both looked pale and half-starved and I suspected that they were giving most of the food they could obtain to their small daughter. They insisted on my coming to a meal and I saw no way of refusing without hurting their feelings. Luckily, I was able to bring with me a substantial quantity of chocolate which, with my English money, I was able to buy at black market prices. In spite of the prevailing semi-starvation, profiteers and foreigners could get most things in Berlin by paying for them.

On my way back to England I spent a night in Leipzig and had very pleasant interviews with Dr. Otto, head of the firm of Tauchnitz, and with Dr. Kippenberg, of Insel Verlag. Dr. Otto published four of my novels in the Tauchnitz edition. His liking for England and hatred of the war were obviously sincere. The great international library built up by his firm was ruined by the fluctuations of the valuta, and I saw in the paper some years later that he had taken his life.

Dr. Kippenberg showed me his famous Goethe library and subjected me to a friendly cross-examination on the subject of current English literature. This enabled me to do some unofficial agency work on behalf of D. H. Lawrence which bore fruit later. After dinner that evening, when I was sitting in a large café listening to the excellent band, the waiter who brought me my beer, seeing that I was alone, asked if he could take me round the town and show me the sights. He was, he said, just going off duty, and it would take him twenty minutes to go home, change, and return to fetch me. He was a boy of about twenty, spoke English fluently and had charming manners. I accepted his proposal gladly and spent several hours in his company, learning much about the conditions in a German working-class family during the war years. Throughout my stay in Germany I never met with anything but courtesy and friendliness from the hotel employees, waiters, cab-drivers and other members of the common people with whom I came in contact. The victims of the hunger blockade were not the Junkers and the profiteers, but the impoverished middle and lower classes, and, in particular, their young children, who were no more responsible for the war than were the victimized plain people of our own or any other country.

To base any generalization on my experiences, in view of my ignorance of the German language and of what was really going on behind the scenes, would be absurd. By dint of much study during the intervening quarter of a century, I have gained a clearer idea of the situation as it existed in the summer of 1919 than I had at the time. The conviction I then formed that anything might have been done with the German *people* had we acted with humanity and justice, permitted the German revolution to succeed, supported the peace-loving elements in the population and cracked down on the Prussian military caste, Junkers and big industrialists, has been fully confirmed by subsequent events. Our ruling clique, however, terrified by the spectre of what they are pleased to call " anarchy and chaos", acted in defeated Germany precisely as they have since acted in " liberated " Italy, Belgium and Greece. The record of Amgot, the support given to Balkan quislings, the bouquets to General Franco, the respect accorded to Hitler's Papal ally and the licence permitted to the Polish émigrés all show that the type of reactionaries whose treatment of Germany made the present war possible still exert a powerful influence behind the scenes and have learnt nothing from the past.

One of the principal causes of the war's renewal in 1939 was, unquestionably, the fact that the public was completely misled as to the behaviour, policy and secret motives of the British Government in their handling of the situation in Germany after the Armistice. Even skilled observers and experts in Foreign Affairs were unable to ferret out the facts and, in consequence, built up a whole edifice of logical argument on premises which later proved to be unsound. It was not until I read " Need

Germany Survive", by Julius Braunthal (Gollancz, 1943), and "World in Trance", by Leopold Schwartzchild (Hamish Hamilton, 1943) that I realized the close connection between what happened in the past and what is happening today.

The situation in Germany in the summer of 1919 which my ignorance of what the Allied authorities were really up to prevented me from understanding, is thus summarized by Braunthal :

" The revolution was from the very beginning frustrated by the hostility of the victorious powers. They refused to recognize the revolutionary Government elected by the Workers' and Soldiers' Councils ; they refused to negotiate peace with the representatives of the German revolution ; as a preliminary condition for peace negotiations they insisted on the election of the Government by a duly elected National Assembly. They further prohibited the maintenance of diplomatic relations between the German Republic and Soviet Russia. When, in November 1918, the Soviet Government proposed an exchange of Ambassadors, the German Government felt itself bound, under the pressure of the Entente, to reject the Russian suggestion. The blockade against Germany was still in force ; the country was threatened with famine and chaos and, worse than that, by an armed intervention by the victorious Powers hostile to a Soviet revolution."

This hostility to Socialism, the only economic system which has the remotest chance of ridding the world of the scourge of recurrent wars, was the dominating motive of the British plutocratic oligarchy in 1919, as it still is in 1944. Then, as now, their sole aim was to return as far as possible to the economic *status quo*. Equipped as we now are with penetrating " hindsight ", only conscienceless parents can fail to realize that it was to their fear and hatred of Bolshevism that the Conservative Caucus, by which we are still so largely governed, sacrificed a generation of young Englishmen who were then in their cradles.

Having totally defeated the German Empire and taken the necessary powers under the Peace Treaty to ensure its disarmament, the Allied reactionaries proceeded to support all the aggressive elements in Germany which had plunged Europe into a morass of mud and blood. On the usual pretext of suppressing " anarchy and chaos " they forced back into servitude the pacific and oppressed majority of the working-class population of the Central Empires. From the first, British diplomatic and military agents in Germany got into friendly contact with the German

Junker aristocracy, the military caste and the big industrialists—on a class basis. Gentlemen dealing with gentlemen. The butcher Mannerheim had successfully massacred the Finnish " Reds " with the aid of a German free corps : this incident undoubtedly predisposed the British wire-pullers to consider a reconstructed Germany in the light of a useful Bulwark against Bolshevism. The murders of Karl Liebknecht, Rosa Luxemburg, Kurt Eisner, Haase, Rathenau and others, and the scenes of which I was an accidental witness in Munich and Berlin, thus aroused not horror but secret approval in the British Government and its military advisers. In 1919, according to Herr Schwartzchild, " it was estimated in Paris that the disarmament of Germany would be accomplished three months after the conclusion of peace ". That this would be done was naturally taken for granted throughout Great Britain. All the arguments of the pacifists regarding the treatment of Germany were based upon this assumption. " But 1920, 1921, and 1922 went by and Germany was still ' disarming.' " . . . The Allies had to fight and argue every step of the way. Often a matter seemed settled and the Control Commission checked it off in their files, but a month later it would have to be reconsidered. The German courts meted out draconian sentences against anyone suspected of aiding the Control Commission. When a hidden store of cannon barrels was discovered in an armaments factory in Berlin, the stock manager was accused of having revealed it to the Commission. A German tribunal sentenced this alleged traitor to life imprisonment. " How do you know that the Control Commission was informed of this by the stock manager ? " the director of the armaments plant was asked. " An English member of the Commission told it to me confidentially." The Conservative " anti-Bolshevik " Fifth Column was thus already in action.

At the time of the " Kapp Putsch " the German people and the parties of the " Weimar Coalition " roused themselves to resist the militarists, but the only weapon they could use effectively was that of the general strike. " Strike leaflets ", says Schwartzchild, " were dropped on Berlin from planes, and the capital, although under martial law, obeyed. Everything came to a standstill. Only one institution in Berlin functioned as usual—the hotel where the members of the Inter-Allied Military Control Commission resided. The waiters and chambermaids of the Adlon wished in this way to show their solidarity with all the forces which opposed the return of the militarists. They made only one exception to this exception. While continuing to serve the French, American and Belgian officers, they refused to serve the British. They had observed the social life of the British members of the Commission. Although there was no truth in Trebitsch-Lincoln's fairy-tale about London's support of the *putsch*, and we have no proof that General Malcolm and his staff knew anything about it or encouraged it, the waiters and chambermaids had witnessed too much cordiality between the British and German officers."

During this extraordinary period, Lloyd George seemed to be as much under the influence of Francophobia as President Wilson, and his conversations with President Millerand at San Remo in 1920 were the reverse of cordial. " His attitude was that the German nation was not responsible for the war, the Junkers have been ejected and that, generally, the Germans should not be regarded with suspicion."

Lloyd George's fears that the French would get above themselves, and disturb the historic Foreign Office policy of maintaining the " balance of power " in Europe, were hardly calculated to ensure the effective working of the Military Control Commission and the Officers' Corps skilfully took advantage of them.

After the Locarno Pact an " Admission Committee " was set up to consider Germany's application to join the League of Nations. The Inter-Allied Military Control Commission was ordered to undertake a " final inspection " of the state of her armaments. Briand and Sir Austen Chamberlain expected the Commission to supply a reassuring report that German disarmament had been effectively carried out. The preliminary report, however, completely upset all their calculations. In their dilemma, the French and British Foreign Ministers decided that " higher interests " required that the people of France and Great Britain, and the Admission Committee of the League, should be kept in the dark. They accordingly shelved the disquieting preliminary report and a few months later relegated the 504 pages of the definitive report to their secret files. " This incident," says Herr Schwartzschild, " would have remained a secret if a British member of the Military Control Commission had not violated military discipline and made the extraordinary transaction public." (In *The Times*, November 4th, 1933.) General John H. Morgan, Adjutant-General of the Commission, gave the whole game away by declaring that the sense of the suppressed final report had been that " Germany had never disarmed, had never had the intention of disarming, and for seven years had done everything in her power to hinder, deceive and ' counter-control ' the Commission appointed to control her disarmament." The course followed by the British Foreign Office was to strengthen Germany as a counterweight to France and, more particularly, to the dreaded U.S.S.R. As early as 1922, General Morgan had revealed to his superiors that by an ingenious system of organization the Reichswehr comprised 250,000 men instead of 100,000 men as the Treaty demanded. When he made a report to this effect, " he received," says Schwartzchild, " a telegraphic order from Lloyd George to resign, and only Marshal Foch's personal intervention saved him from outright dismissal."

In this fashion, by means of these methods of fraud and deceit, were the million men of our race who had given their lives in " a war to end war," betrayed. In this fashion—by concealing from us essential facts—was another massacre more frightful than imagination could then conceive, rendered inevitable. The fathers of boys who will be of military age in the next ten years can no longer plead ignorance as an excuse for evading their responsibility as parents or their duties as citizens.

For twenty-five years successive Parliaments, under Tory domination, have betrayed the electorate by failing to lay bare the real basis of British Foreign Policy and by failing to exercise any effective control over the Foreign Office. The lesson of the past which today is clear as daylight is that any vote cast for a Conservative, " National " or Coalition candidate is a vote for secrecy. A vote for secrecy about the causes and conduct of the present struggle can only be regarded as a vote for its continuance after another period of armistice. Mr. Churchill's fond belief that this war is becoming " less and less ideological " is a clear enough indication that a Conservative victory offers more prospects of revolution than of peace.

How far away, and yet how near, seems the Peace Conference at Versailles ! What fears, what longings, it aroused in Europe's martyred millions, what wild indulgence in wishful-thinking it occasioned ! In 1919, the intellectuals thought the " dawn " was breaking at last. They were filled with hope. They believed passionately in what they supposed to be the ideals of the Labour Party and actually thought Ramsay MacDonald the sort of man to see them realized. How many of them are now confident that Messrs. Attlee, Bevin and Morrison will succeed where MacDonald failed ?

CHAPTER THREE

The Nineteen Seventeen Club

I

If the shape of things to come has been made clearer by the progress of the present titanic conflict in Eastern Europe, vague psychic stirrings and premonitions inspired the " mad hatters," and those who listened to them in 1917. When Lenin and his friends made their historic journey through Germany in a shuttered railway carriage, there were a few—outside the handful of Communists—who realized that something had happened of world-shaking significance. The grains of mustard seed lodged in the most surprising bonnets. Cranks of all varieties—vegetarians, conscientious objectors, mystics, progressives of all sorts and descriptions, Quakers, poets and a queer crowd of *avantgardists* of every creed, colour and social and ethical background who had " seen the light in the sky "—gradually found themselves coalescing into a group. What brought them together was partly the instinct of self-preservation in face of official hostility. It was as a persecuted minority that, after the outbreak of the Bolshevik Revolution, they formed themselves into a club which, in Russia's honour, they called " The 1917 Club."

In 1944, with the exception of the Conservative governing class who have never pretended to be anti-Fascist and are solely concerned with the survival of the old system of profit-grabbing, the bulk of the population actively engaged in the war have some conception of what it is about and what kind of world they wish to see resulting from it. A comparatively trifling incident, the release of Sir Oswald Mosley, revealed the unanimity of the people in opposition to the Fascist sympathies of the still unrepentant ruling classes. When war broke out on August 4th, 1914, we were by contrast a nation of innocents. The masses of the people trusted the Government implicitly. The automatic response to superiors, founded on a quasi-religious patriotism of the kind inculcated by Rudyard Kipling, brought the public-school-educated youth flocking to the Colours. The necessary stimulus to emotional idealism—since our island was not threatened and, as Balfour admitted, no British interests were directly at stake—was provided by references to "Brave Little Belgium" and "scraps of paper."

All our previous campaigns, including those against Napoleon —on the successful outcome of which our power and prestige were still mainly based—had been fought for us by a comparative handful of professionals. The excuse and justification of a patrician caste, in England as elsewhere, is that when war breaks out it shall provide leadership in the field. On this under- standing, it is accorded social privileges in time of peace and allowed an easy and enjoyable existence mostly devoted to field sports and other less edifying pleasures. The rank-and-file, in Wellington's day, was mainly supplied by the dregs of the common people, with N.C.O.s selected from the class of gentle- men's servants. It is not recorded that any large number of itinerant preachers, poets, novelists, school-teachers, stage-players, portrait-painters, architects, musicians, male ballet-dancers or university professors were called upon to maintain the thin red line at Waterloo, or to man the guns of H.M.S. Victory at Trafalgar. Our Jane Austens could write their genteel comedies of manners without being disturbed by the world-shaking events which were taking place across the Channel, or being called upon to "do their bit." The commercial classes, including the farmers, since agriculture was our staple industry, naturally looked on wars as a heaven-sent opportunity for getting rich quickly. (They still do.)

The four years' war was the first in our long history in which tens of thousands of completely unmilitary types of men, including many who had been brought up in a religious or political atmo- sphere in which war was held in abhorrence, were coerced into the armed forces of the Crown. Thus the passing of the Conscrip- tion Act of 1916 had the effect of sifting out from the mass of the population our residuum of cranks, eccentrics, political rebels, fanatical Nonconformists and hard-bitten individualists—gritty human material which the military machine was unable to absorb or crush. "The position of the Conscientious Objector," wrote Julian Bell, "was one of simple resistance ; a conviction that it was impossible for anyone of intellectual integrity to surrender to the discretion of fools and scoundrels engaged in the enterprise of destroying civilization."

As the whole military machine, backed by mob fury and class resentment, was set going against a few thousands of "Conchies", the charge that they were "lily-livered" and

actuated by physical cowardice—a charge freely brought by
" home defence " Colonels, " white-feather " spinsters, " indis-
pensable " business executives and elderly journalists, will hardly
stand up, particularly as there were numerous funk-holes in which
the naturally timid could escape the trenches in protective khaki.
At the end of the war, the Conchies were shown to have suffered
as many casualties in proportion to their numbers as the fighting
forces. Most were financially ruined and the widows of those
who died in gaol or as the result of ill-treatment in military
barracks naturally received no pensions. In later years, it is
surprising what a number of war-resisters have made their mark
in politics, literature and the arts. When the first round of the
present " ideological " war started in Spain, some of the younger
political " objectors " volunteered for service with the International Brigade. There was nothing inconsistent in their action.
Socialists who have not repented of their Socialism have proved
themselves, in all countries, veritable ironsides in the struggle
to crush Fascism. They are the men who know what they are
fighting for and love what they know. It is no paradox that the
convinced Socialist-pacifist should today prove the most
determined belligerent. By definition, all Socialists, including,
fortunately for the world, Marshal Stalin, are pacifists, although
all pacifists are not Socialists.

II

The " objectors," many of whom joined the 1917 Club, were
certainly the oddest lot of people ever temporarily united under
one banner. Some of them carried their dislike of killing so
far that they existed only on vegetables. Others would not even
hurt the feelings of a vegetable by cooking it, and lived on unfired
food. Perhaps the strangest figure who ever appeared before a
Tribunal was the late Lytton Strachey. The dignified bearded
historian, on arriving in Court, calmly inflated an air cushion
before seating himself to discuss with the tribunes, in his high-
pitched voice, what he would do if he came upon a Hun in the
act of molesting one of his female relatives. Another Conchy
was a musician who had the honesty to admit his physical dis-
ability. " Quite apart from my hatred of war," he explained
to a friend, " I am entirely devoid of all the more obvious forms
of physical courage. I cannot bear explosions or thunderstorms,
always avoid fields containing cattle, cannot use my fists or order

other men about, have no presence of mind in an emergency, and always feel faint at the sight of blood. It is the way I am made—just as some men are born deaf or short-sighted." The tribunes were, of course, unanimous in refusing him any kind of exemption. Fortunately a sympathetic doctor fitted him out with a pair of flat feet, so he was able to go on playing his piano undisturbed.

The majority of war-resisters were tough men, both physically and intellectually, or they could not have endured what they went through. One, now high up in the Government service, actually had the courage to go on a thirst strike and kept it up for eleven days. Another was a lawyer by profession and, in politics, an old-fashioned Nonconformist Radical. He was always immaculately dressed in top-hat, cutaway coat and sponge-bag trousers and invariably wore a pink carnation in his buttonhole. His manner was dignified and suave ; nothing excited or upset him. He thought this particular war unjust and indefensible. He had not been consulted about it, nor had he been given the opportunity of recording his vote for or against it. He therefore ignored it. He did not appear before the Tribunals and he took no notice of his calling-up papers. He was, in due course, arrested and removed to barracks, where his elegant civilian clothes were stripped from him and a suit of khaki supplied in their place. He continued to smile and took no action in the matter. I believe, eventually, he was forcibly dressed in uniform, court-martialled, and imprisoned " for the duration." When I saw him again, after the war, he had resumed his top-hat, his London clothes, his pink carnation, and looked extremely pleased with himself, as well he might. He had fought the judiciary and the whole armed forces of the Crown single-handed, defied the mob and beaten the lot of them. As he never showed any desire to convert anyone to his views I never discovered exactly what they were. However mad and wrong-headed his ideas may have been, he was a quintessential Englishman : a fine example of the national type which never surrenders and does not understand " appeasement."

Although I have always had a soft spot for eccentrics, I must confess that a good many of the stained-glass window, other-cheek-turning Conchies with whom I came in contact at the 1917 Club, filled me with an un-Christian desire to give them a kick in the pants. Their vanity was colossal, they would not unite with the main body of Socialists or make any attempt to translate their religious attitudes into coherent political action. They preferred to form a number of little societies and " councils," each convinced that it alone preached the true gospel, each suspicious and resentful of its rivals. A handful of earnest Nonconformists and essentially high-minded agnostics, all on intimate terms with one another, would meet in a suburban drawing-room, form themselves into a body, and give themselves some such modest designation as " The World Movement for the Abolition of Warfare." When some similarly composed group, meeting later in a different drawing-room, started, shall we say, " The International Council for the Suppression of Militarism ", the anger of the first group at this attempt to steal their thunder, their subscriptions from the public and, as usually happened, their " vice-presidents ", was apt to be unedifying. These people not only did no good, they did a great deal of active harm by bringing discredit, in the eyes of the mass of the electors, on all progressive or left-wing opinions. Thus they played straight into the hands of the Bolshevik-haunted Tories.

When, like other ignorant and impressionable young men I " got religion " in the political sense, I swallowed what my elders and betters taught me without questioning it. I was as uncritical as a Roman Catholic convert receiving " instruction." In the light of recent events it is easy to recognize where my mentors led myself and others astray. They misunderstood the anxieties of the French, underestimated the power and cunning of the Prussian military caste, were hoaxed by President Wilson and allowed their generosity to blind them to the villainy of British big business and financial pressure groups. When all this has been admitted, the case put forward in 1917 by the Socialist war-resisters for accepting President Wilson's offer of mediation, which the other side had already agreed to, cannot, even now, be lightly dismissed. The Socialists argued that the war was essentially a capitalists' and not a people's war. They maintained that none of the objects for which so many hundreds of thousands of young men had sacrificed their lives would be realized. It was not a war to end war, nor, if continued, would it make the world safe for democracy. On the contrary, it would make the rich richer and more powerful, and the poor poorer. A negotiated peace, if backed by all the might and moral influence of the United States, would, in their view, have more chance of proving durable than any settlement likely to result from the policy of the knock-out blow. Why, therefore, continue the useless slaughter of a whole generation of young men? As Socialists they were aware of the rising strength of Socialism in pre-war Germany, and of the mass-meetings of protest which had been held by the German workers when they realized that war was imminent. Unlike British Foreign Office experts (Lord Vansittart included) they had contacts with the German masses and their leaders and believed that, if the war ended in a negotiated settlement, there was a chance of reconciliation between the workers of all the countries involved. Moreover, they were far-seeing enough to realize that if the United States made an armed intervention in Europe, the results might be unfortunate for Europe. Why should more blood be spilt merely to satisfy the avarice of Anglo-American profiteers?

These arguments convinced me at the time, and the truth of most of them was quickly confirmed after the Armistice. France was bled white, her victory was sabotaged, she was coerced into accepting President Wilson's fourteen points and thirteen supplementary principles and induced to agree to the inauguration of the League of Nations by the promise that her security would be guaranteed by the United States. This promise was repudiated. Too late she discovered that by the American Constitution an American President's signature to a Treaty of Peace is valueless, unless subsequently endorsed by the United States Senate. The Messianic Wilson was disowned by his compatriots, and American big business, gorged with the wealth extracted from Europe, settled down to enjoy the fruits of their triumph over their exhausted Allies. As the Treaty of Versailles had largely resulted from the coercion applied by Wilson and Colonel House, it satisfied nobody except the German Junkers and the Prussian Officers' Corps, who escaped more lightly than they could have dared to hope. The pacifist " idealists " agreed with the British and French " realists "—though for different reasons—in regarding it as making another European war in twenty years inevitable. In the preface to his book " Our Ruling Class ", from which I have already quoted, Francis Francis observes :

" The Peace of Versailles has placed so little restraint upon the future development of Germany—in fact has left her with such enlarged scope in this respect—that the great war is merely interrupted, its recrudescence merely a question of time . . . Circumstances repeat themselves. They are the more likely to do so in the case of our late experiences, since the political system responsible for them remains in force, the warnings they conveyed have been ignored. The war threatened the existence of governments, the fatuities of the Peace Conference threaten the permanence of civilization."

When politicians desert the principles of morality in accordance with which civilized men normally live, says this writer, they leave the safe path of experience and plunge into a maze of gratuitous difficulties. The truth of this remark was to be proved in the two succeeding decades, while his indictment of the corrupt incompetence of the ruling class of the Lloyd George era holds good of the same class at the present day :

" Either their circumscribed vision, their cowardice or their inexplicable tenderness for German interests, prevented them from realizing and boldly preparing for a calamity which over-whelming evidence foreshadowed. Their incapacity or neglect sent armies of Britons upon unfair terms, to an untimely end. Rivers of blood flowed in consequence of their diplomacy. Yet in no sense has it ever appeared that they consider themselves to blame in the matter ! So far from any of them having com-mitted suicide under the appalling sense of guilt which should be theirs, not one of them has decently withdrawn from public life, not one of them has confessed to the least feeling of responsi-bility for their country's misfortunes and its sacrifice of young lives ! On the contrary, one and all, they have clung to office, and there continued to preach policy and their own infallibility."

These words, published in 1922, are a hundred times more true today than when they were written. The reason why the guilty men managed to cling to office, after the last war and, in due course, to land us in the present conflict, was the fact that the presence of a Tory majority in the House of Commons enabled them to pass a sponge over their misdeeds. As no Royal Com-mission of Enquiry into the Causes and Conduct of the War was set up, with power to examine witnesses under oath, the facts were never revealed and the people, confused and ignorant, continued to vote into power the architects of their own destruc-tion. If, after the present European struggle is over, another "Coupon" Parliament burkes enquiry and saves the guilty men from exposure, a third world war in another ten or twenty years can be postulated as inevitable. So much, at least, we have learnt from the blunders and mistakes of 1919. But the third world war, should it break out, will bear no resemblance to its predecessors.

The historic significance of the 1917 Club lies in the fact that its queerly assorted members were the first to realize in this country that the Russian Revolution was the only salient Good Thing which had resulted from the four years' massacre. Today, the Gerrard Street pioneers have been vindicated. Russia has changed the course of history by arresting the rapid descent of mankind to the abyss, triumphantly defending the Life Force against the assaults of the cohorts of Death, preserving the Future against the last desperate onslaught of the Past and thus restoring hope to the common man of every race and colour. The victory of Russia, taking a long view, is of such stupendous significance as, by comparison, to dwarf the importance of the immediate outcome of the present struggle on all the other nations involved in it.

III

The premises of the 1917 Club, at 4 Gerrard Street, Soho, had all the squalor and dinginess associated in the popular imagination with a conspiratorial den of Bolsheviks and thieves. The house, though some two centuries old, was without dignity and emphasized the fact that jerry-building had not been invented by the Victorians. The dining-room was, at first, situated in the basement. From the ground floor a narrow staircase, smelling strongly of invasions by the neighbouring tom-cats, led up to drafty, untidy, badly-furnished sitting-rooms and lounges. The street, one of the most unprepossessing in Soho, was frequented by tarts and souteneurs, contained several second-rate foreign restaurants, but was principally known to the outside world from the presence in it of the first of Mrs. Meyrick's famous night-clubs, "Number 43." This establishment was almost opposite the 1917 Club, and some of the less high-minded of our members used occasionally to pop across the road for a final illicit drink. Generally speaking, however, the club, though tolerant of all forms of revolutionary exuberance, was a home of political idealism, democratic fervour and serious progressive thinking. The highly respectable Ramsay MacDonald was its first President, and various left-wing politicians of equally blameless reputation were among its original founders and frequenters. I wish I had preserved a list of them, as it would now be of considerable interest. Among the more prominent figures who used the club in its heyday were H. W. Nevinson, H. N. Brailsford, F. W. Pethick-Lawrence, Sir Charles Trevelyan, Joseph King, H. G. Wells, E. D. Morel, Clement Attlee, C. G. Ammon, Noel and Charles Buxton, Mary Agnes Hamilton, Stanley Unwin,

K

Leonard Woolf, Evelyn Sharp, Rose Macaulay, Sir Osbert Sitwell, Francis Birrell, Aldous Huxley, and Lord Ponsonby. There were doubtless many others of equal eminence whose names I have now forgotten. Of the younger members, so many of whom have since achieved fame, Dr. C. E. M. Joad, Harold Scott and Elsa Lanchester stand out in my memory.

In 1919, with Harold Scott and two of his Dartmoor friends, I started, among many other activities, a " People's Theatre Society", principally to facilitate a London production of D. H. Lawrence's play, " The Widowing of Mrs. Holroyd." As usually happens when some enthusiast starts a society with a particular aim or object in view, his purpose is promptly frustrated by his colleagues. This occurred in connection with The People's Theatre, when the Committee opposed the Lawrence project and persuaded Harold to put on a translation of a Serbian play called " The Liberators " instead of it. The production resulted in a financial loss, for which, as I had already resigned, I was luckily not responsible. The episode would not have been recalled here but for the fact that, in connection with the Society, Harold Scott interviewed a number of stage aspirants who had been attracted by our announcements. Among them was a girl of about sixteen, with flaming red-gold hair, who had learnt dancing in Paris under Isadora Duncan's brother, Raymond Duncan. Her name was Elsa Lanchester. Out of the wreck of The People's Theatre thus sprang that most amusing cabaret, " The Cave of Harmony," which, under Harold's and Elsa's direction, enlivened our nights in the early 'twenties. It began in a house in Charlotte Street, was carried on for several years at different addresses, and led to a revival of interest in the Victorian music-hall which today finds expression in Ridgeway's " Late Joys."

Elsa became one of the shining lights of the 1917 Club and soon acquired numerous admirers in the world of art and literature. Among them was a young artist, now one of our most gifted painters, whose fidelity made him occasionally visit Gerrard Street in search of her. He was not apparently favourably impressed by her surroundings, as the following ribald and wholly libellous poem, for which he was responsible, perhaps indicates:

> In nineteen seventeen they founded a club,
> Partly as brothel and partly as pub.
> The members were all of them horrible bores,
> Except for the Girl in Giotto-pink drawers.

(I hasten to add that the colour of Elsa's alleged " drawers " was an innocent club joke, the point of which I have forgotten.)

There were a fair number of club bores, chief of them being by common consent our eminent President, Ramsay MacDonald, but the majority of the younger members were too lively by temperament and too heterogeneous in character and outlook to fall into this category. Among us were Hindus, Parsees, puritans, free lovers, Quakers, teetotallers, heavy drinkers, Morris dancers and Folk Song experts (with a fol-de-diddle-ol and a hey-ho for Badley and Bedales), members of the London School of Economics, Trades Union officials, journalists, poets, actors and actresses, Communists, theosophists. In short, every colour and creed, every " ism " and " ist " was represented, and each of us was filled with a burning faith in his particular private gospel. Apart from the fact that all the members could be labelled " Lefties " and were opposed to the reactionary clique in power, there was no other recognizable nexus and no uni-formity of political opinion.

On the first day that my Irish wife and I lunched in the base-ment dining-room, Aldous Huxley and that remarkable figure, Lady Ottoline Morrell, were lunching there also. In any other surroundings they would have looked slightly exotic : in the 1917 Club they passed unremarked. In the course of that after-noon I went upstairs to the large attic at the top of the house to write a letter. On my way I was passed on the staircase by an elderly Quaker company director, who was hurrying downwards with flaming cheeks. When I reached the writing-room I discovered the reason for his agitation. A bearded young " sexologer " in horn-rimmed spectacles was delivering a lecture there to a mixed audience on the subject of masturbation !

Even the most learned members were caught by the post-war craze for dancing. The London School of Economics, then presided over by Sir William Beveridge, to which several friends of mine belonged, provided a band and a dancing-floor, thus enabling future notabilities to disport themselves. Among these were Dr. C. E. M. Joad, then beardless, and the B.B.C. play producer, Barbara Burnham. The 1917 Club got up dances of its own at fairly regular intervals, and after the " Cave of Harmony " was started a large contingent of members became regular frequenters. Evenings at the Cave consisted of dancing from about nine till midnight, followed by an hour's cabaret and further dancing until 2 a.m. In the basement underneath there was a Negro Club which did not encourage strangers. The craze for " duskies " started about the year 1926, when that charming artist, Florence Mills, appeared at the Palace Theatre in a Negro revue which drew " all London."

The cabaret shows put on by Harold and Elsa usually consisted of singing and dancing, but on one occasion a one-act play by Aldous Huxley was produced and drew a semi-fashionable audience, including people like Arnold Bennett. It was at the Cave that Elsa made one of her earliest successes with the touching Victorian ballad, " Please sell no more drink to my father." Among the early frequenters were Mary Butts and her brother Anthony, Pat Kaye, then a pupil of Mme. Astafieva and subsequently known to fame as Anton Dolin, Edgar Jepson and his wife and daughters, Alec and Evelyn Waugh, that genial pundit, the late J. W. N. Sullivan, and a host of others who belonged to the intellectual half-world from which Aldous Huxley derived many of the characters in " Antic Hay."

Many supporters of the Cave and early members of the 1917 Club have, in the past twenty years, achieved wealth and fame ; some have joined the ranks of the " stuffed shirts " and would doubtless not thank me for reminding them of their Bohemian past. Having lived to experience two world wars and preserved to some extent the faculty of detached observation, I regard the vices of Age and Respectability with more distaste than the follies and excesses of youth.

Time brings its rewards as well as its reverses. Elsa and her husband, Charles Laughton, are notabilities in the American film world and have acquired American citizenship. Aldous Huxley, cured of his partial blindness, is said to have become an American citizen and to be pursuing the Way of Perfection in Hollywood, under the religious tutelage of that, to my mind, rather unconvincing mystic, Gerald Heard. Harold Scott's voice comes to us regularly over the air from the studios of the B.B.C. Mary and Tony Butts and Sullivan are dead. The 1917 Club, after degenerating into a cheap luncheon club for civil servants, who reserved for themselves a special table, in order not to be contaminated by " the workers," petered out in the 'thirties after an undignified squabble over the election of its Committee. The Labour Party, confused and frustrated by the weakness of its leaders, soon lost the crusading zeal which animated it in the early 'twenties. When the war, which it foresaw and failed to avert, is over, it now seems destined to

make way for a United Socialist Party which honestly believes in
Socialism and, as in other liberated countries, includes the
Communists.

Like most writers I am a bad Party man and have never found
it easy to toe lines or have my thinking done for me. Moreover,
I was little impressed by the Trade Union stalwarts who frequented
the 1917 Club in its early years, or by the personality of
MacDonald. Ramsay's grizzled hair and handle-bar moustaches
seemed to have a devastating effect on the middle-aged ladies
who fluttered admiringly round him. They thought him handsome : to me his features seemed rather coarse. He was, apart
from the ladies, extremely unpopular in the Club : so much so
that I could never understand why his Party considered him their
inevitable—and only possible—leader, unless it was due to the
fact that he so clearly saw himself in the role of a future Prime
Minister that they accepted him at his own valuation.

After the Election of 1922 when, although Arthur Henderson
lost his seat, there was a tidal-wave of I.L.P. victories, a meeting
of the I.L.P. was held in the House of Commons at which it
was decided to support MacDonald against Clynes, as Parliamentary Chairman of the Labour Party.

Josiah Wedgwood, in his " Memoirs of a Fighting Life." says
that " MacDonald wisely refused to come to the meeting. Philip
Snowden did come, and his was the one solitary voice warning
us that if MacDonald led we should live to regret it. We thought
we knew MacDonald. We ought to have known that none of
us, except Snowden, really understood the man. At the meeting
of the whole Parliamentary Party that followed, MacDonald
was elected by a small majority over Clynes, the only vote I
have ever regretted." Wedgwood was elected Deputy-Chairman
by a small majority over J. H. Thomas.

As no one seemed particularly anxious for MacDonald's
company when he lunched at the 1917 Club, he frequently
sat down opposite to me when I was alone. I was a bit of a fish
out of water, like himself, as he possibly realized, and this may
have accounted for the honour. I regard it as in his favour that,
unlike so many politicians, he went out of his way to be affable
to writers. He was certainly very civil to me, so that I have
qualms in recording my instinctive dislike and distrust of him.
He once told me a long story about his visit to India, with E. S.
Montagu. Arrived in Bombay, they repaired together to the
most famous and exclusive hotel, and were refused admittance,

Montagu on the ground that he was a Jew and MacDonald on the ground that his politics were regarded as untrustworthy. It was clear from MacDonald's account of the incident that he had no quarrel, *in principle*, with the way the hotel-keeper ran his pub.   He could be as exclusive as he pleased so long as he, Ramsay, was not among the excluded.   I gathered that if he had been received with open arms and the respect due to his eminence, humbler colleagues might have been shown the door without his disapproval.   For the Russian Revolution and the régime of Lenin and Trotsky he could hardly conceal his antipathy.   Here again I felt that no question of principle was involved.   All that concerned him, in view of the hatred of Bolshevism among the best people, was that the suspicion of Bolshevik sympathies might adversely affect his career.   That MacDonald must have had qualities which did not appear at the luncheon table, or to which I was temperamentally allergic, is evident from the effect he had on some of the most intelligent of his younger supporters.   It is clear also that multitudes were impressed by his platform manner.   In his book, " So Far . . . ", W. J. Brown, M.P., says, " Mr. Ramsay MacDonald in those early 'twenties, was at the height of his oratorical powers.   His magnificent figure, his finely moulded head, with the black moustache tinged beautifully with the grey which subsequently conquered it, and the grave, dark eyes, all combined to make him an arresting figure to look at.   His voice was, I suppose, one of the most beautiful platform instruments of all time, except when he shouted.   When it was controlled it was capable of every range of expression, from a whisper to the great bass-notes of an organ. He carried himself regally—so regally that at one time he had the nickname of ' Gentleman Mac.'   His most striking asset as a speaker at that time lay in the infusion of a certain poetic quality into his speech and the suggestion he conveyed of vast depths yet undisclosed, at which the spoken word only hinted. On me he made a great impression."

With Mr. Brown's estimate of such figures as Philip Snowden and Robert Smillie I find myself in complete agreement, but I never came under the spell of MacDonald's platform oratory. At private meetings of the 1917 Club over which he presided, he used to grow pink with annoyance when he was heckled by irreverent members, and no poetic qualities or hidden depths were discernible.

The day on which he was appointed Prime Minister—January

23rd, 1924—was bitterly cold. As usual, MacDonald went to lunch at the 1917 Club. The crowd of prostitutes who had been driven by the police from Shaftesbury Avenue and perambulated Gerrard Street, looked like hungry seagulls. The poor creatures were evidently at their wits' end to earn a living and had formed the habit of accosting every man they saw with a hastily improvised topographical appeal. The new Prime Minister's first greeting as he entered the Club was from one of these ladies of mature charm who, with a terrific ogle, murmured " *Hullo, Yorkshire boy !* " as he went in.

The members greeted MacDonald with modified cheers and some clapping of hands as he entered the dining-room, but I never saw him there again. As Prime Minister, he was made a member of the Athenæum, where he was able to shake himself free from his humbler political associates and cultivate the socially established. I don't blame him. As a man gets older he needs the sort of comfort which it is the business of a well-run club to provide. The 1917 Club was shockingly and disgracefully uncomfortable. The gimcrack old house was impossible to keep clean and its situation, opposite Ma Meyrick's " 43," in a street infested by tarts, was squalid and depressing. All the same, it had a certain quality which all the other clubs lacked. When opulent friends took me to lunch at the Travellers, the Reform, the Garrick, the Savile, the Athenæum or the Union, I used to envy them their attentive servants, leather-covered arm-chairs and excellent liqueur brandy. But when I looked about me on these occasions, my professional curiosity alive, I could not fail to observe certain changes, at least in the younger members of these institutions. In chairs which had once supported the posteriors of a Dickens or a Thackeray, lolled smart young literary agents, advertisement touts wearing brand-new " old school ties," juvenile directors of publishing firms, and prosperous-looking manufacturers with safe jobs in the family business. One might have expected that at least ninety per cent. of " West End Club men " of military age would have shown some traces of the strains of trench warfare. Such, however, was not the case, and the impressions I myself formed have since been confirmed by many other observers. The casualties among temporary officers of the public-school class had been devastating. Many of the survivors had been reduced to such penury that they were unable to pay their subscriptions to the clubs they would normally have joined. Others preferred the various Service clubs to which their war records gave them the right of entry. As a result, the ordinary " West End Club " became dominated by " stout fellas," who, in one way or another, had enjoyed a jolly good war, taken no physical risks and come out on top. Provided one was not suspected of being a " Bolshie " or of entertaining " views " of a disturbing nature, these chaps were amiability itself.   As bar companions they were far more agreeable than many of the rather repulsive, angular types of left-wing highbrow I encountered in Gerrard Street.   But what gave the 1917 Club its peculiar cachet was that no one in it had made any blood money, no one had made a good thing out of the four years' massacre, or was prepared to accept a return to yesterday.   Dirty, untidy, despised and poverty-stricken though it was, the 1917 Club looked forward and faced hopefully a changing world.   The more palatial institutions, which catered for the profiteers and bureaucratic yes-men, wanted nothing better than a return to 1914.

CHAPTER FOUR

THE POETRY BOOKSHOP

IT is I suppose inevitable that certain years in a man's life stand out more clearly, in retrospect, than any of the others.   1919 was the fullest and most crowded twelve months I had up to then experienced, or have ever experienced since.   After a period of loneliness in Yeats's flat, when the only callers I can remember were Maire O'Neill, the Irish actress, Franklyn Dyall and Mary Merrall, Paul Nash, who lived near by, and Herbert Read, who was then editing *Art and Letters* with Osbert Sitwell, we suddenly became mixed up in a seething mob of new friends and acquaintances.   In the five years before I went to Sweden to take up a post as Lektor at Gothenburg's Handelshögskola, " wild parties " of the kind so frequently described in the novels of the 'twenties, went on almost continuously.   In spite of them—or because of them—I have never been more productive than I was during this period.

What brought me back into London literary circles after the war was the series of stag parties which Harold Monro gave in his rooms over the Poetry Bookshop, in Devonshire Street, Theobalds Road. At the first of these I met Alec Waugh, who had recently burst into the ranks of best-sellers with " The Loom of Youth." Alec was then about twenty. Outwardly, he seemed a shy and diffident youth, although his war experiences, as with so many other boys of his age, had made him in some ways precociously adult. (In reality, he has never suffered from shyness and is not in the least diffident, as he himself engagingly admits.) This meeting proved a momentous one for me. Not only was he a most lavish and generous host—his frequent parties at his parents' house at Golder's Green were among the best I ever attended—but, on the strength of his appreciation of my " pacifist " war novel, " The Fortune," his father's firm, Chapman and Hall, became for some years my publishers.

I had known Harold Monro in pre-war days and had contributed verses to his " Poetry and Drama," although, somewhat to my annoyance—and to Flecker's, on my behalf—I had been left out of " Eddie " Marsh's various anthologies of Georgian Poetry. The object of Harold's gatherings in the spring and summer of 1919 was ostensibly to inaugurate a new literary periodical called the *Monthly Chapbook*. They formed a meeting place for old friends who had lost touch with one another during the war years, as well as providing those who frequented them with opportunities of making new acquaintances. Almost everyone who had ever published any verse turned up at them. Among those whose appearance I happen still to recall were Osbert and Sacheverell Sitwell, Humbert Wolfe, F. S. Flint, Maurice Hewlett and Ford Madox Ford. Warfare between the Left Wing literary rebels and the " stuffed shirts " of the Establishment, who had formed themselves into a racket and controlled most of the post-war reviewing, was carried on with enormous gusto. Monro published my " Triumphal Ode", satirizing Victory Day, and several of the essays subsequently included in my book " Reputations", which Chapman and Hall published in 1920.

In 1942 I received a letter from a professor of Literature at an American university, asking leave to reproduce a passage from " Reputations " in a history of the contemporary English novel. This aroused my curiosity sufficiently to make me take the half-forgotten volume from my shelves and re-read it. On the whole, I found in it surprisingly little that I wanted to alter or regretted having said. But, in the light of later experience,

I was staggered by my reckless daring. If any writer ever set out to damn himself in mid-career, I was that man.

A marked deterioration in literary manners took place after 1919, and anyone not an established best-seller who dared to challenge the big shots was asking for trouble. When, in 1922, I expanded the essay on Flecker which appeared in " Reputations " into a memoir, the silence with which it was greeted was positively deafening. The only review I remember was contributed by a literary clergyman, to a Church of England periodical, and intimated that my claim to have had any association with Flecker was an impudent piece of self-assertion on my part. Some two years later, when Ford Madox Ford guilelessly published his " remembrance " of Joseph Conrad, he was treated in much the same way. Throughout the 'twenties there was unceasing warfare between the various reactionary cliques of the Establishment and the Independents. Men of genius like D. H. Lawrence and James Joyce held their own, made no concessions, and fought their way through, but weaker brethren, with families to keep and bread and butter to earn, were gradually got under, disciplined and conditioned, until, by the 'thirties, nearly every spark of vitality in current professional writing had been damped down. I shall always be grateful to Arthur Waugh for maintaining the old publishing tradition of allowing the author to say what he pleased over his own signature. My novel, " The Black Curtain ", dedicated to D. H. Lawrence, which I wrote in 1919, would not have been allowed to appear a dozen years later, on account of the " subversive " opinions expressed in it. How commonplace they seem today !

Harold Monro was a good-looking, dark man, with what is officially called a " fresh complexion " and a sudden charming smile, which revealed dazzling teeth. Owing to emotional and temperamental complications, which I only came to understand in later years, he was not a very happy man. Few poets are. By nature rather secretive and suspicious, he was apt to suspect his best friends of harbouring designs against him and to place boundless faith in men who let him down. I know little about his early life beyond the fact that he was at Radley, where he preceded Louis Wilkinson. After leaving school he spent a year in France and then went to Cambridge (Caius College), where he read modern languages. I first made his acquaintance in 1913, but did not get to know him really well until the 'twenties. The letter which began our acquaintance I have accidentally

preserved.   It is written by hand on the notepaper of " Poetry
and Drama," and the date is January 26th, 1913 :

" Dear Sir,
    May I venture to congratulate you on your last volume which
I have just been reading ?   I somehow overlooked ' A Country
Boy ' when you sent it me last year, or rather I think I found it
too derivative, but you are taking on strength in ' Streets.'   It's
not for me to pick faults.   I felt inspired to write a notice of it
for our March number, and have just done so.   I'm going to
give a reading of some of the pieces next Thursday at 5.30.
Do come if you feel inclined.   Open readings take place every
Tuesday and Thursday at that hour.   Rupert Brooke reads this
Tuesday.   I'm going to make a point on the Thursdays of reading
from books lately published.

    I wonder whether you've put everything you've got at present
into ' Streets.'   If not, I should very much like to have the
opportunity of considering some of your new unpublished work
for our March number.

                                        Yours truly,
                                    HAROLD MONRO."

The establishment of the Poetry Bookshop, in a beautiful
Georgian House in a slum street off Theobalds Road, and the
publishing activities and poetry readings connected with it,
had a stimulating influence on creative literature in the years
before and after Great War One.   By a peculiar irony of Fate,
the harder and more successfully Harold worked to establish
the reputation of his brother poets and to make the publication
of new verse commercially possible, the less attention was paid
to his own output.   He was primarily regarded by his colleagues
as a bookseller and publisher, and a source of small but welcome
cheques.   His reputation as a poet—one of the best, least pretentious and most durable of the " Georgians "—was only firmly
established after his death.

    The night life of London in 1919 was carried on with difficulty
owing to the continuance in force of D.O.R.A. restrictions.   When
centres like the Café Royal closed, the artistic and literary element
had to find some place in which to carry on their discussions.   By
chance, some adventurous spirits happened on a low dive behind
the Lyric Theatre, where glasses of " Russian " tea, with a slice
of lemon floating on the top, could be consumed till midnight.

The café was kept by a rather unsavoury Armenian, and was promptly nicknamed by its frequenters "The Armenian's." For about a year the fortunate proprietor made money hand over fist. The place was packed every night with poets, painters, novelists, musicians, and their girl friends. One of its attractions was a tame rabbit which wandered about among the tables and lived in the filthy basement with the Armenian's family. One night I noticed the Armenian eyeing this animal in a speculative way, which seemed to me to bode no good for the rabbit. I said to him, "He's your mascot. If you eat him, your luck will change." The Armenian grinned effusively and protested that the rabbit was his son's pet. All the same, greed got the better of him. The rabbit was in due course killed and eaten. A week later, as a result of one of those unpredictable changes of fashion which used to be the Parisian café-proprietor's nightmare, the place was empty.

One of the chief difficulties of existence, in the period immediately following the Armistice, was to find somewhere to live. Another was, of course, how to pay the rent when a place at last was found. After we left 18 Woburn Buildings, at the end of Yeats's lease, Betty and I spent unhappy weeks in furnished flats in Battersea and Earl's Court. I finally solved the problem by taking a large, semi-derelict house in St. James's Terrace, Regent's Park, and letting off all of it except the ground floor, which my wife and I occupied, to various tenants, one of them being the newly-established "Save the Children Fund." This improvised method of communal housekeeping was adopted by a number of our friends to solve the *crise de logement*. Mary Butts was the tenant of a large house in Belsize Park, 43 Belsize Park Gardens, and a group of amiable " Bloomsburies " developed an elaborate system of communal housekeeping at 19 Taviton Street. The floating population of these three remarkable establishments became to some extent interchangeable. When my marriage dissolved, in the way that so many marriages did in the 'twenties, I took a room first at 19 Taviton Street and afterwards at 43 Belsize Park Gardens, where I was for a time a fellow lodger with Elsa Lanchester. Later I returned to St. James's Terrace and Mary Butts and Cecil Maitland took the floor above me. These constant changes of address, varied by long visits to " abroad," were characteristic of life in the 'twenties. It is fortunate that I am not of sufficient importance to require the services of a biographer, for if I did the wretched man would find it difficult, if not impossible, to keep track of me between 1919 and 1928. Again and again I accumulated furniture, books and pictures and either lost, sold, gave them away, or had them stolen. A perpetual rolling stone in those years of chaos, excitement, mental liberation and abortive effort, I gathered no " moss " in the way of possessions, success or fixed ideas.

What started me on my European wanderings was a chance meeting at one of Alec Waugh's parties, with Hugh Kingsmill Lunn, second son of the famous travel agent and Swiss hotel proprietor, Sir Henry Lunn. The headquarters of the innumerable companies with which Sir Henry, like another Cinquevalli, accomplished his remarkable feats of financial prestidigitation, was at 5 Endsleigh Gardens, Euston, a house once occupied by William Michael Rossetti. The list of people on the pay-roll of the " Banyan Tree," as Sir Henry's younger sons irreverently called it, was surprisingly long and included a strange assortment of penniless peers, down-at-heel Oxford dons, artists, actors, clergymen, and, finally, writers and poets. Hugh Kingsmill Lunn, who had always had a foot in the world of literature and journalism, genially secured jobs for those of his acquaintances who were at a loose end. I was one of these. I was sick of what D. H. Lawrence called " those pamphlet shops," could not get a footing in the Left Wing press, and had an eager appetite for foreign travel.

It was Sir Henry's policy—a policy to which he owed a large measure of his success—to divide his clientèle into separate and more or less homogeneous groups. Those who " travelled with Sir Henry " were not " Lunn tourists," but members of the " Free Church Touring Guild ", " Church Travellers Association", or whatever it might be. Similarly, his Swiss hotels were not sold to the public as specifically " Lunn " hotels, but as public-school and university Alpine sports centres. The chief of them, at Mürren, was presided over by his elder son Arnold, author of " The Harrovians", who had married into the peerage after a successful career at Oxford.

To the list of his religious touring clubs and companies, Sir Henry, at Hugh's instigation, now added a new organization called " John o' London's tours", in connection with the literary weekly of that name. Each tour was to be conducted by a genuine literary man, and the assumption was that he would prove an overwhelming attraction. Actually, the only type of tourists who seemed titillated by the prospect of hobnobbing with novelists or poets, were female elementary school-teachers. On one occasion my party consisted of thirteen of these ladies, with not a single other male except myself. The history of " John o' London's tours", could it be set down in detail, would constitute the wildest farce. I drew on some of my experiences for a chapter in my novel " Nobody Knows", which I once read to a literary society in Copenhagen, the members of which had enough experience of conducted tours to be amused. Once I nearly lost my entire flock by getting off the train at a wayside station in Italy. The train started while my back was turned and I had to race after it, only just managing to leap on board before it gathered speed. On another occasion, I left London in a hurry, to deputize for another conductor, and found, when I got to Havre, that I had forgotten to bring my passport. I only managed to evade the *contrôle* by heavily tipping a porter who guided me behind a goods train to a place where I could slip out and rejoin my flock.

On my personal association with Sir Henry I look back with, on the whole, the liveliest amusement and satisfaction. He is one of the characters I have encountered in my life whom I would not have missed for anything. Half a commercial buccaneer of a familiar type, half a Nonconformist hot-gospeller, and the whole of him flavoured with Gladstonian Liberalism, he was an astonishing example of the Big Business " executive." Whether he possessed a secret sense of humour or was only the occasion for humour in others, I was never quite sure. To watch him at his desk at Endsleigh Gardens, roaring down three telephones and ringing simultaneously for his secretary and his cashier, was a spectacle which, for me, never lost its fascination. Outwardly, I am rather easily browbeaten and intimidated, but though visibly quailing before big noises I usually manage, inwardly, to take a detached view of them. Like most self-made men, Sir Henry had a concealed but really exaggerated respect for anyone suspected of being entitled to wear an " old school tie." No doubt he remembered how hard he had toiled, starting from scratch, to earn the money required to educate his sons as " gentlemen " and had a corresponding respect for the result. In any case, his roars had always rather a hollow sound and were accompanied by a considerable amount of geniality. He was, in some ways, astonishingly broadminded, as well as being enterprising, imaginative, boldly adventurous and not incapable of generosity. I suppose he could be described as a Free Church "tycoon", a peculiarly English blend of sanctimonious Christian and ruthless man of business. I hope Hugh Kingsmill will some day write his father's life and not refrain from blending his characteristic wit and gift for sub-acid comment with his filial piety.

When, after a long absence abroad, conducting Sir Henry's comic tourists to Italy, Normandy and the Châteaux of the Loire, I returned to find that Betty had transferred her affections to my employer's younger son, the farcical aspect of my occupation was temporarily obscured. No member of my family had ever, to my knowledge, been divorced and I was not psychologically prepared for such a contingency. The experience changed me from an immature young man into an adult. Fortunately, my filial relations with Jim and Ellen Duncan remained unimpaired by this family upset, and as Betty stayed in double harness with Brian Lunn no longer than she had with me, there was no reason, after her departure, why our old friendly relations should not be resumed. Years later, when I had re-married, I stayed with Brian at a Lunn hotel at Hastings while Sir Henry was in residence. We lunched with him on Sunday, *à trois*, in his private quarters and the old man behaved to me precisely as he might have done to a son-in-law whom he had not seen for some time. He evidently realized that I was in some way connected with his family, but he had forgotten what exactly the connection was. The humour of the situation was fully appreciated by his guests.

CHAPTER FIVE

E. D. MOREL

I

ON a night of November 1924, after we had dined *chez* Stulik, at the Eiffel Tower, my friend, Cecil Maitland, and I made our way home by Tube. Before we descended in the lift at Goodge Street station, Cecil bought a *Star*, looked at the stop-press column, and remarked : "Hullo. Morel's dead." I snatched the paper out of his hand, gulped painfully, and murmured "Oh God ! Not Morel !" Seeing my obvious distress, Cecil said : " I'm awfully sorry, Douglas. I didn't know he meant so much to you."

I mention this incident to show just how much E. D. Morel *did* mean, to those who knew him. His loss was shattering. He was in the prime of life, just over fifty, and, as all of us hoped, on the threshold of a great parliamentary career. Only a few days before, on the eve of his departure for a well-earned holiday in Devonshire, I had had a long talk with him in the 1917 Club. He had just returned from a triumphal election campaign at Dundee, where he had exposed the " Red Letter " plot and been placed at the head of the poll with the record vote of 32,846. Mr. Seymour Cocks, in his obituary notice in Morel's paper *Foreign Affairs*, records that when he left Dundee " over 20,000 people collected outside the railway station. ' We are fighting,' said Morel . . . . ' an age-long struggle on behalf of the under-dogs, on behalf of justice for the weak and peace among men. Faith will remain with us, because we know that Truth and Justice must triumph in the end.' "

At the end of his speech at the Caird Hall, Dundee, on Sunday, October 25th, 1924, in which he made a detailed exposure of the Zinoviev forgery—the Conservative plot which succeeded in bringing down the first Labour Government—Morel uttered these prophetic words : " My friends, it is a great movement, this Labour Movement of ours. It is greater than any of us who are in it. We come and go as the days pass. It is greater than our leaders. They, too, play their parts : they come, they go, they pass as dust before the wind. Death ? Death is nothing ! Death cannot stop us. It is the cause, the cause which is immortal !"

The following account of Morel's last moments appeared under the heading of " a personal note " in " Foreign Affairs." " E. D. M. went to Devonshire on November 10th for a short holiday to recuperate from the strain of the General Election. On the afternoon of November 12th (having spent the morning writing to many of his friends) he and his sister-in-law proceeded to the Aller Farm, North Bovey, a part of Dartmoor well known and well loved by him. They walked, as a full moon was rising up through the woods, to the heights above the valley, E. D. M. exulting as he drew the moorland air into his lungs ! 'This gives me new life.'

" The next moment . . . ' I feel queer. Don't be alarmed ' and so, lying down a moment to rest, he fainted : did not thereafter regain consciousness, but gently, painlessly, peacefully, fell on sleep."

When I saw him in the 1917 Club, he was obviously tired and, at the same time, emotionally upset and in need of unburdening himself. I have often regretted since that I took no notes of our long and intimate conversation, the subject of which was Ramsay MacDonald's latest exhibition of treachery and double-dealing. After their long association in the Union of Democratic Control Morel had every reason to expect that he would be included in MacDonald's Government—at least in a minor capacity, if circumstances made it impossible for him to be given the Foreign Office before serving an apprenticeship elsewhere—and was justifiably incensed when MacDonald passed him over. But it was not on any grounds of personal animosity that he was now attacking the leader of his Party. It was MacDonald's shuffling over his answer to the " Red Letter " which he considered such a cowardly betrayal of all the principles the U.D.C. stood for. The late Lord Wedgwood, in his " Memories of a Fighting Life", made an interesting comment on this episode which it might be injudicious to quote. Perhaps it is as well that I have forgotten the details of Morel's indictment. MacDonald was no more unprincipled than other careerist politicians in the Labour ranks, before him and after him, but to a man of such unswerving moral courage, of such blazing and incorruptible honesty as E. D. M., the sudden realization of his real character came as an overwhelming shock. In the twenty years which have elapsed we have learnt to shrug our shoulders at each fresh revelation of the fact that it is often difficult to keep a Labour leader straight, once he has tasted the sweets of office. If he was born into the ruling class, he usually reverts to type ; if he started from the proletariat, the first glass of champagne offered him by a toff in a swagger restaurant goes to his head and undermines his virtue. With Morel, the fact that his politics were his religion and that he was faithful till death to the cause to which his life was devoted, made him one of the outstanding figures of his age and generation. Nothing describes him better than the quotation from William Lloyd Garrison which he used in 1906, as an epigraph to his famous book " Red Rubber."

" I will be harsh as truth and as uncompromising as justice.
    I am in earnest ;

L

I will not equivocate ;
I will not excuse ;
I will not retreat a single inch ;
And I will be heard.
Posterity will bear witness that I was right."

II

I first met Morel at a dinner-party given in a private room
of the Trocadero Restaurant in 1919 to inaugurate an English
branch of the International *Clarté* movement, which had been
founded in Paris by Henri Barbusse.   Lord Ponsonby, Sir Charles
Trevelyan, Bertrand Russell, Robert Dell and E. D. Morel
were among those present and the guest of the evening was
Madame Madeleine Marx, a friend and disciple of Barbusse.
Madeleine Marx was a chic, very attractive Parisienne, in her
middle-thirties and made full use of her sex appeal.   After being
introduced to Morel, whose books had made him one of her
heroes, she could hardly take her eyes off him.   " Ah, comme
il est beau ! " she murmured, at intervals.   There was plenty
of excuse for her enthusiasm.   Morel was a tall, broad-shouldered
man, whose snow-white hair, dark eyebrows and moustache and
piercing eyes made him strikingly good-looking.

Clarté had been represented as an organization of European
intellectuals—novelists, poets, painters and so forth—who believed in peace, international brotherhood and the dawn of a new
era.   I became its English secretary probably owing to the
fact that my novel, " The Fortune " had been read and praised
by such international figures as Romain Rolland, Henri Barbusse,
Dr. Georg Brandes and Ellen Key.   So far as we, in England,
were aware *Clarté* had no defined political background.   At
that stage in my education, I had no clear ideas about Communism, could not have explained the difference between
Communism and Fabian Socialism, and had neither knowledge
of, nor any particular interest in, political theory. On the other
hand I believed as firmly as Ford Madox Ford that literature and
art were international, above frontiers, and that those who
practised them should establish such close relations as would
enable them, in future, to work together in defence of civilization.
On this firm and sure foundation, Mrs. Dawson Scott, with John
Galsworthy's invaluable aid, afterwards built up the still flourishing
P. E. N. Club.   The English section of *Clarté* came to an end

for two main reasons. In the first place, once it was established the Committee could not decide to what form of activity it should devote its energies. Public meetings, " drawing-room " meetings, pamphlets ? All of these seemed equally futile. In the second place, it became increasingly clear that the parent body in Paris was concentrating on international Communist propaganda and was trying to use us to further its unavowed objects. As none of the English writers who lent their support to the movement were Communists, while its political sponsors were orthodox members of the Labour Party, its collapse was inevitable. If I remember right, Robert Dell finally handed over the corpse to his friend, Mrs. Corbet Ashby, for decent interment.

The attitude of many of the younger writers towards *Clarté* was summed up by Siegfried Sassoon, who, in writing to tell me he was unable to attend one of our meetings, added : " To be perfectly frank I do not see that anything is likely to be accomplished by *Clarté* in England unless it is directly supported by men like Wells and Shaw." However contemptible this may have seemed in the eyes of Wells and Shaw, who have been urging their juniors for over half a century to stand on their own feet and acquire some moral guts, it was, from the practical standpoint, plain commonsense.

As I was incapable of any form of public speaking and detested meetings, I suggested that we should follow the lead of Paris and Brussels and start a paper of our own. Fortunately for my professional career, this proposal set up the usual reactions in the minds of the Committee—" Of course, he wants a job " —and was rather rudely rejected. Nothing will ever teach the Left that writers have everything to lose—financially and in every other way—by working for causes in which they believe, instead of for their own advancement. D. H. Lawrence, whom I had long admired but met for the first time in 1919, used to foam with rage at Betty and me for getting ourselves mixed up with " fusty-musty peace cranks " and their loathsome " pamphlet shops," and was delighted to hear of my escape from " that Bertie Russell crowd."

My chief source of income at this period came from the New York publisher Thomas Seltzer, who, besides issuing my own books in the United States, had made me his London agent. In this capacity I got him to produce the first edition of Lawrence's " Women in Love " which, after " The Rainbow " prosecution, had failed to find a London publisher. Seltzer held advanced political views and until he went bankrupt—a fact of which I was only made aware when my salary suddenly ceased—showed remarkable courage in launching books which, in a politically backward country like the United States, might easily have got him into trouble. As a result of my meeting with E. D. Morel and Madeleine Marx at the *Clarté* dinner, I was able to open negotiations for placing an edition of " Truth and the War " with Seltzer and to get him to publish a translation of Mme. Marx's feminist novel, " Woman." How daring it was of Seltzer to sponsor " Truth and the War " was revealed after Morel's death by an American contributor to *Foreign Affairs*, who stated that " the first light that came to our country (on the war guilt question) was the great work of E. D. Morel, ' Truth and the War ', yet so intense was the hatred of the new opinion that mention of this book was practically stifled. It could be found only by those who took great trouble, like myself, to seek a copy."

No doubt, Morel realized more clearly than I did the difficulties to be overcome before he could get a hearing in America and was, for that reason, the more grateful to me for my efforts to persuade Seltzer to take the risk. In any case, a friendship sprang up between us, only terminated by his tragic death, which I have long regarded as one of the outstanding privileges of my life. For some months, before Betty transferred her affections and broke up our marriage, we lived in rooms at Rickmansworth, not far from Morel's house at King's Langley. This enabled me, with the aid of a push-bike, to ride over to see him on several occasions. Many others, who knew Morel much more intimately than I did, have described the home surroundings which strengthened him to endure the almost unbelievable campaign of obloquy and insult to which for years he was subjected. His house and garden, his wife and family, his roses, and the man himself all combined to create an atmosphere of peace, love and loyalty which must have impressed everyone who visited them. Not for the first time, I realized that the happiest men and women are those who devote them-selves, wholeheartedly and without self-interest, to the service of humanity. I have certainly never met a business man or any inheritor of great possessions who had anything like the inner serenity which radiated from Morel. His tall and handsome daughter Stella, who, later, married a Polish historian but died before witnessing the martyrdom of her adopted country, was his constant companion, comrade and fellow-worker. His study, with bookshelves filled with row upon row of documents all neatly bound up in brown paper, was such a model of orderliness that he could lay his hands on anything he wanted at a moment's notice. In Stella he had a perfect secretary for one endowed with such an enormous power of work and concentration as he possessed.

Apart from our meetings at King's Langley, I used to see E. D. M. and Stella at the evening parties given by the Charles Trevelyans at their house in Great College Street, at the 1917 Club and elsewhere in London. Unfortunately, my divorce for a time put an end to my normal social activities, as I was too badly hit to care to show myself in circles which Betty and I had frequented together before our parting. But I always kept in touch with E. D. M. and, as recorded above, was honoured with his confidence a few days before he died.

Morel combined a Voltairian Frenchman's love of liberty and justice with an English Quaker's courage in the cause of peace and in defence of civil rights and freedom of conscience. In an age of pre-revolutionary corruption when, for a time, the principle of Evil seemed likely to predominate, Morel, had he been spared to us, would have proved a shining example and a tower of strength. For while we have among our politicians many passably good and well-intentioned men, there are few who have so far shown themselves both good and great.

III

For the following details of Morel's career I am indebted to the obituary notice by F. Seymour Cocks, which appeared in *Foreign Affairs* for December 1924.

Edmund Dene Morel was born in Paris on July 10th, 1873. His father, Edmond Morel de Ville, was an official in the French Ministry of Finance. His mother, Emmeline de Horne, was an Englishwoman and a member of a Quaker family long settled in East Anglia. The de Horne family came to England from the Netherlands in the reign of Queen Elizabeth to escape the persecutions of the Duke of Alva. Morel's father died in 1877 as the result of hardships endured during the Franco-Prussian war. His mother was bent on educating her son in England and sent him first to a private school at Eastbourne and later to Bedford Modern School. "It was during his schooldays," says Mr. Cocks, "that Morel first exhibited and developed that love for the countryside, for flowers and insects, birds and butterflies, which lasted him all his life. Those who knew Morel only as a political controversialist may be surprised to learn that he was a keen entomologist, and was an authority upon British moths as well as upon secret diplomacy."

After leaving school, in 1889, Morel spent some time in a Paris bank and later obtained a clerkship at Liverpool in the office of Messrs. Elder, Dempster and Co., which was the centre of West African interests in Britain. The subject of West Africa interested Morel and with characteristic thoroughness he set himself to find out all about it. He mastered it in every detail, then sat down to write about it and soon became recognized as an authority of unquestionable accuracy. His period of journalistic activity, during which he was a regular contributor to the *Daily Chronicle* under Robert Donald, lasted from 1893 to 1913. He married in 1896. "Morel and I," writes M. Réné Claparède, "were walking up and down the railway platform at Dijon. Suddenly he said to me, 'I should never have done what I have without my wife's help. I was often discouraged. It was she who invariably made me strong again by saying to me, 'Go on'."

Morel, from the first, became a champion of the rights of the West African natives. As a result of paying frequent visits to Belgium in the course of his duties, he heard stories which aroused his suspicions about the so-called Congo Free State. At that time, the vast Congo territory was despotically ruled by Leopold II for his personal financial profit, and that of approved concessionaires. Morel discovered firstly that the natives were being robbed, secondly that, as they naturally wouldn't work voluntarily for nothing, they were being enslaved. In proof of these two points, he amassed an overwhelming volume of direct evidence.

"Morel," says Mr. Cocks, "was only twenty-seven. He had not been married long. He had no capital, no powerful social influences behind him. And against him he had the wealthiest, the most astute, and the most unscrupulous monarch in the world and social, political, and economic forces of a Continental magnitude. Yet not for one moment did he hesitate. The voice of Truth called him and as always throughout his life, he followed that high command. He sat down and penned a series of articles on " The Congo Scandal" for the *Speaker* which attracted the attention, and brought to Morel the co-operation, of the late Sir Charles Dilke. He threw up his position at Elder Dempsters and almost single-handed, impelled by his passion for justice, he went forward to battle for the lives and freedom and happiness of 15,000,000 African natives."

In 1903 Morel started a weekly paper called *The African Mail*, which he edited for a dozen years with great success, and in 1904 he formed the Congo Reform Association.

Mr. Cocks says : " It is not possible in a few short paragraphs to describe the heroic and historic conflict which now ensued between Morel and the reformers and Leopold and his con-cessionaries, a conflict which ended in the total abolition of the hideous system of oppression and extortion which was desolating the heart of Africa. . . . Over three Continents the con-troversy raged, and scores of newspapers and magazines in France, Belgium, America, and Britain printed contributions from Morel's untiring pen. Morel's activities were amazing. Every move made by King Leopold or his agents was instantly countered ; every statement made by apologists for the Free State was answered with that wealth of detail which, always apparently at Morel's command, made him one of the most formidable controversialists of modern times. Pamphlet followed pamphlet and book succeeded book in rapid succession. Visits to America, visits to France, visits to Switzerland, to the leaders of all the churches, speeches at the Sorbonne and at the Inter-national Peace Congress at Boston, all formed a part of his campaign and he took them all in his stride."

In 1906 Morel published his *Red Rubber* which even the *Daily Mail* described as " the most appalling indictment of personal rapacity, cruelty, expropriation of life and labour, maladministration and tyrannical atrocity ever recorded on irrefutable proof against any one man in any country or in any age."

At last the British Liberal Government began to exert its influence. Reforms were gradually conceded. The atrocities ceased. An honest Belgian administration replaced the domina-tion of the concessionaires. Native rights were restored. And on April 23rd, 1913 Morel was able to announce to the world that victory had been won.

To-day, especially if the reader was born after 1913, two points about Morel's Congo campaign must stand out with special significance. The first is that little more than thirty years ago the civilized world still had a conscience which could be stirred to action. The second is that a large part of the " capitalist " press of Great Britain and other countries was still unmuzzled, fearless, responsible and capable of a crusading zeal to right wrongs, defend the weak and expose injustice. The lesson to be drawn from it is that, in the years to come, restoration of the freedom of the Press is an essential preliminary to any recovery of our sense of right and wrong.

Morel considered that his fight against slavery was, in a very real sense, a fight against war. " This crusade," he said at the final meeting of the Congo Reform Association, " has been a great peace crusade." His efforts therefore, to bring about a better understanding between France, Germany and Great Britain were, as Mr. Cocks points out, " in logical succession to his Congo campaign." In his book " Ten Years of Secret Diplomacy " he did his utmost to open the eyes of the public to the catastrophe which threatened Europe. In it he pointed out the danger of secret commitments, proclaimed the necessity of international co-operation, and showed how essential it was for Parliament to secure effective control over foreign policy. The warning was unheeded. Asquith and Grey assured the country that the secret understandings with France, at which Morel had hinted, did not exist.

On the outbreak of war Morel resigned his position as Liberal candidate for Birkenhead and joining with his friends Charles Trevelyan, Arthur Ponsonby and Norman Angell, helped them to form the Union of Democratic Control.

" Its first and dominant principle," wrote Mrs. H. M. Swanwick, who succeeded Morel as editor of *Foreign Affairs*, " was embodied in the name taken by the new organization. We believed that the causes of war went far back into the policies pursued by the various Governments concerned for many years past and we believed that publicity would have made those policies impossible. It was the object, successfully pursued, of all the governments to concentrate popular attention on the last-hour negotiations, which they were able in every case, by judicious editing, to commend to their politically excited peoples."

The demand for " open diplomacy", ceaselessly reiterated by Morel and his friends, probably caught the ear of President Wilson who, although not averse from carrying on negotiations behind the backs of his Allies, fully realized the difficulties which had been created by the Secret Treaties. In 1919 those who, like Morel and Philip Snowden, realized what would be the effects of the Peace Treaty, were able to forecast with melancholy conviction that the Second World War would break out in 1939. The writer, at that time the father of a son a few months old, said to himself, with clairvoyant foreboding : " My God, that means that Hugh will be caught." Within twenty years and one month the prophecy came true.

Morel's investigations into the causes of World War One, proved that the responsibility for its outbreak was distributed, and " that the belief in the sole culpability of Germany was a crude, unscientific and unfounded legend." This view, confirmed by subsequent knowledge of the parts played by Isvolsky, Count Berchthold, Grey, and others, was set forth in his book " Truth and the War", published in 1916, and has since been accepted by most serious historians.

Additional proof of Franco-British diplomatic culpability was supplied by Wilfrid Scawen Blunt—who was Morel's precursor in exposing what he calls " our infamous Foreign Office "—in his two-volume work " My Diaries", which appeared in 1918.

Blunt, a poet, ex-diplomat and ex-Catholic, a High Tory, a Sussex landowner, a close friend and relative of George Wyndham, an intimate of men like Winston Churchill, Balfour and Asquith, yet an anti-imperialist who fought for the liberation of Ireland, India and Egypt, was one of the most remarkable Victorian survivals. He had numerous bees in his bonnet, but no man had a deeper first-hand knowledge of the secret history of his time. He started his campaign against secret diplomacy in the 'eighties of the last century and carried it on with relentless vigour up till 1914. Blunt and Morel, however, lived in totally different worlds and approached the same problems from different angles although they often reached the same conclusions. I cannot find any evidence that they ever met. This is not really surprising because when " Truth and the War " was published Blunt was 76 and had been living in retirement for several years.

The publication of " My Diaries " caused a considerable sensation in political circles, but for " Truth and the War " Morel was " attacked, vilified and maligned as few public men have been", Mr. Cocks records. Finally he was, as the Americans put it, " framed."

" In 1917 Morel was sentenced to six months' imprisonment

under D.O.R.A. The charge against him was that he had attempted to send two of his pamphlets by hand to the distinguished French author, M. Romain Rolland. Had M. Rolland been living in France, no offence would have been committed. But he happened to be living in Switzerland, a fact of which Morel was unaware. Therefore Morel was morally innocent even if technically guilty. Nevertheless, the magistrate, who had obviously never heard of the author of *Jean-Christophe*, sent Morel to herd with criminals for six months."

" This disgraceful prosecution," says Mrs. H. M. Swanwick, " showed how formidable Mr. Morel had become and how anxious the Government was to put him out of the way. He emerged seriously weakened in health . . . and there is too much reason to believe that irreparable harm was done to him physically by semi-starvation, cold and insomnia."

Vernon Lee, in an obituary tribute, wrote : " With his curious mixture of very British with very French, Morel was not unlike Romain Rolland's war hero, Clerambault, the sort of man who, on the Continent, would have been assassinated like Jaurès, Rathenau and Matteotti. In our law-stickling England of the war years, he was merely put in a convict's jacket for infringing unwittingly a regulation against sending pamphlets to neutral countries ; and was employed for half a year sewing mail-bags with a burglar (as he told me) for his right-hand neighbour, and a violator of little girls on the left."

His imprisonment undoubtedly sowed the seeds of the illness which caused his premature death, but Morel still had six years of successful activity left to him. In March 1918 he joined the I.L.P., and in July of the following year founded the monthly journal *Foreign Affairs*, which has only recently ceased publication.

At the General Election of 1922, when the Tories conducted a campaign of incredible virulence, in which Lord Birkenhead surpassed even his own previous records for vulgarity, Morel defeated Winston Churchill by no less than 10,000 votes and was returned, with Scrymgeour, as Member for Dundee. " The election of 1924," says Mr. Cocks, " was perhaps an even greater personal triumph for Morel than that of 1922. Throughout the country the tide of reaction reached its high-water mark. But Morel surpassed himself."

The obituary notices which appeared in the press after Morel's death, were characteristic of the 'twenties. Hardly one outstanding figure in politics, literature or art, who died during that decade, escaped the posthumous vilification of journalists whose excuse was that they "had to earn their bread and butter." Lowes Dickinson, a man not often given to such comments, felt forced to remark that, "I read with disgust the kind of articles (about Morel) published by *The Times* and even the *Daily News*."

CHAPTER SIX

A VISIT TO A. E. HOUSMAN

In that charming book of his old age, "From a Paris Garret", Richard Le Gallienne makes an observation the truth of which was borne in on most artists and novelists in the early 'twenties. "However bad business may be," he writes, "whatever the distressing fall of the pound, the franc or the mark, the publisher and the dealer always go about in their cars. The artist, without whom they could not exist, goes about on foot, glad that he has a pair of old shoes for his weary feet." As I was a publisher myself up till August 1914 and even later—in 1915 I gave birth to the firm of Selwyn and Blount, before handing it over to Roger Ingpen—I have always had a friendly feeling for publishers, and have usually got on well with agents. I therefore do not grudge them their comforts, although I sympathize with Le Gallienne. As Ford Madox Ford used bitterly to lament, the status of the author had been steadily declining in England since the last decades of the nineteenth century. During the early 'twenties the descent was, for some of us, catastrophic. On the other hand, publishers, most of whom had done well during the war years, and literary agents with good American connections, seemed to be flourishing more than ever. As middlemen became richer, and authors poorer, the agents began to assume a new importance in the literary world. You always found them in the best "West-End clubs", their sons began to sport the most expensive "old school ties", and their wives wore strings of pearls, became literary hostesses and dispensed cocktails to the more remunerative clients. The deference to their authors shown in pre-war days by veterans like J. B. Pinker—the famous "Jye Bye"—was replaced by a distinct air of patronage on the part of their post-war successors. Some started giving us kindly advice about what books we should write and even how we should write them. As many of us were wondering how we should eat, this advice was listened to with eagerness and humility, even if it was not always followed. In my own case, although—through lack of talent as much as lack of inclination—I regretfully had to decline my agent's suggestion that I should write detective stories, I was glad of the crumbs which, in the way of odd jobs, occasionally fell from his opulent table. In association with a new firm of publishers, he organized a first-novel competition and engaged me, for the modest fee of £4 a week, to weed out the MSS sent in. This kept me going for nearly a year. As I spotted Ethel Mannin's first novel as a potential winner—not, I may add, a very difficult task—and she became in consequence one of his most valued authors, I can safely claim that I earned my money. The manager of the firm at this time was a go-getting young Irishman engaged in writing the official biography of one of our less blown-upon generals and thus himself a potential, if not actual, " author." He was a breezy fellow, with black curly hair, thick glasses and a useful fund of pep and self-assurance. Discovering that I was a member of the P.E.N. Club, he asked me to take him to one of its monthly dinners. As Mrs. Dawson Scott, the founder of the club, had, quite rightly, set her face against the admission of publishers and agents, the request put me in a rather a quandary. However, the dividing line between the professional writer and the literary tradesman was already hard to trace, and since my employer was at least " almost an author " and a fairly presentable chap, I eventually allowed myself to be persuaded.

On the following day he summoned me from my small office into his more imposing apartment, and beamed at me genially. " I was pleased with you, Goldring, last night," he observed. " Yes, I was pleased with you." I gathered from his sub-sequent remarks that he had noticed that I was able to tie a tie and had refrained from attacking my soup with a knife and fork. This managerial approval of my deportment in my own club aroused mixed feelings, but writers tend to have an exaggerated respect for those who possess qualities in which they believe themselves deficient. I therefore assumed that my temporary boss at least knew his business. The novel on which I was engaged had stuck, I needed money and the only way to get it was to make a contract for a bread-and-butter book which would tide me over. In my capacity not as employee but as a client of the firm, I explained the position and asked him to do his stuff. A few days later, he sent for me and said : " Look here, Goldring, if you'd care to do a book on A. E. Housman—brief biography and critical appreciation, like your book on Flecker —I can easily get you an advance of £100." He mentioned the name of a " literary " publisher, whose imprint at that time had acquired a good deal of prestige. " Why don't you run down to Cambridge and see the old boy ? " he went on. " He'd probably give his consent."

I asked for time to think about the proposal and the more I thought the less I liked it. I did not know Housman, and apart from having sent him a copy of my little book on Flecker which elicited a brief but flattering reply, saying that " it contains, if I may way so, discriminating criticism", I had never had any contacts with the poet who, in my youth, had influenced me more than any other contemporary writer. By all accounts he was reserved and not easily approachable, in fact a don of the austere, headmasterly type, in no sense a " mixer." The mere fact that I had so much respect of him increased my disinclination to force myself on his acquaintance and make a request which he might well consider impertinent. On the other hand, if I secured his permission to write the book and signed the publisher's contract, I had no reason to suppose that I should make a worse job of it than any other hack. Meanwhile, the £100 dangled in front of me meant at least three months' security, at a time when my financial outlook was, to say the least of it, bleak. It was all very well for my bouncing, eupeptic agent to say : " Run down and see the old boy." He himself would not have hesitated a moment. He was made like that : I wasn't. To my nervous protestations, he impatiently rejoined : " What's the matter ? He can't eat you." I knew, only too well, that he *could*. And, as will afterwards appear, he *did*.

Finally, I overcame my tremors and wrote to ask Housman if I could call on him. He replied making an appointment for 6 p.m. on January 2nd, 1923. As I had never been to Cambridge, I thought I might as well make a day of it. A friend, whose father was head of one of the smaller colleges, kindly met me at the station, took me home with her to lunch and afterwards showed me the sights. Although it was pouring

with rain, I enjoyed our walk and my loyalty to Oxford did
not prevent me from appreciating the mellow beauty of the
Backs and the grandeur of King's College Chapel. But, as at
a dinner after which one knows one will have to make a speech,
I should have enjoyed myself more but for the thought of the
ordeal ahead. My friend and I had tea together, after which
she went off in the rain, wished me luck and left me alone.   When
six o'clock came I enquired at the Porter's Lodge at Trinity
College for Professor Housman's rooms. He sent me across
the road to Whewell's Court, a depressing block of buildings
in the nineteenth century " collegiate " style, where a second
porter told me I should find the Professor's rooms at the top
of the last staircase. Somewhat out of breath after my climb,
I reached a green baize door and gave a deferential knock.
The door was opened almost at once by an elderly man, gray-
haired, with a drooping gray moustache who, probably because
he leaned backwards, gave the impression of being even taller
and more formidable than he actually was. There was a
bright fire burning in the otherwise dreary room, the centre
of which was occupied by a square dining-room table covered
to the height of two or three feet with learned tomes. My
host ushered me into a shabby armchair and sat and blinked at
me, while I struggled to make the usual small talk. After
a pause, in the hope of recovering my aplomb, I felt for a
cigarette and asked : " Do you mind if I smoke, Sir ? "   To my
increased embarrassment, he only too obviously did, and the
packet slipped back into my pocket. Perhaps to ease my
discomfiture, he then proceeded, in an agreeable voice, and
with an occasional rather wintry smile, to go through the
required motions of a Master who is being interviewed by a
disciple. No doubt it bored him to have to do it, but at least
he did it graciously. Steering the conversation towards modern
verse—he cheered me by mentioning that he had read some of
my efforts in Harold Monro's " Chapbook "—he asked what
I thought about " The Georgians," what school (of poetry)
I belonged to and if I was one of J. C. Squire's " little band."
After I had assured him that I had no connection of any sort
with the " Squirearchy", he mentioned Osbert Sitwell's squib on
" Jolly Old Squire and Shanks's Mare " which he had just
been reading with amusement. He expressed great interest in
the Sitwell family, particularly in Osbert. A sudden gleam
came into the old veiled eyes as he enquired if it was true that

Osbert Sitwell had been an officer in the Guards during the war. When I replied in the affirmative he relapsed for a moment into what seemed pleasurable rumination. The Guards! What memories did that magic name recall? Afterwards, reverting to current literary journalism, he praised the musical criticism of W. J. Turner and expressed the view that T. S. Eliot's paper, the *Criterion*, " seemed rather thin for 3s. 6d." While I sat wondering how on earth I was to broach the subject I had come to discuss with him, he made the conventional enquiry as to what I thought of Cambridge. Apologizing for repeating a chestnut, he then told the story of an Oxford man who ordered his scout to pack for him as he was going to Cambridge. " Cambridge, sir? " said the scout. " Yes, sir. I 'ave 'eard of it. Something in the Keble style, I think, sir." I tittered dutifully, like a sixth form boy at a headmaster's dinner-table.

My first introduction to " A Shropshire Lad " came through my Felsted housemaster, the Rev. R. B. Clark, who lent me the volume with some reluctance on account of its " morbidity." Clark claimed to have been at St. John's, Oxford, with Housman and told an amusing story about the poet's horror at hearing a don deliver himself, at a lecture, of a false quantity. It occurred to me to ask if he remembered Clark, but my query only elicited a sharp denial that he had ever heard of him. Clearly I had made a *gaffe* : Oxford memories were not encouraged !

The conversation now turned to the safer and less personal topic of English " public school and University " education which, then as now, was coming in for sharp criticism. I suggested that like the English climate, which enabled Englishmen to endure all degrees of temperature from the Tropics to the Arctic, so our public school training, though it did not teach us how to make a living, enabled us to enjoy existence at almost any income level from extreme wealth to poverty. In particular, I added, a liberal education equipped a man to be profitably idle. " The education must be good to achieve that end successfully," Houseman replied. " I remember," he went on, " that in my native town there was a tallow-chandler who sold his business, making the proviso that he should always have the right to call at the shop and spend the day there when the tallow was melting—thus ensuring one day's pure joy a week, so long as he lived."

The " interview " could not be continued like this indefinitely. At last, with considerable trepidation, I forced myself to explain the real purpose of my call. The flush of annoyance which immediately came into the old man's cheeks gave me my answer before he opened his mouth. The suggestion horrified him. He considered " that kind of writing most impertinent. A man should be judged solely by the value of his work." He added that he did not imagine that after his death one person in ten thousand would appreciate what had been the *real* achievement of his life—his edition of Manilius.

In saying this, I thought at the time, and have been certain since, that he was consciously " putting on an act." No one could have known more clearly than himself that his labours in editing this little-known astrological poet—apart from the opportunities afforded of engaging, by means of foot-notes, in violent warfare with rival scholars, principally German—were no more than what Freudians describe as " escapism." Seeing my serious distress at having unintentionally offended him, he softened the blow by observing that Disraeli—he pronounced the name Disreeli—had been pleased by a book written during his lifetime. The author of it was T. P. O'Connor. The precise implications of this remark he left me to work out for myself. As the nature of his personal views about " that kind of writing " was, however, not left in doubt, I took my leave after blushingly murmuring my apologies and thanking him for having so kindly received me. At the station I bought a stiff whiskey to pull me together and chain-smoked all the way back to Liverpool Street.

By temperament I belong to those who are happier if they remain poor and—at least as regards their main function— honest. Instinct warned me from the start that the idea of my writing a book about Housman was a mistake. I ought to have obeyed this inner prompting and told my man of business to get me a commission for a travel book. The writing of travel books is, as a rule, the most unremunerative of all forms of literary activity, but at least it enables one to travel and that was, for me, a paramount inducement.

After this embarrasing and abortive adventure, I did some agency work on my own account and fixed up with Chapman and Hall the book subsequently published under the title " Gone Abroad." I made scarcely any money out of it, but I enjoyed every moment of the wanderings it records and even the writing of it was more of a pleasure than a burden.

CHAPTER SEVEN

GONE ABROAD

ONE of the circumstances which enhanced the rapture of being alive in the 'twenties and young enough to enjoy oneself was the opportunity created by the high value of sterling of going abroad. Life was cheaper almost everywhere in Europe than it was in England, and in congested Paris—in spite of the Yankee invasion—an English pound note went three times as far as it did in London. The great advantage which a painter or free-lance writer has over those who enjoy the financial security of a " regular " occupation is that they are free to do their work wherever they choose. No office ties them to one particular town or to one country more than another.

After the Armistice those who could do so had every induce-ment to cross the Channel. London was grim, gloomy, depressed, shabby, overcrowded and expensive. Dora and her misbegotten progeny reserved most of the good things of life for the profiteers, who could evade her restrictions, drinks were dear, pubs opened late and closed early, and financial depression soon followed on the brief post-war boom. The intellectuals contrived, it is true, to ignore these drawbacks, to get together, indulge in wild parties, and generate a collective excitement. But the friendships and associations, the loves—and even the hates—which started in 1919 could be carried on much more agreeably in sunny climates where the drinks were cheap. At the beginning of 1922 I had an additional reason for leaving London behind me. My divorce, although divorces were common enough in those days, hit me so severely that, like any chorus girl or Hollywood film star, I just wanted to go away " and forget." From a letter written to me in January 1922 by Wentworth Lewis, then Paris correspondent of *The Times,* it seems clear that I must have made at this period one of several abortive efforts to get a newspaper job. Lewis was at Felsted and at Oxford with me and by way of being an " old school chum." I had run across him again on a Channel packet, in 1919, and spent a rather hectic night with him in Paris at the Café Napolitain, then the haunt of boulevard journalists. " Please forgive me for having delayed so long in answering your letter,"

M

he wrote. " Cannes (he had been covering a conference for *The Times*) was a hectic rush when one could find time for nothing but drink and work. Still I showed your letter to Tuohy but he fears there is nothing doing on the *New York World* which already has more staff correspondents than it knows what to do with. Incidentally the man to see would not be the Tuohy you met with me (Ferdinand) but his father, J. M. T. who lives in London and is the head of the N.Y.W. foreign service. . . . I am very sorry indeed for the reason which makes you want to get out of England and you have my sincerest sympathy." Although baulked in my effort to join the well-paid press gang, I managed to spend a large part of the 'twenties wandering in Mediterranean countries and writing novels and travel books. My most interesting and valuable experiences were gained in Italy and the South of France, where I was fortunate enough to stay with friends who taught me what, for Anglo-Saxons, is the most difficult art to acquire, the art of " going native." My wander years proved to me what I already guessed by instinct, that the common people, in Latin countries especially, are the salt of the earth. It was Tina and Luke Hansard who carried on my education in this important matter, laughed me out of the remaining remnants of my " old school tie " prejudices and—though they themselves were unaware of any political implications in what came to them so naturally—showed me the basic solidarity between " intellectuals" and workers and peasants. Although, at that time, there were no visible barricades in Western Europe, my experiences left me in no doubt as to which side of them my sympathies would lie.

Luke Hansard was one of those English eccentrics who escape fame only through an accidental shortage of literary talent. His qualities found their expression in the sort of life it amused him to lead, which was that of a rather bogus " propri taire-agriculteur " in the village of Mougins, between Cannes and Grasse. He suffered, like Byron, from a club-foot, though whether this was due to an accident which occurred during a legendary period of service in the R.N.V.R. or to some form of infantile paralysis, I never discovered. His parents were well-off and lived in Cadogan Gardens, where I dined with them once or twice and was thus able to observe Lukey in surroundings which to some of his meridional friends might have seemed incongruous. His father, Colonel Hansard, was

an expert in ballistics, a clever amateur wood-carver, a loyal
" old Wykehamist " but far from being the conventional Blimp ;
his mother was a charming and cultivated woman, well-read,
much-travelled and more broad-minded than most of her class
and type. Luke adored her, but this did not prevent him from
feeling a misfit in the home circle. Early experiences at
Winchester, where he had been ferociously bullied, had given
him a permanent distaste for the English pukka sahib. He was
proud of his family and his name—which he once told me meant
in French, a " butcher's cleaver "—but he did not look English
and always asserted that he must be a throwback to some
Italian ancestor. At Cambridge he read Romance Languages,
and on this foundation he soon acquired, after he settled on his
Provençal *mas*, " Lou Miraclé," an extraordinary knowledge of
local dialects. When I first stayed with him at Mougins he was
in process of being divorced from his first wife, a South African
lady, and was living alone. Pietro, his man, slept under a
tree in the garden, and Pietro's " woman", who lived in a
nearby cottage, did the cooking and looked after us. Luke's
acquaintance in the department of Alpes-Maritimes was probably
more extensive and certainly more peculiar than that of any
other English ex-patriate. All the local characters, including
the bandits and the smugglers who brought gunpowder across
the Italian frontier, knew " Mestre Louko " and his seven-
year-old Ford. Wherever we went remarkable " types " came
up, exchanged gossip in their, to me, incomprehensible patois
and were stood drinks which they never failed to return. They
accepted Luke as one of themselves. Even the hard-boiled
porters at Cannes railway station would go out of their way to
do him a good turn. Compatriots, especially the synthetic
" majors " and usually bogus pukka sahibs, who began to
infest the Riviera after the Armistice, viewed these hob-nobbings
with a distaste which was actively returned. Among the few
English people of whom Luke seemed to approve were his
neighbour, the Comtesse de Pourtalès, and Sir Hugo de Bathe,
once the husband of the Jersey Lily. " Shuggie " de Bathe,
lean, spare, well-preserved and still good-looking—Ouida's
conception of the English aristocrat—used to dash up and
down the Croisette in a blood-red Bugatti, wearing a béret
and a silk shirt open at the neck. When Lukey's battered Ford
drew up by the side of Shuggie's spotless racer, the contrast was
remarkable. The numerous social impostors who figured as

leaders of English snob society at Cannes, used to fill Luke with combined amusement and contempt. We both became experts at picking them out : how they ever deceived anyone passes understanding. On one occasion we were introduced to a gentleman with scenic titles like " Prince d'Istria and Duc de S. Giovanni di Medua " ! Our hostess addressed him as " Prince " after every second word. Luke and I looked at each other, with difficulty restraining our giggles. Afterwards, exchanging notes, we both remembered having had our hair cut by the " Prince " at a shop in Bond Street. As a " tonsorial " artist he was first-rate : even as a Riviera " prince " he displayed considerable native talent. He must have invited us to call, for I recently discovered a large ornate visiting-card with his titles displayed on it, but we did not avail ourselves of the honour.

On a later visit to Mougins, I found Luke in the throes of a *grande passion* which he dramatised with true meridional flamboyance. He had fallen in love with the English wife of a blameless White Russian general who was the mother of two grown-up children and ran a boarding-house, if I may use such a vulgar term, at La Napoule. She was a few years older than Lukey and came of one of those English aristocratic families who, if not stationed abroad as military attachés or diplomats, became expatriates in the nineteenth century from choice. She was the granddaughter of an English Duke and half-sister of a Marquess, but had lived nearly all her life abroad, much of it in Cannes. Like Lukey, she understood and loved " the natives", fully appreciated his attitude towards them and detested the English and American nouveaux-riches who swarmed on the Côte d'Azur and prided themselves on being unable to speak a word of French.

The only obstacle to Lukey's happiness was the Russian general. Night after night I used, so to speak, to hold Lukey's hand, as the saucers piled up in front of us in the Taverne Royale and his rage increased.

" I'll shoot the fellow. Shoot him like a dog. It's the only way. I shall *have* to do it."

" Now don't be an ass, Lukey. Don't be impatient and ruin all your chances of future happiness. You are civilized people. It will all work out quite satisfactorily if you keep your hair on."

" Grrh. I'll shoot him."

This sort of dialogue used to continue by the hour together. Finally I had to leave Cannes and return to my work in Sweden. Some time later, I heard from him in reply to a letter of inquiry and found that everything had worked out as I anticipated.

" Dear old Friend,

Your letter of the fifth reached me yesterday. . . . It goes well. At last I have ' crossed that last blue mountain barred with snow.' In other words, I was married by the British Consul at Cannes, Jack Taylor, whom I think you know, to my Sweet Lady on November the Fifth last : and we drank to the health of the immortal Guido ffoulkes—surnamed by the vulgar : ' Guy Fawkes '—an honest man, perhaps the first who realized the futility of our modern outlook. From the above address you will see that after much wandering I have come back (to St. Basile, Mougins) . . . . And I never believed it possible to enjoy a ' coming back ' so much. After many moons in strange places, to meet the old friends—and never till now did I realize what friends they were—and to hear and speak the old jargon again. A few are dead : and a few in Gaol ! But what matter. I doubt if you will remember where St. Basile is. It lies on the other side of Mougins from my old home. Some five or six kilometres away in fact ; a sufficient distance. I have a dear, comfortable house, if simple. Also I have bought the very latest kind of Ford, an interior drive saloon, which gives me that millionaire feeling. . . . You ask me ' if I know of a cheap winter place that isn't Paris '—I know of but one : St. Basile, Mougins. Here is a cook far better than I have met in all my wanderings, and a ' home from home.' Superb view over the mountains, marvellous excursions, etc., etc. In other words, Dear Lad, why not come and spend a little while with us. My dear one wants so much to meet you and she asks me to invite you when you will and for as long as you can ; any day from now onwards. . . . Come and see ' the prophet who can understand.' In other words, come along as soon as you possibly can, and enjoy the stimulation of sunshine after your Northern mists.

Ever your old friend,

LUKE HANSARD."

Poor Luke did not long enjoy his new-found happiness. I went to St. Basile on two or three occasions within the next twelve months. On my last visit, I found Luke in a nursing home, with some internal complaint. It seemed preposterous that anyone so vital, in his own way so "dynamic" as Luke, should be laid up for long. Luke himself had no illusions about his condition. He knew that his number was up. As I rose to leave, he called me back. "Come here, old lad." I went to his bedside and he kissed me on both cheeks, in the French way which came natural to him but the very idea of which sends the average Englishman into fits of laughter. I didn't, however, feel much like laughing. "We've had some good times, old boy," he said. "Don't forget me when I've passed out." He was quite philosophical, almost gay, took a few cigarettes from me, and gave himself about seven days to live. His guess was accurate. Exit Lukey.

II

Tina, the other formative influence in my wander years, like Lukey, put all her talent and originality into life itself, although could she have canalised her gifts and found means of expressing them in one of the arts, she might have been hailed as a genius. She was, by her own account, the love child of an Irish wine merchant and a Spanish girl of an "aristocratic" family—possibly a Jewess, though this was not admitted. Her first husband was a journalist and minor poet, who dabbled in occultism and was mixed up with a society of Rosicrucians. When I first met her she was married to a solid, kind, understanding and infinitely long-suffering artist to whom she had borne two delightful children and for whom, in spite of her tempestuous and erratic temperament, she had a deep affection and respect. (As a couple, they reminded me very much of Grahame Brown and Marie Tempest : Tina's husband had the same gentle resilience as that of our great comedienne's stage and domestic partner.) Tina was tubercular, like D. H. Lawrence, and her latent illness no doubt accounted for many of her vagaries as well as for her hectic vitality. As I was more than usually inexperienced and obtuse in these matters, I found her alternately infuriating and fascinating, never made allowances for her affliction, quarrelled with her finally over something which seemed important at the time but which I have now totally forgotten and, to my lasting regret, took no steps to make it up before her death.

She was a friend of G. B. (Peter) Stern, who, with her then

husband Geoffrey Holdsworth, had gone to live at Diano Marina, on the Italian Riviera. To be near them, Tina had taken a furnished villa in Diano and had installed herself there with her two children and a nursery governess. There was a spare room and, in response to her invitation, I occupied it for several weeks, of which some chapters in my " Gone Abroad " give only a pale and sober reflection. In my novel " Cuckoo", one of the characters is partly based on Tina, but I failed to do justice to her inspiration. Nor has she been satisfactorily " caught " in my account of our subsequent visit to Mallorca and Ibiza. As a character she always defied my limited powers of portrait-painting. In appearance she was a thin wisp of a woman, with an unruly mop of dark hair cut in a straight fringe over the forehead. She usually dressed in flaming red, had a hoarse, husky voice—not improved by excessive cigarette-smoking—and a gurgling, chuckling, derisive laugh. She was the only woman I have ever met who could use a man's uncensored vocabulary, and cap his stories, without—paradoxical though it may sound—ever making an error of taste. She had, moreover, an unerring eye for the comic side of every human being, young or old, male or female, with whom she came in even momentary contact. Her men friends, whom she chaffingly referred to as her " lovers," she relentlessly turned inside out, punctured, debunked, unstuffed and mocked at. No weakness or folly, no secret pomposity or strain of conceit escaped her psychically disrobing glance. As for the Ligurians, a sly, deceitful, hard-boiled but humorous race, she saw through them in a flash, picked up their dialects with ease, got on with them, understood them and even revealed them to themselves. They loved her for it and though they could not occasionally restrain themselves from robbing her, nearly always returned what they had stolen.

A letter, undated, headed " Villa Miramare, Diano Marina," runs as follows, and evidently preceded my visit to Diano.

" Dear Douglas,

Peter Stern and Geoffrey are going to Rome to-night. I was going but M. (her husband) said I wasn't to. Never mind, the weather is lovely. I have won £4 10s. at poker in two weeks : I am wearing a lovely dress bought with my winnings : X (an Italian soldier married to an English wife) and his cretina signora are back : and I am quite happy. I'm even beginning to like Diano. So you'd better come out. Peter says so too. She'll be back in 5 days.

I've been really putting in some good work lately, Douglas. I can't write but *can* criticize—say what you like—and Peter's new book, ' The Matriarch,' which is nearly finished, is really enthralling me. It's the thing I like best about Peter. We have nearly bust twice over it—we haggle like a couple of Whitechapel Jews over values. We've (she) has dismissed a secretary and taken another over it : but I've been enjoying myself well. It's a fine book . . . . but not a seller, I'm afraid : a muddled, flamboyant Jewish family chronicle of a decade and a half.

As for you, you write me nothing itself. I gather you are eating the husks that the swine did eat ; I also gather it's no use saying don't : and as, besides the knowledge that it is impossible to frown darkly at you, I also want to see you, I am, as gentlemen occasionally are in golf circles, whatchermite call 'andicapped.

But—have you heard this one. . . . You asked me about my lovers. I have none. Mine, dearie, she said soberly, 'ave all either gone west or else 'ave been aleniated away from me. There is, however, still hope that a disillusioned, jaded, purblind blighter of 75 may court me in a high falsetto and false teeth. . . . There's a very large bedroom, facing the sea—one window : the other, the hills. The food, too, is extremely good because Cesira, the cook, is in love with me. She kisses my underclothes and washes and mends them. She's a cantankerous, ugly bitch, too. . . .

Do you want my poem beginning

' How it stuck in Sally's gizzard
When her brother found a lizard ? ' ''

In another undated letter written after our joint exploration of the Balearic islands, Tina refers to her life in Diano.

" Dear Duggy,

I was awfully glad to get your letter, and simply disgusted with the American guy who sloped off. Perhaps he has turned up since with much monies and our little Duggy is already the victim of a nasty headache over the first few dollars. . . . I'm not mad on Italy : I love the dancing at Alassio, where chauffeurs, ham and beef men or their counterparts in Italian, hairdressers, soldiers, wine-sellers, and oddments—all clean and springy and smelling of pomade—come up, bow, and whirl you off : I *love* my little partner who is a dancer born and who spins me round like a Dervish. I like and love and admire Peter Stern more than I can say : I adore Pino and Bianca and Dr. Watson [Peter's dog] and Peter's secretary Vera (you'd love her) : I don't think the Italians, as much as I've seen of 'em, in the same street with Spaniards, and I can't abide the La Carruba cat. . . ."

Diano Marina remains in my memory as one of the most odious little places on the Ligurian coast. It was completely destroyed in the earthquake of 1887 and rebuilt on hygienic lines, with broad shadeless streets and adequate drainage, possibly in the hope that the notoriously mad English would desert nearby Alassio for the pleasure of walking in its noonday sun. At the time of my visit only a handful of seedy compatriots, attracted chiefly by low rents, had availed themselves of these advantages. Their sole diversion was to take the morning train into Alassio to drink cocktails at one or other of its American bars and enjoy the coolness of its crowded " Main Drain."

The Stern-Holdsworth villa, La Carruba, was prettily situated in an olive grove, on a low hill behind the town, with grand views of the mountains and the sea. Peter and Geoffrey had a remarkable butler and cook and several literary dogs of which " Dr. Watson " became the most famous. They entertained the local notabilities and were lavishly, if rather nervously, hospitable to Tina and myself. I say " nervously " because, although Tina and I were too busy enjoying ourselves with the " natives " to be aware of it, what may be termed the social aspect of the present European conflict was already discernible. In the first brushes between the " respectable " and the " emancipated ", the bond and the free, the free enjoyed a short-lived triumph. In the 'twenties, the internationally-minded writers and artists, assisted by Transatlantic good-time-seekers and the exuberant English young (some of them with " backgrounds ", some without) successfully cocked snooks at the inhabitants of all the snob-ridden Continental " English colonies." In Alassio, Tina's " goings-on " horrified and disgusted the Blimps and their wives, but greatly intrigued their daughters, who saw Tina and her friends enjoying fun from which they were excluded. The position was further complicated by the fact that a retired Admiral, one of the acknowledged social leaders of Alassio at that time, was Tina's uncle by marriage She was, therefore, so to speak, " all right " ; she possessed a " Service background." Invitations to their ghastly bridge-parties, odious tennis and sepulchral dinners would have been showered on Tina by all the best people had she given the least indication that their advances would be welcomed, had she in fact behaved " suitably." When, instead of behaving suitably, they saw her hobnobbing with all the local " dagoes", as well as with writers, artists and *people of that sort*, they regarded her with the same distaste as that which the Cannes " majors " felt for Lukey and consoled themselves by indulging in malicious gossip at her expense. Even her daughter Sally, a three-year-old enchantment, contrived to shock them. Sally was an enthusiastic nudist and was once observed toddling across the sands, dressed only in a broad grin, pursued by an outraged carabiniere.

When Tina, chaperoned by a girl friend, joined me in Mallorca, we pretended, for some wholly idiotic reason, to be brother and sister. This was, in a sense, an accurate description of our relationship ; but as I was an obviously " Anglo-Saxon " blond and Tina, in colouring and appearance, took after her Spanish mother, a certain suspicion was noticeable in Palma and its English suburb, El Terreno. My memories of the El Terreno English, five years before the rush of cocktail-drinking tourists disturbed their calm, enabled me subsequently to understand the reason why the more cretinous section of our Conservative middle-class supported General Franco. What poisoned all the " English colonies " in Mediterranean resorts was the fact that the colonists lived entirely segregated from the main body of their compatriots, were oblivious of all fresh developments in their own country, impervious to all ideas which conflicted with the sort of prejudices acquired in their youth and had nothing whatever to do except play golf and re-hash their pre-war gossip. They came in contact with no English shop-keepers, railway porters, bus conductors, artisans, farm-hands, or " common " people ; took no interest in English politics, and, like embryo fascists, actively detested art, literature and every form of intellectual activity. Once, when travelling in Corsica, I found myself alone in a railway carriage with an English naval officer. He tried, with obvious unsuccess, to " place " me, looked at my hand luggage for signs of sporting activities—fishing rods, golf-clubs, etc.—and, finding none,

did not venture on conversation.   After long experience of these
arrested adolescents, I amused myself by trying an experiment
on him.   I dug up from among my youthful memories some
of the jargon of fly-fishing and otter-hunting.   It worked like
a charm.   When I was able to refer, quite truthfully, to a
" day with the Culmstock ", the barriers fell down   We lunched
and shared a bottle of wine together—at Vizzavona, if I
remember right—and, by the time we got to Ajaccio were almost
bosom pals.

Tina and I soon escaped from the English colony atmosphere
of El Terreno and proceeded to a then tiny and unknown
fishing village, Puerto de Pollensa.   It afterwards became, to
my horror, a crowded resort with swank hotels and American
bars.   I have always had it on my conscience that my book
" Gone Abroad " may have contributed towards this lamentable
decline and fall.   In the 'twenties, the impoverished artists and
writers who collected in unknown European villages, where
they could live very cheaply because such places were " off
the map", found themselves the unwilling pioneers of "Tourism."
The travelling public, Americans particularly, developed a
positive rage for " Bohemia", regardless of the fact that Bohemia
has no geographical location, but is merely a way of living
and a state of mind.   As a way of living, it eludes, of necessity,
the tourist approach.   In Paris again and again a handful of
painters and writers would collect round the *zinc* in some shabby
out of the way *bistro*.   They acquire fame : their " haunt "
becomes known and the tourists hurry along to invade it.   Long
before their approach, the painters and the writers have received
warning and fled.   The *bistro*, however, remains.   The proprietor, having amassed a new clientèle by the drawing-power
of its original frequenters, rebuilds his premises to suit it.   The
prices go up, a brand new " American bar " replaces the shabby
zinc, and any writers or artists foolish enough to return are
promptly shown the door.

In 1922, Puerto de Pollensa was still an unspoiled fishing-
village.   The inhabitants—technically " Anarchist-Communists"
—ran their fishing industry on co-operative lines.   The secretary
of the " Posito de Pescadores", a Venezuelan, was almost the
only man in this Arcadian village who could read and write.
He transacted all the business for the community and, by ex-
plaining their illiteracy, sent the tax-collector empty away.
As there was no Law and no Order in the village, there was

no crime. The honesty of these people was absolute and instinctive : no one ever tried to get the better of anyone else. If one of the men stayed up too late drinking with the foreigners, his wife appeared and dealt with the misdemeanour so drastically that it was never repeated. Everyone had enough to eat, wine was plentiful and everyone was happy. The nearest church was five miles off, in the town of Pollensa, and I never saw a priest in the village. (Fifteen years later, perhaps because they were considered " anti-clerical ", Franco's death-carts carried many of them off to "les grands cimeti`res sous la lune ", with the Archbishop of Palma's full approval.)

The little foreign colony we found in Puerto de Pollensa consisted of an elderly Spanish painter, Llangada, an Argentine ex-pupil who had gone to say with him for a fortnight nine years ago and had remained ever since, painting trees, a Danish baron who wrote poetry and translated the works of Oscar Wilde, and two Danish artists, Jan Willumsen and Ivan Opffer. The language question presented no difficulties to Tina. She picked up enough Mallorquin, in a week, to be able to converse fluently with the inn-keeper, Antonio Borras, and invented a kind of lingua franca to establish communication with the others. Ivan spoke American-English and, when necessary, interpreted for his brother Danes. We all swam, sailed, fished, walked, talked and drank together, in perfect international amity. Later, when Tina and I went to the then unexplored island of Ibiza, she picked up Ibicenco with the same ease as she had picked up Mallorquin. As she could take down tunes in a sort of musical shorthand of her own devising, she came away with a large collection of Spanish popular songs, heard one starry night when we entertained a trave ling concert party in the balcony of our ramshackle inn. Had I gone to Ibiza by myself, I should probably have got no further than taking an external view of those of the inhabitants with whom I came in contact. Accompanied by Tina, I got to know almost intimately a whole crowd of fruity local characters. But for her illness and the resulting inability to settle down and " do the actual writing", she could probably have produced a much more entertaining record of our joint experiences than my own can claim to be.

After our return from Ibiza, Tina went back to her home in Hammersmith, while I continued my Mediterranean wanderings, landed up once again at Diano Marina and stayed for a few days as Peter's guest at La Carruba. A letter, as usual undated, has reminded me of this visit.

"I am writing—amazingly—by return of post, but don't let that shake you too much, and disturb the perfect peace that must have set in since my departure. Forget Ibiza and forget Puerto de Pollensa, for it's a far cry from both places to Hammersmith and probably Hammersmith will smudge much of my recently acquired excrescences (unless of course the reverse applies, and Hammersmith did the smudging that Puerto de Pollensa and Ibiza washed clean). . . . . I'm awfully glad that Gladys Stern is affable and hospitable. . . . I can place you all quite clearly here in Hammersmith and imagine a conversation : three voices, " Pantomime", " The Fortune " and good old journalese. I really think you want a little Bull s Blood to add the necessary lust to the otherwise intellectual story. Que vida ! and here am I doing things with mutton fat in Hammersmith.

Four days have passed—three and a bit—and there's devastating news for you. I have as yet no lover. All the possibles have been to see me (about 2 1/4) with the result only that they depart to a pretty tune I learnt in Pollensa . . . and I know that, even if they ate the stomach contents of an egg-bound hen, or the delicacy presented to the guests in the Presidential box in the Plaza del Toros, the song would be the same."

Peter, in her Italian setting, was her witty and amusing, that is, her true self. In London, later, she became a fashionable literary figure. I have always thought " The Matriarch " the best of her many books. Like so many other successful novelists of the period, she accepted her world as she found it, without, perhaps, realizing what a doomed and worthless world it was. The branch on which most of the popular novelists and playwrights of the later 'twenties and 'thirties sat so pretty was already three-parts sawn through. On September 3rd, 1939, it crashed, and they fell with it. We rebels, who shocked our handful of readers, were boycotted by the middle classes, denied a decent living and heavily denounced by respectable reviewers, were more fortunate. We had nowhere to fall, no vogue to lose, no coats to turn. The Standard of Values in which we believed was vindicated by events, and as we never trusted the Armistice interim, the future held few surprises for us.

Tina's illness got a firmer hold on her and exaggerated a failing which she was unable to resist—an impish love of making mischief by repeating what so and so had said about one, or even inventing it. Like Violet Hunt, she was always ready to sacrifice her best friend to her worst epigram. I was singularly naif in those days, always believed what I was told, always rose to every fly and was thus an easy victim of what was, in reality, no more than a rather perverted form of humour. On one occasion Tina recorded, with earnest solemnity, a story about my divorce which she alleged was being told in literary circles by a publisher friend of hers. As I was conscious of having, from the conventional standpoint—since I was the " innocent " party—behaved rather decently in the matter about which I was, apparently, being traduced, I was furious. If I had stopped to think, I should have realized that in " literary circles " it is, after all, common form to suggest that a distinguished colleague has murdered his mother, forged a cheque, or had incestuous relations with his daughters. No bones are broken. Everyone repeats such fairy-tales for the purpose of getting a laugh and no one believes them. At the worst, their effect is merely to create a profitable " legend." Most of us would prefer to be libelled than ignored.

Tina's story, however, made me seriously angry and I returned to London vowing vengeance. It was a case of " just let me get at him", or " hold him back there, you fellows, hold him back." In the midst of my wrath, I happened to meet Charles Scott-Moncrieff, who asked me to lunch at the Savile Club, then situated in Piccadilly. After lunch we repaired for our coffee to the billiard room at the back of the house and the first person I saw was my calumniator. As I could hardly abuse my host's hospitality by rushing at the villain—who was, in any case, armed with a billiard cue—I poured out my grievance into " Scomo's " receptive ear. He at once twisted round the accusation, said, " Oh, look here, that's really shocking, an insult ! " completely guyed the story and reduced me, finally, to fits of helpless laughter. To see the funny side of oneself is a handicap, in a literary career, but the ability to do so on this occasion obviated an unseemly fracas. Some incident of this kind, coupled with my long absences from London, must have caused Tina and I to drift apart. I am thankful that all memory of it has now been obliterated. Tina had a spice of the devil in her, but her intuitive perceptions, her enchanting wit and gay courage more than atoned for it. Even in the reckless 'twenties there were few to equal her.

CHAPTER EIGHT

PARIS IN THE 'TWENTIES

I

PARIS, which for me meant chiefly Montparnasse, recovered its natural gaiety and its position as the cultural centre of Europe with remarkable speed after the Armistice. It was a necessity. Europe found it could not think, create or exist without it. It will recover again, for the same reasons. No other city can take its place.

The hordes of statesmen, bankers, industrialists, journalists, secretaries, trained seals, " suckers " and sharks who descended on the French capital for the Peace Conference brought plenty of money with them and they were soon followed by an invasion of tourists from all over the world. As the French exchequer needed all the pounds and dollars it could get, the fact that the operation of the Volstead Act in the United States led to a prodigious influx of thirsty citizens with well-lined pocket-books, doubtless had its advantages.

Thanks to the legends, largely self-created, surrounding the unfortunate Modigliani—that " Prince of Bohemians " who died of drink and T.B. in 1920—Montparnasse quickly became one of the foremost European tourist resorts. Montmartre, from which all the serious painters and indigenous " types " had long since fled, thrived equally on earlier legends. Frédé was still alive and the " Lapin Agile " struggled to maintain the old traditions, but the Place du Tertre was given over almost entirely to catering for the night pleasures of gaping mobs of Transatlantics. From a seat under the plane trees, I once watched a party of American tourists, roaring drunk, amuse themselves by throwing handfuls of coins and paper money at the feet of a crowd of " natives." " We won the war, didn't we ? " they shouted. " Here's your cheap franc ! " The Montmartrois looked at each other, shrugged, spat, made obscene remarks and picked them up. After all, the money represented food which many of them badly needed. The incident was characteristic. The conquerors could buy surface civility in the swank hotels ; French industrialists " collaborated " with American capital as readily as, later, they " collaborated "

with the Nazis; but the common people were not deceived
and nursed their anger. They had bought security with rivers
of their blood and the once idolized American Messiah, who
had made promises he did not keep, had intervened to rob
them of it. Lloyd George, being a tough bargainer, brought
back from Versailles, for the benefit of Britain's imperialists,
" trophies for his country such as even a Chatham might have
envied ", while the French recovered Alsace and Lorraine, had
the League of Nations foisted on them in place of an alliance
defending them against aggression, and pie in the sky in the
shape of Reparations it proved impossible to collect. True, they
had memories of " inexpugnable Verdun " and, at the cost of
five and a half million casualties and a falling birthrate, could
still sing :

> Madelon, emplis mon verre
> Et chante avec les poilus ;
> Nous avons gagné la guerre,
> Hein !   Crois-tu qu'on les a eus !

The Americans, on the other hand, gathered in the cash
with a minimum loss of American lives, extended their financial
grip on the heavy industries of victors and vanquished alike,
found a world market for their surplus foodstuffs and, like
England's profiteers, could afford to be indifferent to the fact
that they were loved more for their money than for their
contribution to peace and progress.

The sore feelings of the French fortunately did not extend
to impoverished writers and artists or to those of their British
comrades-in-arms who crossed the Channel to drink their
gratuities. In France, respect for art and literature is not, as in
England, confined to the few, but is general among all classes
of the population. This fact creates the intellectual climate
which has made Paris the chief international art centre of Europe
for generations and made it the Mecca of the best creative minds
as soon as the war ended and communications were restored.
Most English writers and painters could make themselves understood in French, many could speak the language fairly fluently.
This capacity—nothing much to boast about in view of our
geographical contiguity and the cultural links forged during
centuries of family quarrels and reconciliations—acted like a
charm and was enough in itself to separate the intellectuals from
the mere tourists. The fact that the former were poor operated

strongly in their favour. No one who has ever " gone native " in France is foolish enough to complain of French avarice. Such complaints merely reveal the ignorance of those who make them. The French are careful of money, despise those who throw it away, and respect the thrifty.

II

In command of our " bridgehead " in Montparnasse was the lively and stimulating figure of Nina Hamnett, who knew everybody who wrote or painted, introduced newcomers to each other as well as to earlier arrivals and generally acted as informal hostess at the Café du Dôme, the " Select " and the other cafés which acted both as meeting-places and clearing houses. She had been a pre-war inhabitant of Montparnasse, in the days when Modigliani, Ortiz de Zarate, Zawado, Mme. Vassilieff, Picasso, Pascin, Kisling, Foujita, the models Kiki and Aicha, and various other figures connected with the " Ecole de Paris " were still struggling for recognition. When I first met her, in the early 'twenties, she was sharing Modi's old studio at 8 rue de la Grande Chaumière, with the Polish landscape painter Zawado. Thanks to Nina and to other old friends already established in the Quarter—among them Ford Madox Ford, Ezra Pound, Mary Butts and Jim and Ellie Duncan—I soon found myself as much at home in Montparnasse as in London, although I never stayed there long enough, at any one time, to be described as a " denizen." The English " Montparnos " of my acquaintance very soon collected into a comparatively small group, with Irish, French, Scandinavian, Central European and certain transatlantic affiliations. The latter were mostly limited to those Americans who were " serious " writers or painters, or genuinely cultured cosmopolitans. With the horde of Volstead refugees, playboys and good-timers who thronged the larger cafés and more expensive restaurants we had few contacts. Most of us rarely strayed outside our Quarter, ate where we were known and drank in whatever bar Jimmy Charters—the famous "Jimmy, the barman "—happened at the time to be functioning. Jimmy, in his youth, had been a feather-weight pugilist and, like most professional pugs, was a temperate, tactful little man, the reverse of aggressive. But on the rare occasions when he permitted himself a night out he made a thoroughly good job of it and frequently got the sack in con-

N

sequence. Wherever he went, however, his faithful clientèle followed. The American " Dingo " knew him for a time, but the English, at least, were glad when he returned to Europe and officiated in succession at Pirali's in the rue de Vaugirard, at the Falstaff in the Boulevard Montparnasse, at the Parnass Bar in the rue Delambre, at the Swedish Strix in the rue Huyghens or wherever it might be. With Jimmy we passed our most intimate and most memorable hours. We used the big cafés mostly for our morning café-crême and croissant and for the purpose of spotting newly-arrived friends. For this the Dôme was particularly useful, as most Londoners of our group made it their first port of call, drove there direct from the station and put up at one of the small hotels in the immediate neighbourhood.

By tacit consent, none of the Dôme frequenters ever used the garish " Rotonde," at the opposite corner of the Carrefour Vavin. The " Rotonde's " new proprietors had cashed in on Modigliani's notoriety, rebuilt the place, taken in one or two neighbouring *bistros*, established an expensive restaurant and " cocktail-dancing " on the first floor and laid themselves out to attract the numerous American tourists who wished to claim that they had visited the far-famed Bohemia. In the days of its fame, under the régime of the silver-haired Libion, it was shabby and uncomfortable, consisting only of a *zinc* with a few tables at one side of it, and a long room on the walls of which the clients exhibited their pictures. Libion, whose racial origins were enigmatic, had a natural sympathy for artists, understood their ways and realized that even if he had to give them credit or take pictures in exchange for drinks, their presence would, in the long run, attract profitable custom. In 1912 a group of young poets, the chief of whom was André Salmon, finding Paul Fort's " Tuesdays " at the Closerie des Lilas too heavy and respectable for youthful exuberance, formed a circle there. They were quickly joined by the Picasso gang—Derain, Vlaminck, Mac Orlan, Max Jacob, Kisling, Guillaume Apollinaire, Zadkine and Vaillant—together with the girl sculptor Taya, Foujita and the poet Olivier Hourcade. Other eccentric types soon followed them. It became one of Modigliani's favourite haunts after his return from his last visit to Italy, but though he frequently made himself a nuisance by getting noisily drunk, the long-suffering Libion never threw him out. Later, when Libion, after being harrassed by the police, retired to a quieter café near the Lion de Belfort and the new proprietors took over, the atmosphere changed. As Charles Douglas records in his "Artist Quarter," Modi was disgusted with the new "Rotonde," with its swagger grill-room and dance orchestra upstairs, its bourgeois clientèle and the cold reception accorded to the artists who had made the café famous. One evening, after he had been celebrating with a party of friends, he returned there and did not deny himself "the pleasure of informing the world what he thought of the whole outfit. There was no direct opening of hostilities, but gentle overtures and fatherly protests. Nevertheless, the manager darted upon him instantly. Modi expressed his parting feelings by the classic French word, launched by General Cambronne, and with a single sweep of his hand, brushed everything on his table on to the floor. So he didn't have to wait long before renewing his acquaintance with the police station round the corner."

Although this incident had occurred some years before I knew the Dôme, the memory of it had created a tradition of hostility against "the place opposite" which was strictly maintained throughout the 'twenties. In the long run, I think the Rotonde must have suffered financially from its affront to artists. Its *terrasse* always seemed to be deserted when the other cafés were crowded.

The interest of Montparnasse in the 'twenties was chiefly literary. Most of the painters fled from the tourists, as they always do. Picasso, already fashionable and well-off, was never seen in his old haunts and preferred the sober respectability of the Deux Magots in the Boulevard St. Germain. I used to see him occasionally when I went to call on my ex-brother-in-law, Alan Duncan, who, like his parents, had settled in Paris and spent much of his time either in the Deux Magots or the adjoining Café Flore. The latter café became a recognized headquarters of Irish literary expatriates.

The twin constellations of the English-speaking literary group in the Paris of the 'twenties were Ford Madox Ford, who started his *Transatlantic Review* at the end of 1923, and James Joyce. Joyce, on the only occasion when I saw him, was living in the rue Jacob and laboriously correcting the proofs of "Ulysses", subsequently published by Miss Sylvia Beach from her Shakespeare Bookshop in the rue de l'Odéon. Ford, as I have elsewhere recorded,* lived in succession in a studio off

* "South Lodge," by Douglas Goldring.

the Boulevard Arago, at 84 rue Notre Dame des Champs and at 32, rue de Vaugirard. He usually took his apéritif at the historic Closerie des Lilas, opposite the now vanished Bal Bullier, and regularly lunched and dined at the *Nègre de Toulouse*, between the Closerie des Lilas and the Carrefour Vavin, of which his friend the amiable M. Lavigne was the proprietor.

During my frequent visits to Paris in the 'twenties, the figures who remain most clearly in my memory, besides Nina Hamnett and "Jimmy the Barman" and more or less permanent residents like Jim and Ellie Duncan, Ford Madox Ford, Sisley Huddleston, Duff Twysden, Pat Guthrie, Mary Butts and the painter Zawado, are Tommy Earp, the poet and art-critic, Philip Heseltine, Anthony Butts, and a variety of girl friends, but, at the D me one was likely to meet, sooner or later, any writer or artist one had ever known or heard of.

One or two occasions stand out with special clarity. I have a particularly pleasant memory of a Christmas night at Pirali's, where Jimmy was officiating, on which I made the acquaintance of Tommy Earp, Frank Dobson, and the composer Constant Lambert. Others present on that mellow but festive evening were Mahony—then the acknowledged Queen of Bloomsbury—the ubiquitous Duff Twysden and Pat Guthrie, Nina Hamnett and the painter Cedric Morris.

Another party, which illustrates the hard lot of painters in Montparnasse in the 'twenties, deserves recalling. There were thousands of visitors to Paris only too ready to buy Nina a drink : very few who would provide her with the money for food, rent, canvases and drawing materials by purchasing her work. Consequently, when Tony Butts, who was staying in Paris with his mother, invited Nina, myself and Harry Jonas to lunch at Foyot's, her hopes ran high. Tony was then well-off and, though he had not yet begun to paint, had a wide acquaintance among artists and ought to have realized Nina's circumstances. The fact that he failed to play up as we anticipated was due not to lack of generosity—he was extremely generous —but to sheer thoughtlessness.

The luncheon was superb. The champagne and oysters and the dishes that followed were fully worthy of Foyot's culinary reputation and left little change out of the *billet de mille* which Tony produced, from a well-filled pocket-book, to pay for them.

Harry Jonas left us after luncheon, but the rest of us drove off in a taxi to Nina's studio in the historic rue de la Grande Chaumiére. A reasonably clean chair was discovered for Tony's mother (who was wearing a new and extremely chic green hat) to sit on while Nina displayed the contents of her portfolio. After a while, when still no purchases had been made, Nina whispered : " Douglas, for God's sake go out and get some champagne." I hurried to Damoy's in the Carrefour Vavin, acquired a couple of bottles of the best they had and hurried back with them. Glasses were produced, the bottles were emptied, the conversation became lively, but still no sales were effected.

At last the distinguished guests rose to go and, with the manners of a duchess (which she has always at command) Nina bowed them out.

I was on my honeymoon in Paris in September 1927 when the great Franco-American " victory " celebration was staged for some now obscure political purpose. The moment was not well-chosen.

Earlier in the year an event had occurred which, at all events in the eyes of the masses, displaced official " England " from its proud position as the world's most hated nation in favour of the United States. The belated execution of the two Socialists, Sacco and Vanzetti, which millions regarded as a judicial murder of the foulest kind, gave the pent-up rage against the Yankee " conquerors " a chance to explode. Demonstrations outside American consulates occurred in almost every country. Even in stolid, " bourgeois " Gothenburg, the effect on public opinion was amazing and hostile crowds had to be dispersed by the police with drawn sabres. As usual, only " England " stood by the United States in this affair. Our rulers had, perhaps, too many similar incidents on their consciences, which had occurred in India and Ireland, to enable them to be censorious without hypocrisy. In any case, as always, our Tories stuck up for their " American cousins " and—as always—they got no thanks for it.

In France, where bitterness against the United States on account of the Peace Treaty had long been smouldering, feeling ran high, particularly among the Communists and Socialists of the Parisian " Red belt." The triumphal march of the American " veterans " through Paris enabled them to stage a typically French revenge.

For weeks in advance the cafés buzzed with rumours. It

was known that only a small proportion of the " veterans " had ever before crossed the Atlantic, and Paris had already had opportunities of noticing the prodigious thirst for hard liquor which Prohibition had engendered in American citizens.   The prospect, therefore, was that the whole capital would be invaded by roaring drunks, that cafés would have their glasses stolen and their windows smashed, in short that Hell would be let loose. One of the most circumstantial rumours was that the authorities had cleared the brothels of respectable French citizenesses and imported trainloads of prostitutes from Eastern Europe to take their places for the occasion.   For several days before the veterans arrived, refined and cultured Americans thronged the railway terminals to escape from their compatriots.   The English were not concerned in the affair.   The fact that they also had played some part in the " Great War " was officially ignored.   No English generals, unless my memory is at fault, shared the honours with Foch and Pershing, and no English troops paraded through the streets.   In view of what happened, this was, perhaps, just as well.

My wife and I managed, without much difficulty, to get a close view of the triumphal march past.   The procession led off with the celebrated mounted band of the Garde Républicaine This was a swell affair : the Third Republic's best effort in the way of military pageantry.   The horses, the uniforms and the music were all superb.   They were followed immediately by a little group of middle-aged men, some rather pot-bellied, dressed in shabby civilian suits, one of whom carried a small, unimposing flag on which was inscribed the magic word " Verdun."   After them came the " veterans," preceded by a band playing what must have been the " world's largest "— and loudest—brass instruments.   What the monstrous things were called I never discovered.   The veterans were arrayed in uniforms of a splendour never seen in Europe except on commissionaires of super-cinemas.   Some of them had " juniors " marching with them, in miniature magnificence.   The male veterans were followed by females, similarly accoutred, wreathed in smiles and shouting hilariously.   (Some of them, if I may be forgiven for saying so, seemed to be in a condition of which Lady Astor would scarcely have approved.)

After them came another little group of *poilus* in civvies, carrying another little flag, which bore on it, unobtrusively, the names of historic battles.

The laughter of the crowd was of the kind that cuts like a knife. The Parisian sense of the absurd has nothing in common with the good-humoured satire of the Cockney. On this occasion it was like a corrosive sublimate.

While the American warriors were parading through central Paris, with flags flying and blaring brass, another American procession, of a more impressive character, was winding its way through half-empty streets to an outlying cemetery. This was the shabby little funeral cortège of the great American dancer, Isadora Duncan, who had met with a tragic end on the Riviera. She died in poverty and few followed her coffin to the grave.

In the evening, my wife and I escaped from Montparnasse with Mary Butts and other friends, made our way to the Bastille quarter, dined at a Bouillon Chartier and afterwards proceeded to the Rue de Lappe. This narrow, stone-flagged street, was lined on either side with queer proletarian " dancings," frequented by the hard-working boys and girls of the quarter, sailors on leave and other genial " types." It was a pleasant change from the tourist centres and it seemed inconceivable that the veterans should discover it. Alas, just when we were beginning to enjoy ourselves in one of the dives, called, if I remember right, the " Brousca Bal," someone rushed in from the street and shouted : " They're coming ! " We went outside to look and sure enough they were. Some traitorous renegade had given the Rue de Lappe away ! Advancing from the end of the street came a procession of hilarious invaders, headed by a huge woman in nurse's uniform accompanied by a military cop. Our party promptly turned and fled.

IV

Of the serious literary activities of Montparnasse in the 'twenties, I saw little except through Ford. For some reason or other I failed to present the introduction given me by Ezra Pound to Gertrude Stein—although I had met her brother Leo in Florence, through Norman Douglas—and never, in consequence, came in contact with the groups who contributed to such periodicals as *transition*, and *This Quarter*. I heard much from Mary Butts and others, about the Dadaists, from whom originated the first Surrealist movement, but never to my knowledge met any of them. Their alleged disgusting vices profoundly shocked

Mary, who was usually tolerant in such matters.   About modern Surrealism of which Herbert Read, surely the most innocent and high-minded of idealists, has become the principal English prophet and exponent, I retain an open mind.   I dislike some of the rather pompous and pretentious French Surrealist verse I have read, because I can't help feeling it ought to be funny and isn't.

Surrealist poetry has deep roots in England, where in the form of what are called " nonsense verses " it may be said to have firmly established itself.   Few writers are quoted more frequently in epigraphs than Lewis Carroll and Lear.   Lewis Carroll prepared the way for the " Magenta Minutes " of Sandys Wason which was first published by Max Goschen, when I was in charge of that firm, and is still cherished by the few.   To the modern ear such lines as :

> There sat a muffin, tinged with pink,
> Upon a kind of form it brought
> And thought of Nothing.   Only think
> What Nothing means to men of thought —

have a particular appeal.

There was what can now be identified as a touch of Surrealism in the Cockney Music Hall and this thoroughly English tradition has been carried on in the cinema by Charles Chaplin and, more particularly, the Marx Brothers.   Old Londoners will easily trace a connexion between the humour of Dan Leno and Groucho Marx.   In a book of reminiscences called " The Days We Knew " by J. B. Booth of the *Pink 'Un*, I have come across a quotation from a melodrama by Dan Leno which well illustrates this point.   Here are three scenes in full :

Scene : The Docks.
Enter : Sailor.
Sailor : Here's a fine go.   I've been and lost my bacca box !
Enter Press Gang.
They take no notice of him, so he volunteers.
Curtain.
Scene : *A Fried Fish Shop.*
Enter a Crowd, who *borrow eightpence and exit.*
Enter Villain.
Villain : I know not how it is with me, and I'm blessed if I know how it would be without me.
Exits.

Scene : *Italy, or as near as possible.*

Enter Maiden and Sailor, *followed by* Brigands, armed with bowls of soup.

Maiden : At last we meet !

Sailor : Yes, but I wonder why we walked here from Swansea ?

All exit, wondering.

This Surrealist fragment was discovered among casual jottings in a notebook, after the comedian's death, and seems to me to deserve careful study by pontiffs like Herbert Read. The stage directions—" they take no notice of him so he volunteers " and " all exit, wondering "—besides being masterpieces of Cockney humour seem to me to reveal a psychological insight which has a quality of genius. In the first, the pathetic vanity of *homo sapiens* is guyed to perfection, in the second, the mindless folly of the crowd is touched off with side-splitting effect.

I must not, however, digress from the main theme of Anglo-American literary activities in our only international metropolis.

Several small publishing firms and private presses sprang up in Paris during the 'twenties which issued " advanced " books in English, including various works which had been banned in London by the police. Apart from James Joyce's " Ulysses ", the novels of that now eminent figure Henry Miller found a Paris publisher and are still unprocurable in England. Robert McAlmon, who issued his " Contact Editions " from the Three Mountains Press on the Quai d'Anjou—where Ford produced his *Transatlantic Review*—published works by Ford, Mary Butts and others. McAlmon and Ford were, I believe, the earliest literary sponsors of Ernest Hemingway.

A whole volume waits to be written on the Anglo-American-Irish school of writers who made Paris their headquarters in the 'twenties, and wrote and published books there. The names already mentioned—James Joyce, Ernest Hemingway, Henry Miller, Ford Madox Ford, Mary Butts, Gertrude Stein, and Robert McAlmon—indicate the scope and interest of such a survey. When the present war is over, no doubt some American professor of literature will be handsomely subsidized to undertake it.

CHAPTER NINE

LITERARY EXPATRIATES

I

IN the course of the present war I was discussing the literary output of the 'twenties with an opulent friend, when he surprised me by making a venomous attack on the literary " expatriates " of the period.   His idea seemed to be that if they had stayed in England they might have done something to " save their country." I thought this unjustified at the time : after further reflection, I am convinced of its absurdity.   As such influence as they had was exerted through their books, whether they wrote them in Mexico or Montparnasse, in Italy or Mayfair was immaterial. As I have already indicated, one of the reasons which drove writers abroad was our poverty.   No one who has not actually been through the experience of dropping suddenly from middle-class comfort to the income level of a farm labourer, can understand its effect on men old enough to have acquired certain regular habits, such, for example, as changing occasionally into evening clothes, taking cabs . . .   In 1919 I used to be genially mocked by Alec Waugh, who had gone straight from school into the Army.   " Look at Douglas !   If he's only got half-a-crown in his pocket, he hails a taxi ! "   It took me several years to train myself to tubes and buses, to adjust my way of living from that of an Edwardian " young gentleman " to that of a middle-aged member of the neo-Georgian proletariat.   The process, though it had its spiritual and political compensations, was neither painless nor easy.   In the interim period, when owing to the cheap franc, a taxi ride which cost half-a crown in London cost only sixpence in Paris, going abroad broke the shock.   Cheap hotel accommodation, cheap—and delicious—food and even cheaper drinks also made it possible for the depressed *intelligentsia* to enjoy for a while the indulgences and *menus plaisirs* to which, in pre-war days, they had been accustomed.   Quite apart, however, from the financial question, was the very strong feeling of international solidarity among civilised Europeans, which burgeoned immediately after the Armistice.   The English literary expatriates were, for the most part, ambassadors of reconciliation, who did their best to undo the harm caused by the non-combatant profiteers, political reactionaries and virulent " anti-Bolshevists " who secretly supported Prussian militarism while sabotaging the Weimar Republic. The pretence, so often heard nowadays from extremely guilty sources, that the youth of post-war Germany and the German workers and intellectuals were already plotting a war of vengeance in 1920, can be dismissed with the contempt it deserves. Before the Wall Street crisis plunged the world into financial chaos, thus giving Hitler his opportunity, almost anything could have been done with the German and Austrian common people, particularly with German youth. How strong and how courageous was the resistance of the German workers to Hitler was proved by the fact that the Nazis never received a majority in a free election and could only maintain their hold over the country by the organised tortures in the concentration camps.

It was precisely their strong-arm methods which excited the admiration of the British Tories who had never concealed their contempt for and distrust of the Weimar Republic. From 1933 onwards, British statesmen like Lord Halifax and Lord Londonderry eagerly courted the friendship of Hitler and Goering and a whole stream of titled tourists of both sexes flocked to Munich, Berlin and Berchtesgaden. The Anglo-German Fellowship, the Link, and the Anglo-German Kameradschaft were significant indications of the sympathy felt by the British ruling class for Hitler's brutal suppression of all his opponents.

It is to the credit of English " expatriates " that, almost alone, they fraternised in the 'twenties with those German artists and writers who were " good Europeans." As for the Foreign Office gang, what they did was well described by Rudolf Olden before he was drowned en route for America.

" Enquire all over Europe, among the peoples which after the Great War, wanted to establish a democratic order, or have actually done so ! You will get the same answer everywhere : the diplomats and generals sent to us always dine with our enemies, hunt with our enemies and believe what our enemies say. Because our enemies, even if they were often murderers, were ' Gentlemen.' But we were no gentlemen, we were schoolmasters, manual workers, labourers—often even Jews . . . It was quite a subordinate consideration that we should have been glad to establish a peaceable Europe. Moreover, there was sometimes a gentleman to be found among us, an aristocrat. But that only made matters worse, because he was a traitor to his class and accordingly the other gentlemen, the real ones, told the foreign gentlemen, the diplomats and generals, when they all went hunting together, that that apostate gentleman was a gentleman no longer."

The leading literary figures of the 'twenties were not, of course, those engaged in any direct way with repairing the broken cultural links between Great Britain and her continental neighbours, although their sojourn abroad aided this process indirectly. Most of them were indifferent to politics. They were bursting with the creative activity which the war had bottled up, hungry for the sights and scenes which had been so long denied them. In Italy, where Norman Douglas was already established, Aldous Huxley, D. H. Lawrence and Compton Mackenzie produced much of their best work ; Ford Madox Ford divided his time between Paris, Provence and New York ; James Joyce remained faithful to Paris. Ernest Hemingway and lesser-known writers like Mary Butts and Robert McAlmon wandered where the fancy took them. Even the towering figure of Somerset Maugham, who defies all attempts at classification except that of being, both as novelist and playwright, the supreme technician of our age, was an expatriate.

II

I had known Norman Douglas in the *English Review* days and was delighted to see him again in 1920 when I was conducting a pioneer party of Lunn tourists to Florence, Rome and Naples. My flock looked after themselves in Florence and I was thus able to spend an unforgettable week in his company. In some way or another, perhaps because of my connexion with the New York publisher, Thomas Seltzer, I had got into communication with Douglas's friend, Maurice Magnus. This unfortunate figure has found his niche in literature as a result of the battle over his memory which broke out after his death, between D. H. Lawrence and Douglas. Magnus sent me a number of MSS. which I tried, unsuccessfully, to place for him, with Douglas's encouragement, in London and New York. Finally, just before he ended his life, although he had made Norman Douglas his literary executor, he made over the rights of one of his books, " Memoirs of the Foreign Legion ", to D. H. Lawrence who was then staying in Malta. Poor Magnus was almost everything that Lawrence disliked and disapproved of. He was a decayed " gentleman," incapable of earning his living, always in debt, always borrowing money, and homo-sexual into the bargain. Lawrence on the other hand had all the financial self-respect and scrupulous honesty in money matters which are among the basic virtues of the thrifty working-class. If he had £2 a week he could live on it with ease, and save. Magnus, on the other hand, was the kind of man who, if he was given £2 would spend it at once on a good dinner and then starve. He had borrowed a considerable sum of money from a Maltese friend of Lawrence's. Lawrence therefore determined to secure the publication of the Foreign Legion MS., in order to get this debt repaid. After Stanley Unwin, to whom I had offered it, finally turned it down it was published by Martin Secker, prefaced by a long, brilliant and merciless account of the author by D. H. Lawrence. In a letter to Curtis Brown, printed in " The Letters of D. H. Lawrence ", Lawrence records the circumstances. " Magnus," he wrote, " was a man I knew in Italy. He committed suicide in Malta, after borrowing money from a nice and not rich Maltese whom I knew. Magnus left several MSS. of not much value : one about his experiences in the Foreign Legion. In order to get some money back for Michael Borg, the Maltese, I wrote a long memoir of Magnus to go before the Legion book." The dispute with Douglas was on two main points. In the first place Douglas, as literary executor, had, with my active help, taken an infinity of trouble, though without success, to get the MSS. of Magnus printed and published, and therefore should, at least, have been consulted. Secondly, Douglas, who probably knew and understood Magnus much better than Lawrence, thought that Lawrence's bitter portrait of his friend was grossly unfair. He replied to it in a pamphlet which in its way is as brilliant as Lawrence's memoir. As I never personally met Magnus I am not in a position to judge whether Lawrence's depreciation, or Douglas's appreciation, was nearer the truth. It was in any case a duel between masters of their craft. The fact that his personality produced such a memorable literary combat is my reason for quoting the letters from Magnus which follow.

" Notabile P.O.,
Malta.
June 25th, 1920.

Dear Mr. Goldring,

D. H. Lawrence writes me you liked the the Legion. I am very glad. Mr. Unwin writes him it isn't. going to pay—

"American edition—buy sheets for English editions." That of course I will *not* do. Done that before and it forms a chapter in my memoirs (not yet printed). Most subtle way of receiving money and not receiving it ! If Mr. Unwin wants the British copright—O.K.—if not I have asked him to return MSS. The American rights are ' spoken for ' and a copy of the entire manuscript in U.S.A. at this moment.

I am sending you under separate cover by registered post ' Love's Tragedy,' by Knut Hamsun. I saw this first in the Moscow Art Theatre years ago. Wonderfully produced—and was much impressed—applied for the English and American stage and book rights from Hamsun and got them translated. The original title is ' The Gamble of Life,' in Moscow they called it ' Love's Tragedy.' Alice Kauser, dramatic agent in U.S.A. had the play for some time, but did not do anything with it—no wonder—after I saw the shocking state of the American stage last year.

Also I am sending you ' To the Stars,' by Leonid Andreyeff. This is probably too literary and subtle for the Anglo-Saxon theatre-going public. It is very readable. Have all the rights. I should be delighted if you could do anything with either—if not for stage then for publication.

The little one-act play ' Twilight ' was written by an amateur —I touched it up. It is very charming. The man who wrote it is the son of a Governor (ancient régime) in the heart of Russia, who owned and lived in Turgenieff's house there, which he kept as Turgenieff had left it.

If you do anything with ' Love's Tragedy ' I should want to go over it once more before going to press.

Many thanks for your interest,
Faithfully yours,
MAURICE MAGNUS.

The Legion book is to be called ' Dregs ; a Foreign Legion Experience,' by an American."

" Notabile P.O.
Malta.
August 10th, 1920.

Dear Mr. Goldring,
The manuscript and book came yesterday. I commenced reading ' The Fight for Freedom ' and didn't lay down the book

until I had finished. It is one of the strongest plays I have read in modern literature—in fact, one of the strongest plays I have ever read. The characters are splendidly defined—there isn't a vague person in it and the dialogue is a masterpiece. The dramatic technique shows the actor—you must have had good theatre training. As to the subject it is the one vital thing at present—and I think you express the ideas of thousands, no, of the majority not only in England, but *everywhere*, where I have been within the last few years : Italy, America, France, Germany, here, Greece, etc.

Our battle will be largely against the Margarets who just complicate things—they are not one thing nor the other—they are just in the way.

I'd like to read ' The Fortune.' Will you send me that ?

Of course I must seem impertinent to write you so frankly and very likely you were not asking for criticism, but were just nice in sending me one of your books. I thank you for the great pleasure your play gave me.

Did you ever read ' Tizer,' a play Mitchell Kennerley N.Y. published some years ago ?

Did you ever read ' Fate ' by Louis Couperus ? Both the play and the novel will interest you, I think. In each the authors are striking out from the terrible rut of the Victorian influence and facing us with very actual problems. I grasp your hand.

MAGNUS."

" 1 Strada S. Pietro,
Notabile,
Malta.
Sept. 2nd, 1920.

Dear Mr. Goldring,

Thank you very much for your kind letter. I fear you will find America worse than England. But try. Fifteen years ago the drama and literature there gave great promise : on my recent trip I found that the good germs had been smothered by a luxuriance of weeds.

I am just retiring from any further effort to do anything but write the stuff I want to, and live cheap in a decent climate. I have reduced my necessities to a minimum.

It is good of you to recommend my stuff to Alec Waugh and I shall send him the final part by next post. Too late today. The agents—alas—my experiences have been so painful. The best have usually succeeded in doing one-fifth of what I did from a thousand miles distance, both in N.Y. and in London. Ask Waugh to show you the MS. I shall send—if you care to see it. Don't forget to send me ' The Fortune ', *please.*

Never mind the attitude of the B.P. and you are doing big things—and that is the main issue. People never do like to hear the truth, and especially in England those who tell it, or do something beautiful, end in exile or prison. However, there are exceptions where England has appreciated her sons of the muses *via* the Continent. That may be your fate. I am glad you are being translated."

(Last page missing)

" Notabile,
Malta.
October 31st, 1920.

Dear Mr. Goldring,
' The Solvent ' is very clever and a wonderful propaganda book—dreadfully inhuman. I think the only human person is Margaret, and one doesn't see too much of her. You don't mind my saying this—I hope—since it is not all yours. In ' The Fight for Freedom ' and ' The Fortune ' you are so infinitely human and so very real to life—without any frills—so absolutely sincere—depicting strength and weakness as it comes that somehow I don't recognise you in ' The Solvent,' except here and there. Will you do me a favour ? X, the publisher, accepted two of my Andreyeff translations. I wrote and agreed to his terms, asking [him] because I am simply up against it, to give me an advance and to send contract. A postcard, dated September 1 arrived saying my letter was received and will be attended to in a day or two. No other communication has reached me although a month ago I wrote and said so. Probably you will be able to find out the mystery of this. I should be most grateful.

I am sitting here on this rocky islet gazing at the deep blue sea . . . yes, and that is all . . . one mail a week . . . and the rest you can imagine.

Fraternally yours,
MAURICE MAGNUS."

I should like to believe that Magnus's references to my play " The Fight for Freedom," and to " The Solvent," were genuine criticisms, not merely the flattery doled out by a struggling writer to one from whom he expects reciprocal benefits. Unfortunately, I am not capable of this amount of self-deception. The central incident in the play and the whole theme of "The Solvent" were not so much suggested as forced upon me by one who, at that period of my life, exerted a dominating influence. By instinct, I disliked both. Most writers resent being told, by amateurs, what to put in their books. Both plots are curiously old-fashioned, almost Victorian, while the whole idea of "The Solvent" was based upon the fallacy that "money" and "gold" are synonymous. I hated being forced to write this novel in collaboration—which meant, of course, that I had to do the "actual writing"—and was relieved when it failed. "The Fight for Freedom" is in a different category, as the characters, the dialogue, and the message—it was what Lawrence called a "pamphlet play"—are, for better or worse, my own. Had it been translated from German or Hungarian, instead of being translated into those languages, it might have made a hit in advanced circles and secured, at least, a Sunday production.

In search of further references to Magnus I have come across a bundle of old letters from Norman Douglas, written from Florence at various dates between November 1921 and April 1922. In them he refers to the fact that he was Magnus's literary executor, and asks me to rout out the MSS. which Magnus sent to me. Some of these, including a volume of Russian Memoirs, I must have forwarded to America and never recovered; others I was able to find and forward to Douglas, in spite of the fact that the people in one of the London houses of which I was an occasional occupant had a tiresome habit of destroying stray papers while " tidying up " !

The correspondence reminds me of a periodical called *Broom*, which had migrated from Paris to Rome, where I asked Douglas, for some now forgotten reason, to run it to earth. *Broom* was one of several short-lived literary periodicals produced by American expatriates after the Armistice. The editor and proprietor, one Loeb, claimed to figure in Hemingway's first novel, " The Sun Also Rises." In Montparnasse, where *Broom* first originated, he was amicably nicknamed Low Ebb. Associated with him was the American poet, Alfred Kreymborg, who promised to publish some MS. in which I was interested, which may account for my enquiries.

As far as I am aware the " Memoirs of the Foreign Legion,"

with Lawrence's introduction, was the only one of poor Magnus's literary remains which ever saw the light.

Douglas was as great an authority on South Germany and Austria as he was on Italy, and when I asked him for advice as to where to go in these ex-enemy countries, he recommended places in the Black Forest, Munich and St. Anton, in the Arlberg Valley.   Mary Butts, Cecil Maitland and I followed his directions faithfully, to our great advantage.   In the early 'twenties some of my happiest (as well as some of my unhappiest) days and nights were spent in South Bavaria and Tyrol.

III

For a full-length portrait of Mary Butts, one of the most characteristic as well as the most " colourful " figures of the 'twenties, I must refer the reader to my book, " South Lodge." For most of the decade she was an expatriate, but she did not " go native," like Lukey Hansard and Tina.   She was a typical member of what New Yorkers call " café-society " and used " abroad " merely as an amusing background and meeting-place for her literary friends, many of whom were Americans. She was a great admirer of T. S. Eliot and her earliest published work had appeared in the American " Little Review," with which John Rodker, her first husband, was connected.   She also contributed to Ford Madox Ford's *Transatlantic Review*, which enlivened Paris throughout 1924.   The following extracts from her letters may give some indication of her remarkable personality, as well as throwing light on our wandering habits. Mary treated Europe, as she treated the London of the Bright Young People, as a wild lark ;   she carried her almost overwhelming " personal atmosphere " about with her wherever she went, and derived little or nothing from the towns and countries she visited or from their inhabitants.   Her interest in places was confined, almost entirely, to her native Dorset.

The first of her letters I have managed to unearth is on scarlet notepaper and headed " Hotel Titisee.   Titisee bei Freiburg. Baden."   The date is the 9th of April, 1922.

" After some crowded hours of glorious life in Paris, we found this place.   Hundreds of miles of black trees and snow, very quiet, which after unlimited cocktails in Freiburg at one penny each, is just as well.   It costs half-a-crown a day to live in the solidest comfort and we shall stay a long time and work.   Let me know if anything happens about the books and Cecil [Maitland]. The very best of luck to you.

"If I hear from you, please include a little gossip—Harold and Elsa for instance."

Four months later, probably on Norman Douglas's advice, transmitted by me, she and Cecil Maitland were at St. Anton in the Arlberg. The reference to " 43 " is to her flat in Belsize Park Gardens, in which Elsa Lanchester and I were intermittent lodgers.

" My dear Douglas,

Good luck and blessings to you ! Details as to the journey— (I will add details of the place you mention at the end of this letter. I can't at the moment see anyone to ask). The —— [a firm of travel agents] are a set of dud devils. They have muddled dates, prices and distances—everything—and let us in for endless trouble and expense.

Once you are over the German frontier you spend very little. Be careful that the lunch car which is hitched on at the frontier is not unhitched while you are peacefully eating so that your luggage goes one way and you another. That happened to us. You'll have a four-hour wait at Frankfort. Opposite the station, between the theatre and the Hotel Bristol is a majestic pub called, I think, the ' Hotel of the English.' The lift-boy is a dream of classic beauty and nearly lost us our train . . . Between this hotel and the theatre there is a large street, and about 100 yards down on the right a lovely little dancing-cabaret. It says Amer-Drinks on its window, and has a jolly band and pretty boys and girls. Very simple and merry and *cheap*. You might do worse than put in an hour or so there . . . Try and reserve a place in the Munich train. We had to sit up half the night and stand the other half.

The trains were late. We arrived S. Anton about seven o'clock on Wednesday evening, found the party stuffing chicken and champagne . . . The place is glorious. So is the whole valley. We shall probably not stay in S. Anton but move two or three miles down the valley to Petneu, where there is a jolly, simple *gasthaus*. The hotel here is frankly profiteering without being really comfortable, let alone chic.

We play beaver everywhere—Sheila [a friend] champion— and we're always hungry and we drink Tokay at a shilling the bottle, and tramp all day and get hot but never dirty and in the

intervals I read Jung's ' Psychoanalysis of the Unsconscious '
and draw [out] a young English terror. Here is a specimen.
' Quite a formal little dinner, you know, in South Ken., at
Watson's, the President of the Gas Light and Coke.'   Not Cecil's
Scotch arrogance nor G's Oxford snobbery can quell it, and
Sheila sets her cap adorably and goes off with her tongue in her
cheek, and we've all bought broad leather sandals at 5 sh. the pair,
and in the whole hotel no one enjoys themselves except us . . .

My dear Douglas—how I hope the publishing will go—I have
a feeling that your luck has turned, at least your individual luck.
I know that meeting you has been coincidental with my luck
turning.   It has been more than incidental—you have done so
much for my shaky belief in myself.

Could I ask you to bring letters from 43 with you ?   They
could be re-posted from Kufstein.   Also Cecil wants a bottle of
strychnine pills—Easton's syrup pills is the family brand—but
he says you know of another.   Either would do . . .   Forgive
this scratch, but I'm unsettled with heat and drink.

Our love to you,
Mary."

I had succeeded in interesting Alec Waugh in Mary's work
and early in the following year Chapman & Hall published her
first volume of short stories, " Speed the Plough." Alec was one
of the most lavish literary hosts, in the days of the Bright Young
People, and he and his brother Evelyn—at that time still at
Oxford—conceived the idea of throwing a super-colossal party
in the huge rooms of Mary's flat.   The guests were more or less
evenly divided between the " respectable " and the Bohemian
members of Alec's vast acquaintance.   The former, who included
Peter Stern, Rebecca West, and similar notabilities, left comparatively early, followed by the butler who had been hired for
the occasion.   The others kept it up until breakfast-time and
closed the proceedings, to the fury of their neighbours, by lighting a bonfire in the garden.

The following undated note from Mary, perhaps refers to this
festivity :

" Dearest Douglas,
What a party ! A fruity mixture indeed : we were all so
happy. We owe you a bottle of drink which shall not be forgotten, but we haven't bought it yet—because we're starting out
in much the same condition as you when you left for Minorca !

If you feel you could, would you send us an introduction to
Norman Douglas ?   I know it is the sort of thing you are perpetually asked, but we are likely to be in Florence some time.
Poste Restante there, till we have a settled address.   All love
and good luck—from us both.   I ticked Alec off superbly when
he came back here.   ' Superb ' includes his not hating me,
either.

What a party !   What drink !   What company !   It will
become a classic example—Christmas near Cannes, I hope."

On reflection, I think this may be a letter of thanksgiving not
for Alec's unforgettable gathering, but for one of my own more
modest " evenings " in my house in St. James's Terrace.

Mary and Cecil duly departed for Italy, and, as I see from
another undated letter, stopped at Rapallo, Ezra Pound's home
town.

> " Pension Select,
> Rapallo.

Dearest Douglas,

How good it was to see your blessed handwriting and your good
meaty letter full of real news.

Until the day before yesterday, there was no need to envy us
for climate.   It rained and rained and rained, winds howled,
several at once, and that tactless brute of a Mediterranean that
never goes in and out soaked us both with iced spray every time
we put out noses out of this anything but Select Pension.   Also
I've been wretchedly, unspeakably unwell.   I ran down like an
overworked mainspring and am only just beginning to feel
better.   Also I missed my dear friends, tho' we've made some
new ones, and a precious queer lot they are.   No ' damned
nonsense about art,' but chunks of life.   It's a long story to be
told when we meet.

Our Christmas plans are in a bad way.   We're horribly broke.
If you go to Luke Hansard, we'll make the effort and come too,
and stay as near as we can—I suppose there's a village pub—but
we daren't attempt a town like Nice.   If not, we shall probably
stay here.

I've begun something rather good and magnificently unsaleable.
If we meet, bring the MS. of ' The House.'   Ford's Review (The
Transatlantic) paid me £4 for a 3,000-odd word story, and since
then I've heard no more.   He was in magnificent fettle, but I

always behave stupidly with him and fear that the impression I left was none of the best.   Paris was a dream.   We didn't go to bed for a week, and spent *all* our money on such binges !   The last thing I remember was dancing solely supporting myself by the lobes of Cedric Morris' ears.

I'm expecting an addition to the family.   *Not* another Camilla, but an enormous, savage, exuberant Alsatian wolfhound, who picked up Cecil the first day we walked over to Rapallo, and now loves but him alone.   It's a lamb with him.   It's owner is madly jealous because Cecil can control the beast and he can't, and he's an American just out from a two years' sentence for man-slaughter because he got D.T. and shot and killed three men. He has nearly got them again !   He continually prophe ies a fresh attack, and I've never seen him anything but completely blotto.   Also, he ill-treats the dog.   It's very complicated.   But I jes' don' nacherly see what's to come of it.

We have also picked up with a nun and a gentleman, here for reasons too difficult to enquire into.

By the way, my dear, has there been recently published in England ' An Anthology of English Ghost Stories ', edited, I think, by Eliott O'Donnell ?   If there has, could you get it for me up to 7s. 6d., and bring it out ?   I want to get ideas from it. I could pay when we meet, but it's no good sending you liras. The ghost-story is a form with which there remains a lot to do.

Darling Douglas, let us know your plans.   Luke Hansard said something about our staying with him too, but it was never con-firmed.   Naturally, we should like that, but can't very well re-suggest it.   Anyhow, where you go, we'll try to follow.   All our loves.

MARY."

Shortly after this a friend got me appointed English Lektor at the University College of Commerce in Gothenberg, Sweden. The work was light, the vacations five and a half months in the year, and the pay, particularly when translated into francs, generous.   In spite of these advantages, I found enforced existence, for half the year, in a bourgeois provincial town as galling as Ovid must have felt his exile at Tomi.   How different my life in Sweden would have been had I been stationed in Stockholm ! I should have been happier, no doubt, in that enchanting capital. On the other hand, in all probablity I should not have met my wife, so I can only thank my Guardian Angel for sending me to

Gothenburg instead. Malin and I were married there on April 4th, 1927, having already matured our plans for escape at the end of the summer term. I had received an invitation from the Boston publisher of my travel books to visit the great United States in the fall, for the purpose of writing a travel book about America " in my usual vein." Fame and fortune at last ! In those days New York and Hollywood seemed like veritable El Dorados to all the writers, artists and film stars of impoverished Europe. The result of this was pernicious on all concerned. English literary careerists turned out a flood of sycophantic tributes to the Great American Dollar, and masses of snob-stuff designed to titillate café-society and to impart " sophistication " to the American social climber. In the film industry, which was making great strides in Sweden during the years I spent there, I do not know of one actor, actress or producer whose artistic integrity survived the " dollar embrace." Charlie Chaplin, as a world genius whose international fame brought so many millions to Hollywood, would seem to be one of the exceptions to this, perhaps, rather too sweeping generalisation. All the same we note, in 1944, that for the crimes of remaining an Englishman, ridiculing Hitler and speaking up for the under-dog, even he has been framed and put on the spot in God's own country.

While it was arranged that I should start my married life by making the famous " trip to the States ", Malin was to go to the South of France, where we intended to live on my return, to stay with Lukey's widow, Evy Hansard. We planned a honeymoon in Paris, where Malin's sister Stina was living with her elderly husband. My mother-in-law spent half of every year in her daughter's flat in Passy, so that it seemed certain that Malin would be well looked after during my absence and would not feel a stranger in a strange land. In addition, although with some misgivings—as Mary was strong meat for babes—I was able to introduce her to my circle of friends in Paris. The first part of the programme went off satisfactorily. We had our Paris honeymoon. I departed to the States in the *Leviathan*, together with Llewellyn Powys and his wife, Alyse Gregory, and in due course Malin went to Cannes. I had not been more than three weeks in New York when I received a cable from my wife to say that her sister and brother-in-law had died in tragic circumstances and that she was returning to Paris to look after her mother. I was sufficiently clairvoyant to imagine the whole situation ; I saw that my presence in Paris was essential and despite the protestations of Ford Madox Ford and other friends who were hoping to see me launched, I hurried back to Paris.

I have never regretted this decision. Even if I had made good in the United States, which for temperamental reasons was exceedingly unlikely, the Wall Street crash, which broke two years later, would have hit me as heavily as it hit Ford. For better or worse, I do not write the sort of books the average American likes. Even in England, which is at least half a century ahead of the United States in its political thinking, I was considered advanced, so that in America I should have been regarded as a subversive "Red", or dangerous " Bolshevik." I therefore lost nothing by leaving half my letters of introduction unpresented and scurrying—if that is the correct term for a slow voyage in a superannuated British liner across the detestable Atlantic—back to Europe. I was just in time to deal with the situation, save my wife from a breakdown and carry her off to recuperate in Cannes. Few marriages can have had a less auspicious beginning. It seemed as if we were under some appalling voodoo, with no protection against the black, enveloping cloud of ill-luck except our feeling for each other and the loyalty of a few friends of whom Mary Butts was one. The following letters from Mary, all undated, cover this period of my life and bring back grateful memories.

> " Hotel du Coteau,
> Tréboul,
> Finistère.

My dear Douglas,

Overjoyed to get your letter, and long to see you and Malin, and love her as much as I love you. I shall be back at the address crossed out (14 Rue de Monttessuy, Paris VII) in about ten days ; at present am seeing a sick friend through his troubles in the middle of three superimposed Atlantic gales and a hotel full of arch-deacons.

News brief : novel in U.S. coming out in January ; another book with illustrations by Cocteau in Oct. in Paris with an American editor called Titus who should be black-listed from Hong Kong to Aberdeen. [As far as I can discover this book never appeared.] Cuddy [her daughter, Camilla] recovered from her illness and safe at Cannes. We've just passed a month together in the Midi. Divorce absolute from J.R. Alimony not yet settled. Finance awful, but prospects bright. Working

very hard, figure down to the fashionable proportions at last·
Lots of news I could tell you.   Longing to see you.   Bless Evie
[Hansard] for me when you see her.   I hope to come South soon
to Camilla, and shall find you all wherever you are.   Anyhow
we shall meet in Paris.   Our last meeting was so terrible [I had
broken the news to her of Cecil Maitland's death]—but of course
you don't know what happened later, the thing that nearly
killed me about C.M.'s death, and the blessed thing that came
after.   I think I'm being and doing everything you'd wish,
especially my work.   The new novel is rather a beauty, and
there are poems and stories and ' big thinks ' by the score.
Dear, dear Douglas, the best of everything to you.   Don't worry
about U.S.   We'll find people you'll love there, and they will
all adore you.   What have you been writing ?   God bless the
hot milk.   I practically ' never touches a drop ' now myself.
How lovely to write ' till about the 10th ' or ' au revoir.'   Embrace your wife for me.

MARY."

The next letter is from her Paris flat.

" O Douglas, O Moron, O low-grade intelligence !   You
gave me a *crossed* cheque on London, untouchable under a fortnight ; open would have been all right.   Anyhow (everyone was
broke) Phil Lasell came to the rescue and Malin got safely off,
plus the 100 francs you so kindly lent me.

I found the child fretting for you, intending to do an after-
noon's shopping and a journey on one cup of coffee absorbed hours
previously.   So took her by scruff of pretty neck and fed omelette,
beer, hot biscuits, melon and bénédictine, all she would look at.
Funny meal.   Take care of her.   She needs it.   Beauty, sweet-
ness and intelligence like that must be cherished, and it all lies
in your hands.   She is a priceless treasure for you to ' perfec-
tioher,' and she's clearly had too hard a time.   Do, do take care
of her and forgive my impertinence for saying what you know
far better than I . . ."

Mary evidently soon left for the Riviera.   Writing from the
" Hotel Antipolis, Antibes," she says :

" Douglas dear, just got your p.c.   Matrimony indeed !
10,000 of fat book finished.   Several poems, and another of my

perennial worryings at the origin of Greek civilisation ; a fruitful one this time, only I haven't half the books I need. Came down on the first. Sported with Cuddy. Then, nearly a week ago, pitched over on one of the infernal cobbles of the old town and did in my knee. Am just about to crawl again.

Hid because, in a way, Malin was right. My last night in Paris I thought I'd do the round and landed up in the *Boeuf* [the Boeuf sur le Toit in the rue Caumartin]. There was J.R. changing colours like a well-managed stage sunset . . ."

For most of the two years which my wife and I spent at Juan-les-Pins and Nice, Mary was our near neighbour, at Villefranche. When we hurried to London, after the Wall Street crisis, she followed, with other expatriates, and soon afterwards married for the second time. Her husband, a charming, frail and rather ineffectual artist named Gabriel Atkin, became a great friend of mine. Although for the past ten years or more Mary had been carrying on a violent and noisy quarrel with her long-suffering mother, her brother Tony had patched up things sufficiently for the wedding reception to be held at her mother's flat, 3 Buckingham Gate. They went for their honeymoon to a house lent them by Gerald Reitlinger, the painter, at Iden. From here, we received an invitation which we were unable to accept.

> " Thornsdale,
> Iden,
> Rye.

Douglas and Malin—my dears,

This is to wish you every good Christmas thing for always, with all our loves.

We are exceedingly happy here, in more sun than I've ever known in England and with all Romney Marsh to play with. Come down and see us when you like.

In London the Fall of the House of Usher [the reference is to the financial situation of the Butts family] is at the point where— if I remember right—the whole edifice crumbles into the lake. I should like to talk to you. Meanwhile, blessings on you both for ever. MARY."

Shortly before, or after, her marriage—Mary's letters were seldom dated—she wrote asking leave to dedicate a volume of short stories to me which was published by Wishart in 1932, under the title " Several Occasions."

" My dear Douglas,

For a long time I've wanted to ask you if I might dedicate my next book to you, only for so long there wasn't a new book published.   Now Wishart is bringing out a large-ish collection in a proper edition of stories in January and I'd be so very glad if I might have the honour of dedicating it to you, in memory of our long friendship and of all I owe you, and all my work owes you, and all that the people I love owe and have owed to you.

Let me know if I may—as it's just about to be printed.   Always,

MARY."

Mary and Gabriel settled at Sennen Cove near Land's End in a rough-cast bungalow to which they gave the name Tebel-Vos. Here I paid them long visits, sometimes alone, sometimes with my wife and sons.   Her years in Cornwall were the most productive of Mary's life.   She got her foot well on to the ladder of success, secured a first-rate imprint for her books and began to write for the high-brow weeklies.   But I imagine the strain of her hectic life during the 'twenties had proved too much for her originally robust condition.   She died on March 5th, 1937 at the age of forty-four and Gabriel, from whom she had been separated, followed her into the grave a few weeks later.

I learnt recently, with great regret, that her brother Tony Butts committed suicide in the early years of the present war. He was a marked contrast to his sister.   Quiet, unassuming, brilliantly gifted, he once admitted to me, with a sad smile, that he had the temperament of " a Victorian spinster."   Mary's much publicised quarrel with their mother, to whom he remained devoted, caused him the more distress from the fact that the quarrel was largely about himself.   " A struggle between two determined women for Tony's soul " someone described it. Tony's blessing, or curse, was his critical faculty.   He was an excellent painter, and had received much friendly encouragement from Sickert, but as soon as he realised that he would never be in the first rank, he gave it up.   Towards the end of his life, he became art critic to *The Listener* and showed himself a writer of distinction.   He had fastidious taste as well as exceptional knowledge of his subject.

Mary, Tony, Gabriel—the 'twenties gave them a good run for their money.   They were " period " figures, products of an upheaval which first liberated and then destroyed them.   Whether

Mary's books will last is no more predictable than the survival of the poetry of T. S. Eliot, by whom she was greatly influenced.

IV

Malin's first encounters with her compatriots by adoption, must have given her a queer impression of the Anglo-Saxon world. In Paris she met Mary Butts, Nina Hamnett, Stella Bowen, Lady (Duff) Twysden, my festive American crony, Porterfield, my old friends Louis and Nan Wilkinson, even, on an unforgettable occasion, that great artist and attractive human being, Paul Robeson. They were an odd bunch of " contacts " for a young and inexperienced Swedish girl, who had spent much of her childhood in a remote island off the West Coast and most of her youth in a smug, " bourgeois " and intensely respectable provincial town. But, no doubt, it was a good preparation for the Riviera—that sunny land of shady people—to which we soon repaired.

CHAPTER TEN

THE GENERAL STRIKE

I

" I FEAR the situation in England is very black," said Professor Otto Nordenskjöld, the Rector of Gothenburg's Handelshögskola, on the morning in May 1926 when Europe read of the outbreak of the General Strike. The Professor pulled his beard thoughtfully and looked away from me, He was a kindly man, full of sympathy and distress on my account.

" It looks," he went on, " as if the British Empire is now doomed."

My reply was a deep chuckle of laughter, which appeared to disconcert him. My laughter was spontaneous, almost automatic. I did not, at the time, attempt to analyse it. Looking back, I can see that its basis was, first of all, absolute confidence in the traditions, guts and staying power of the British racial group, in any forseeable set of circumstances ; secondly, the instinct to stick up for one's own country before foreigners ; thirdly, the private conviction, arising from more knowledge of British Labour and its leaders than the Professor possessed, that the Strike was, in some way, "phony". Had it been the reverse, had it proved successful, my confidence in my compatriots would have been increased, not diminished, though this was a point which I could hardly expect my chief to understand.

In private, what authentic news I could gather about the Strike, its causes and its consequences, aroused apprehensions of a kind which I was not disposed to discuss with my Swedish colleagues. Like the publication of the forged Zinoviev letter in 1924 and the attribution of the miners' strikes in April 1944 to alleged "Trotskyite" activities, it was too convenient to the Conservative oligarchy to ring true. Winston Churchill's return to the Gold Standard in 1925 at Montague Norman's instigation had led both to an all-round increase in unemployment and to an attempt on the part of the coalowners to reduce wages and lengthen hours in the mining industry. As Churchill and Baldwin must have foreseen, the miners resisted. Their slogan was "not a minute on the day, not a penny off the pay." The T.U.C. was forced by its rank-and-file to support them. This was so exactly what the Government wanted that it is difficult to believe that they did not, themselves, help to engineer the situation that arose. All their plans for accepting Labour's challenge and dealing the whole Trade Union Movement a crushing and decisive blow, had evidently been matured in advance. They knew, far better than the rank-and-file of Labour, the weakness, timidity and selfishness of the "leaders", they knew that, under such generals as Ramsay MacDonald and J. H. Thomas, the fight would only be a sham fight and that victory was " in the bag " from the start. Under the pugnacious influence of Winston Churchill, whose hatred of " Bolshevism " and dislike and distrust of the masses were at that time unconcealed, the Baldwin Government rejected the last-minute offers of the miners' delegates and awaited events, secure in the certainty that the whole of the middle and upper classes would rally to the defence of " King and Country."

The T.U.C. announced a General Strike for May 3rd, and the event was dramatised throughout the world as a "revolutionary " outbreak. All Union labour ceased work except for those engaged in public health services. The Government answered with an "organization for the maintenance of supplies", enlisted from middle-class volunteers. Wearers of " old school ties ", inflamed with patriotism, drove trams and buses. Troops were stationed in Whitehall and employed in convoying food, while Hyde Park, as on previous occasions, was closed to the public and used as a milk depot. The first fatal blunder made by the T.U.C. was to call out the newspaper operatives, thus shutting down the Press. Churchill replied by taking control of broadcasting and issuing a Government newspaper called *The British Gazette.* Meanwhile the *Daily Mail* was printed in Paris and flown over to London. On May 3rd, under the heading " For King and Country ", its leading article declared that " A general strike is not an industrial dispute. It is a revolutionary movement intended to inflict suffering upon the great masses of innocent persons in the community and thereby to put constraint on the government . . . This being so, it cannot be tolerated by any civilized government, and must be dealt with by every resource at the disposal of the community." When, on May 12th, the Labour leaders surrendered, it headlined the news : "Surrender of the Revolutionaries ", "A Triumph for the People ", and assured its gullible readers that Zinoviev had planned the strike in 1918 and that 500 Soviet agents had helped to foment it ! Sir John Simon, although out of office, distinguished himself by declaring the strike illegal, on the ground that it was " not covered by the Act of 1906 which rendered trade union funds immune from claims for damage caused by industrial disputes." The judgment was contested by other legal authorities ; but Sir John was soon back on the nation's pay-roll.

In the light of later events, perhaps the most important incident in the whole ten days was the Government's treatment of religious opinion. The Bishops of Winchester and Southwark held the view that Christian principles called for further negotiations, not open strife, and urged that a further subsidy should be given to the coal industry. The Government, however, refused permission for the broadcasting of an appeal by the churches for the resumption of peace negotiations, although the appeal was backed by the Archbishop of Canterbury and the Free Church leaders. On the other hand, Cardinal Bourne's contention that the strike was a " sin against God " was given the widest publicity. This open identification of " God " with " Mammon ", on the part of the head of the Roman Catholic community in England, was destined to have far-reaching political consequences.

Two years before the signature of the Lateran Accord between Mussolini and the Vatican, Winston Churchill was already

enamoured of Fascism and convinced of its efficacy as an antidote to Bolshevik bestiality. On January 20th, 1927, fresh
from his triumphs over the miners and the T.U.C., Churchill
delivered an address in Rome to the Italian and Foreign Press,
in his capacity as Chancellor of the Exchequer. " I could not
help being charmed," he said, " like so many other people have
been [the relatives of Matteotti, Amendola and the Rosellis were
presumably not among them] by Signor Mussolini's gentle and
simple bearing and by his calm, detached poise in spite of so
many burdens and dangers. Secondly, anyone could see that
he thought of nothing but the lasting good, as he understood it,
of the Italian people, and that no lesser interest was of the
slightest consequence to him . . . If I had been an Italian I
am sure that I should have been wholeheartedly with you from
start to finish in your triumphant struggle against the bestial
appetites and passions of Leninism." Churchill then continued :
" I will, however, say a word on an international aspect of
Fascismo. Externally, your movement has rendered a service
to the whole world. The great fear which has always beset
every democratic leader or working-class leader has been that
of being undermined or overbid by someone more extreme than
he . . Italy has shown that there is a way of fighting the subversive forces which can rally the mass of the people, properly
led, to value and wish to defend the honour and stability of
civilized society. She has provided the necessary antidote to
the Russian poison. Hereafter no great nation will be un-
provided with an ultimate means of protection against the
cancerous growth of Bolshevism."*

Mr. Churchill's infatuation for Mussolini was shared by all his
Conservative colleagues, as well as by Lord Rothermere . . .
On June 11th, 1924, the Socialist Matteotti had been murdered
—at the Duce's instigation as many believed—with the result
that the Fascist régime was shaken to its foundations and would
probably have been overthrown if British Conservative opinion
had not been mobilized in its support. The first Labour Government was then in office, though not in power, and Arthur
Henderson, a member of it, had openly stigmatized Mussolini
as " the murderer of Matteotti ". Later in the year the Government fell and was replaced by a Conservative administration
which immediately reversed its foreign policy. Sir Austen
Chamberlain became the new Foreign Secretary. In this capacity

* Quoted in *The Twenty Years' Truce, 1919-1939*, by Robert M. Rayner, 1943.

one of his first actions was to pay an official visit to Rome, from December 6th to 12th, 1924, to establish friendly relations with the gangster whose hands, in the eyes of every decent Italian, were still dripping with blood. Sir Austen fawned on the murderer and his wife, who was destined to play a sinister part in the Appeasement era, was photographed in the act of shaking hands with him. A million and a half copies of this photograph were printed by Mussolini's orders and distributed throughout Italy, in proof of the fact that " Great Britain " was firmly on his side. In an interview with the *Tribuna*, Sir Austen said : "Signor Mussolini is a wonderful man and a formidable worker. I cannot enter into the internal policy of foreign countries, but I must say Signor Mussolini is working for the greatness of his country, and is bearing a tremendous weight upon his shoulders."

Such speeches were regarded throughout the Continent as the veritable voice of " England ", depressed the millions of Europeans who still looked on England as the traditional stronghold of liberty and progress and had a dispiriting effect—in view of the Corfu incident in the previous year—on the struggling League of Nations. There is also little doubt that the cordiality of Sir Austen Chamberlain and Winston Churchill, combined with the activities of the reactionary Roman Catholics in the Foreign Office, facilitated the signature of the Lateran Accord in 1929.

This disastrous event, which provided the Fascist gangsters in all countries (including the United States) with a cloak of " Christian " respectability, gave the Vatican an enormous financial interest in the stability of Mussolini's régime—to which Italian priests were required to swear allegiance—and paved the way for such a sacrifice of innocent lives as made the massacre of St. Bartholomew seem like a schoolboy prank and the action of Judas Iscariot a mere error of judgment. Today, all uncorrupted human beings, including genuinely religious Catholics, have more reason than Voltaire to cry : " *Ecrasez l'infâme* ! " The conversion of the Vatican to the elementary principles of Christianity is as much a necessity for world peace as the conversion of Nazi Germany to the standard of ethical values which is the basis of our civilization. The Pope's messages to General Franco and his congratulations to Hitler on his escape in July 1944 were a challenge to the conscience of the world. In view of the endless strife and bloodshed, past and present and to come, which can be traced back to the alliance between Fascism and Catholicism, the day on which the Lateran Accord was signed must be regarded as one of the blackest days, not only in the present century but in the whole of European history since the dawn of the Christian era.

CHAPTER ELEVEN

PLAYBOYS OF THE WEST-END WORLD

I

LACONIC references in a small engagement book for the year 1927 remind me of the fact that, in spite of visits to Paris and the Riviera and months of exile in Sweden, I contrived to put in some crowded weeks in London. 1927-1929 may be considered the heyday of the Bright Young People, the Wild Party's crescendo, the final binge before the slump. In the ensuing 'thirties some of the good-timers died of exhaustion, some became Roman Catholic converts and subsequently Fascists, a few developed social consciences and turned Left. The vast majority settled down, got jobs and faded out of the limelight. There could be no worse misuse of the " personified state " than to refer, as some do, to this boisterous little gang of publicity-hunters as the " England " or even the " young England " of the 'twenties. There were, perhaps, a couple of thousand of them all told, with a fringe of socialites and intellectuals of the kind portrayed in the novels of Michael Arlen, Aldous Huxley and later, Evelyn Waugh. Plodding Germans, like von Wedderkop, editor of *Der Quers hnitt*, and in the 'thirties, Ribbentrop, who drew conclusions about " England " from the behaviour of small unrepresentative groups, had surprises in store for them.

The real interest—and it is a considerable and legitimate interest—which the period of " wild parties " retains for the social historian is that it brought into the open tendencies in human behaviour which had previously been politely ignored. It was the age of debunking, particularly in regard to sex matters, and thus a wholesome and necessary prelude to what Dr. Buchman, stealing a useful phrase for questionable purposes, has called "moral rearmament ". Debunking preceded revaluation.

One of the results of the war which had a most disturbing effect on girls of the upper classes was the number of young men of their own age and social status, from whom normally they would have chosen their husbands, who were either sexually indifferent or ostentatiously homosexual. This upset the entire basis of feminine sex technique. Even if the sophisticated products of the more fashionable schools did not use the phrase " Men are such beasts ! They all want the same thing", they neverthe-less subconsciously worked on this very natural supposition. Victorian grandmothers, reproving errant husbands, would murmur : " Remember, Algernon, *I gave you myself*." Although this was a joke in the 'twenties, girls still expected young men to display a masculine eagerness to undress them, to show a proper degree of excitement at the charms revealed, and some gratitude for their surrender. When epicene youths resolutely declined to be " beasts ", even exhibited polite and supercilious disgust at what should in any normal he-man arouse a flattering violence of desire, they were disconcerted and bewildered. In vain they flattened their chests and cropped their hair in the effort to compete with " pansies " and " tapettes ". I remember a young lovely confiding to me, tearfully, at a party, that " Nigel ", a youth at whom she had been setting her cap, " is nothing but a heart-less he-vamp ". This state of things had consequences which need cause no surprise. In the first place, older men, accustomed to the theory that, in sex matters, man is the hunter, now found themselves the quarry. If they fell, " pounced " or merely made passes, the facts were published to the world by the maiden concerned with whoops of triumph. A well-known painter told me that he was once sitting on the top of an omnibus when he chanced to hear his name mentioned by two girls, neither of whom he had ever set eyes on before. " Oh, yes, dear," said one of them to the other. " I know X. You see, I was his mistress for two years."

A wealthy young woman of my acquaintance once found herself alone in her bedroom while the windows were being cleaned by a good-looking young workman. With instant presence of mind she affected not to notice him, began to take off her outer clothes, displaying in the process a shapely pair of breasts, and then looked up and caught his eye. The effect was so shattering that the young man nearly fell off his ladder, so to avoid accidents, she beckoned him inside. Charmed by this adventure she took a flat in an obscure street and had her windows cleaned twice a week. When the neighbours at last became censorious, she retired in good order and handed over the flat to a struggling and extremely virtuous artist.

The female Don Juan was a familiar type in the 'twenties but "new moralists", who had no objections to their adventures with proletarian Adonises, rightly condemned their attacks on the virtue of Negro artists. In the middle 'twenties Negro revues of the "Blackbirds" type, had an enormous and deserved success in London. (In Paris, where colour prejudice is practically unknown, Josephine Baker made a similar sensation.) The casts of these revues were composed of talented and hardworking Negro actors and actresses, most of whom were happily married and contented. I doubt very much if any of them had any particular desire to be taken up by London's Bright Young People. When, however, they found themselves invited after the show to what appeared to be the homes of London socialites, they naturally accepted. I attended several of these "secret parties", which usually started after midnight, and my sympathies were with the coloured artists, who behaved much better than their hosts. The Negro craze infected several women of what Victorians would call the "highest ranks of society", and some unpleasant scandals, due to the natural anger and jealousy of the wives, were only narrowly averted.

I must have written about these occurrences to my festive American friend, the late George Alexander Porterfield, who during the 'twenties created a "legend" in London, Paris, and New York which is not yet forgotten by any of those who came in contact with him. Porter, as he himself admitted, rarely "drew a sober breath", but was hardly ever incapacitated. A perfect example of the playboy, he lived entirely on charm and the belief, prevalent among English people, that all Americans are really rich, even if temporarily embarrassed. Porter, to my knowledge, never had a penny, except what was doled out to him by friends, relatives, wives, and a hard-working mother. Though hardly a moralist, either "new" or old, he found my description of the "secret parties" rather too much for his digestion. Replying from his home in Santa Barbara—whither he had fled to recuperate and escape his creditors—he observed : "I must say the black 'petting' parties sound simply too frightful. It isn't that I mind meeting niggers on terms of social equality so much —though I'm not really fond of it—as it is I can't for the life of me see that simply being black constitutes any particular charm or eminence in itself, but of course, I may be hopelessly oldfashioned. A [his then wife] says I'm getting horribly stuffy, but I'm sure it isn't stuffiness loathing X [an elderly Bright Young

Person]. Dear God ! *What* a woman ! Quite the most revolting of all created beings, she sends a quick sense of nausea through me just as the sight of some infested, dead thing would . . . Niggers *and* X ! That's my idea of horror ' plus.' Your stay in Paris sounded infinitely jollier : lots of drink and (as you say) what's better, lots of good talk. I think I miss that more than the drink out here in this misbegotten corner of the world ; and I'd willingly exchange the comfort and security we have to be able to wander into the first pub we came to and enjoy an hour's good talk with you, old chap." Porter survived, miraculously, until the end of the 'twenties. He died of pneumonia in Paris, leaving behind him a few short stories, published in American magazines, some unfinished novels, and probably a " flock of debts ". Those who knew him forgave him all his offences, up to seventy times seven. From some standpoints he was " utterly worthless " ; he was certainly selfish ; but he had good manners in a period when manners had noticeably decayed and a charm which even St. Peter may, we hope, have found himself unable to resist. I trust he has secured admission to one of the most golden of the saloon bars of Heaven.

The shortage of the kind of men they required led, in the 'twenties, to numerous associations, of a more or less Lesbian character, between intelligent women with intellectual interests and no time or liking for the current forms of dissipation. Unless purposely paraded, such friendships aroused little curiosity or comment, thanks to the debunking of cant on this and similar subjects. Growth of knowledge about sex psychology, on the other hand, seriously disturbed the conventional Tory aristocracy, whose favourite vices, although well-known to Continental observers—Stendhal's " De l'Amour " discusses them in detail— had hitherto been concealed from the public gaze. Hereditary legislators from the " backwoods ", who only attended the House of Lords to vote for the continuance of the practice of flogging small boys, or to prevent the torturing of rabbits being made illegal, were offended by the irreverent sneers which these activities occasioned. The peculiar tastes traditionally associated with the peerage, the squirearchy, with " legal luminaries " and fox-hunting ladies, were publicized, analysed and healthily ridiculed in the 'twenties. Some psychologists, moreover, traced a connexion between the sadism prevalent among a section of our Junker class and the treatment meted out by certain country magistrates to juvenile delinquents. The flogging of working-class children for trivial offences, their classification, often on wholly insufficient grounds, as mental defectives and consequent imprisonment in lunatic asylums, began to arouse angry comment. The arrogance and tyranny of J.P.s in dealing with licensing questions also led to a subdued murmur of resentment among the cowed populace. The fact that the masses were cowed and their complaints subdued was one of the chief signs of national decadence, or at least apathy, in the post-war years.

The attitude of the conventional—and outwardly—respectable members of the plutocracy towards the handful of the younger generation who insisted on " giving the show away " by parading their vices was one of baffled rage. If only the Bright Young People could have been exposed as " Reds " or " Bolsheviks " ! Unfortunately, most of them, in so far as they had any politics, were as devoid of moral sense as their parents, in fact the Fascists of the future. Attempts were made to divert popular criticism from the sprigs of aristocracy to those of the *intelligentsia* who satirized their follies, but they were not very successful. "Jix", however, did his best.

The police took action against the publishers of Miss Radclyffe Hall's "The Well of Loneliness", and against the Warren Gallery for exhibiting pictures by D. H. Lawrence. They also seized a French translation of the Hunting of the Snark and some drawings by Blake ! James Douglas denounced the " ordure and blasphemy " of Aldous Huxley's " Antic Hay " and attacked several other outstanding novels, with great benefit to their sales. Even the " Pink 'Un " raged against the obscenity of " Ulysses ". " What can we do to be banned ? " was the novelists' query as a result.

The practice of any of the arts involves an infinity of labour and the most intense concentration. By contrast, the chief characteristic of the Bright Young People was that they made a business of " pleasure " and hunted the " good time " until exhaustion overcame them. By the end of the decade the Wild Party was over and the Sunday journalists began to look for copy in other fields.

II

One of the penalties I paid for wasting time with playboys and their girls, attending innumerable parties, frequenting night clubs and watching the development of not a few " real life " dramas, in some of which I played a minor part, was that I lost

the habit of going regularly to the theatre. I must have missed
a lot, for it is obvious from the books which have been written
about the stage and the cinema in the 'twenties that the decade
was one of unusual interest and creative activity. It saw the
first productions of Shaw's " St. Joan ", with Sybil Thorndike
as a rather massive Maid and Ernest Thesiger as the Dauphin,
and of Flecker's "Hassan", with a caste including Henry Ainley,
Allan Quartermaine, Laura Cowie and Cathleen Nesbitt, and
incidental music by Delius—two events which were in themselves enough to make it important in theatrical history. As a
friend of the author, I was sent tickets for the premi re of "Hassan"
at His Majesty's, and took with me Elsa Lanchester, who was
then scarcely out of her teens. Her flaming red-gold hair, exotic
costume and *gamine* appearance had—much to my amusement
—a startling effect on all the stuffed shirts who beheld her.
" Who's that girl ? " I heard people murmuring in the entr'acte.
Shortly afterwards Elsa made a hit in a small part in Karel
Capek's " Insect Play ", translated by Paul Selver, and later
scored a success with Harold Scott in Sir Nigel Playfair's production, " Riverside Nights ". (I have already referred to " The
Cave of Harmony ", which she and Harold Scott carried on for
several years.)

Playfair's revival of " The Beggar's Opera " at the Lyric
Theatre, Hammersmith, with Frederick Ranalow as Macheath
and Lovat Fraser's dresses and décor, is one of my happiest
memories of the early 'twenties. I suppose I must have seen it
at least a dozen times. Rutland Boughton's music drama
" The Immortal Hour " at the new "Regent Theatre", formerly
the Euston Music Hall, provided another unforgettable thrill.

The disillusioned, sub-acid comedies of Noel Coward, who
rose rapidly to fame in the post-war years, titillated Mayfair and
pleasantly shocked Suburbia. The same note of cynicism,
blended with half-concealed disgust, characterised the more
mature work of Somerset Maugham and Frederick Lonsdale.
The only one of these plays I can now recall is "Our Betters",
in which Marian Terry had a minor part. It was one of the
very few occasions on which I had the privilege of admiring this
great actress. Even in her old age she spoke the English language
more beautifully than I have ever heard it spoken before or
since.

In the world of pure, or not so pure, entertainment C. B.
Cochran was as dominant a figure in the 'twenties as in the

succeeding decade. Anything good of its kind was seized on by him and brought to London, from the Guitrys to Negro revues, from Raquel Meller to the ever-verdant Delysia, from Russian Ballet and Balieff's " Chauve-Souris " to " No, No Nanette ". Perhaps, on reflection, he was not responsible for quite all these stage joys, though it is natural to give him credit for them for he has been the supreme showman of my lifetime.

Of the cinema in the 'twenties I am not qualified to speak for I have never been an habitual filmgoer. The Film Society, founded in 1926, gave Sunday performances at the New Gallery Cinema which I attended once or twice. For the rest I recall certain German films, such as The Cabinet of Dr. Caligari and Doctor Mabuse, Felix the Cat, some early Chaplin triumphs and numerous Hollywood productions which, stupid and vulgar as they were, did not, in my recollection, touch the " all-time low " of those wished on us in the present year of grace.

CHAPTER TWELVE

" MY BLUE HEAVEN "

THE glutinous notes of " My Blue Heaven " poured out of every Casino ballroom, every cheap " dancing ", every gramophone, when I first arrived in Cannes in 1928 and the syrupy tune was still pervading the Riviera when I left it in March 1930. It was the theme song of the English good-timers in the South of France in the late 'twenties, just as " Any old umbrellas " was the theme song of Chamberlain's England ten years later.

The three years I spent on the physically enchanting but morally enervating Côte d'Azur, taught me more about the Anglo-American ruling class and its continental equivalents than I could ever have learnt in England. At home, the ruling cliques—as the present war has painfully revealed—live in a world of their own, separated by impassable barriers from the broad masses of their compatriots. Angry criticism from the nation reaches the ears of Transport House, the Carlton Club, the Foreign Office or 10 Downing Street in the form of vague murmurs from a distant mob. Our leaders have now almost no social intercourse with the led. Apart from a handful of authors, artists, journalists and priests who are, ex-officio, classless, the English, in their choice of friends and acquaintances, for the most part play for safety by confining their social contacts to people in their own income group, who share their political views and have much the same outlook. In this way it is hoped that unpleasantness of any kind will be avoided. When after the Four Years' War the cleavage among wearers of " old school ties " became pronounced, those who went Left stayed in their own camp. They soon lost touch with former friends and schoolfellows who remained faithful to their Tory prejudices.

On the Riviera in the 'twenties we found a microcosm of English middle and upper-class society the members of which lived at too close quarters to be able to ignore each other's existence. The effect of this accidental contiguity was further increased by the fact that "the Race", as Timothy Shy calls us, was surrounded by foreigners—in short, by " natives "—and thus to a large extent, segregated.

The circumstances of our respective professions—my wife was in practice as a Swedish masseuse—forced us to enlarge the range of our observations among the English residents. Apart from the permanent members of the British colony there was a fairly constant flow of friends from England which gave us numerous contacts with the floating population of *hivernants*, tourists, good-timers and transients. After a short and painful stay in Cannes we settled at Juan-les-Pins for the summer season of 1928, and afterwards took a flat in Nice. We were, of course, poor, but as we both spoke French (of a sort) with tolerable fluency we were able to " go native " and thus had the great pleasure of gaining some inside knowledge of French provincial life. After Luke Hansard's widow, with my full approval and blessing, married his great friend Albert Raynaud of Grasse, we also enjoyed the rare privilege of being included in a French family circle. We had acquaintances among the artists of Cagnes-sur-mer, a sort of Riviera outpost of Montparnasse, and literary friends like Bill Mathers (Torquemada of the *Observer*), Louis Wilkinson and his late wife, Nan Reid, Ethel Mannin, Mary Butts and others paid short or long visits to Nice and kept us in touch with the outer world. Through Louis, we got to know that game old buccaneer Frank Harris, who ended his long and variegated career at Nice.

As General Editor of Harrap's Kit-Bag travel books, I had assigned myself the volume on *The French Riviera*, which gave me the excuse and opportunity to explore the whole coast and its *hinterland*, particularly the enchanting villages in the Var valley, at the back of Nice. These excursions remain among my happiest recollections of the years I spent—perhaps " wasted " would be the appropriate term—as a " prisoner of the sun ". Other literary activities included a novel called " The Coast of Illusion ", and a long, careful but disastrously unremunerative book on the island of Sardinia.

Meanwhile, we established connections with some of the more or less permanent English residents through a friend who ran an admirable circulating library at Juan-les-Pins. Herself a pukka " mem sahib ", with an unimpeachable " Service " background, her business contacts ranged from crusted Tories of the utmost respectability, to American millionaires (who pinched her books), stockbrokers, profiteers, *rentiers*, retired Civil Servants, dubious " majors " and all kinds of Riviera flotsam and jetsam, including one or two well-born crooks. Thus it so happened that, in one way or another, as spectators of the Anglo-American plutocracy on the spree, assisted by its horde of parasites and hangers-on, we may be said to have occupied ring seats. Golly, what a performance they put up !

Compared with the brainless debaucheries of the commercial plutocracy, the private lives of hardworking writers and painters are models of virtuous propriety. The reason why the English *bourgeois* regards the artist as " immoral " was, for the first time, revealed to me on the Riviera. It is not because he " drinks " or is sexually loose—the City of London swims in alcohol and any " big advertiser " can sleep with the daughter of an earl if he agrees to sign a contract from which she will derive a commission—but because he creates ideas and thinks for himself. That is the deadly sin in the eyes of Wimbledon and Woking, Weybridge and Bournemouth, Cheltenham and Bath. As for the rest, snobbery dominates their whole outlook. The rich City business man would rather have his daughter seduced by a peer's nephew than respectably married by an " immoral " poet of origins no more distinguished than his own.

The behaviour of one of the festive *rentiers* I got to know on the Côte d'Azur shocked me as a " new " moralist. He was well-connected, had charming manners and an excellent—and I believe, authentic—war record. His favourite amusement was to take little girls, the younger the better, to see the pornographic cinema at Nice. This practice of his was well-known even to the churchgoing section of the English colony, but involved him in no unpleasant social rebuffs. His position, as one indubitably out of the top drawer, was impregnable. He was just the kind of man that the wives and daughters of any City solicitor, living at Woking or Weybridge, would fight to secure as a guest at their appalling dinners. This " triste monsieur " deliberately robbed adolescents of the lyrical ecsta ies and illusions of young love, in order to get a kick out of noting their reactions. No such crime was ever proved against Oscar Wilde, whose homosexual practices, for which he was imprisoned and ostracized, injured no one but himself. I often wondered what would have happened to this chap had he not been protected by his old school tie.

II

In one way and another, Conservative England, transported to the shores of the Mediterranean, made a poor showing. Its golf-links, tennis-courts, smart brothels, pornographic cinemas, *boîtes de nuit*, gambling hells and " exclusive " clubs, its snobbery, arrogance and selfishness, combined to create a hot-house atmosphere which produced the rankest and most astonishing growths. The English profiteer got together in the baccarat rooms at Monte Carlo with his Transatlantic and Continental brothers and in the intervals of winning and losing on the tables, concocted fresh villainies against the peoples which still tolerated them, and planned new onslaughts on the one nation which had thrown them out. The only political opinions I ever heard expressed were praise of Mussolini, hatred of the working-classes and terror of " Bolshevism ". The latter was brought to fever pitch by the presence on the Côte d'Azur of a horde of penniless White Russian refugees.

It was not the fault of the Russian emigrés that their sad lot created this anti-Bolshevik obsession in the minds of the English nouveaux-riches. On the contrary, those I knew seemed to me to display the traditional virtues of a genuinely aristocratic caste. Even when reduced to semi-starvation by exile, they remained cultured, philosophic, courageous and dignified. I often wondered how our bogus " best people "—this crowd of golf-playing " patriots ", arrogantly ignorant, incapable, as their political record shows, of a single honourable action, of any unselfish and uplifting thought—would comport themselves if they were ever forced, by some outburst of popular indignation, to leave their country for their country's good. Every time they tipped an ex-colonel of the Russian Guards for performing some menial service they must have shuddered with internal apprehensions. Oddly enough their efforts to get the Russian " Whites ", even those who had been imprisoned and tortured by the Communists, to join in hymns of hate often fell flat. I listened to several conversations in the course of which the Russians, while deploring the new régime and wishing to see it overthrown, displayed a genuine devotion to their country and a pride in the genius of their race which obviously discomfited their interlocutors.

The literary flunkeys of the Baldwin plutocracy swarmed on the Riviera and were lavishly publicized in the Society columns of the local snob press. Fashion experts abounded, writers of popular novels describing the amours of the Anglo-American " Tatler set ", crowded the casinos in search of local colour. In those days it was hardly possible to open one of the shiny magazines without finding stories of love and laughter in the world's " most fashionable " pleasure ground, illustrated with drawings of sun-bathing lovelies, opulent restaurants, smart cars, yachts, palm-trees, and all the other familiar adjuncts of a musical comedy décor.

While we were at Juan-les-Pins, a friend of my Edwardian " dancing days " who had studied the contemporary fiction market with a sharp eye to the main chance and had successfully exploited his social advantages in highly-paid magazine stories, made an impressive début on the *plage* in a purple silk bathgown. The airs he gave himself convulsed us with laughter. He was tremendously the " distinguished " author, travelling incognito to avoid the autograph albums of his admirers. These must have been numerous for there was no denying the good looks of which he was so obviously conscious. His lean, bronzed figure, beautifully shaped head, fine eyes and clipped dark moustache, might have made even a Rudolph Valentino envious, but I doubt if any intelligent girl would have fallen for him, except for impurely physical reasons. Even the " debs " in his days of pre-war splendour, used to complain that he was '" eaten up " with conceit. Women are quick to realise that those who too wholeheartedly love themselves, have nothing to give in return when they are loved by others.

I have no doubt that in a small place like Juan, Basil—this was not his name—caught sight of me as frequently as I caught sight of him, but we contrived to avoid openly cutting each other. It would have embarrassed me if he had made a move to renew our acquaintance. We worshipped different gods and had never had sufficient mutual respect to bridge the ever-widening gulf between our opposed political camps.

Among the many illusions cherished in English suburban homes about " The Coast of Illusion " was the idea that the Riviera was a paradise for lovers and the place in all Europe where a pretty girl could most successfully exploit her sex-appeal. Nothing could have been further from the truth. The Riviera, especially in summer, should be avoided by honeymoon couples. Not only has the climate a disastrous effect on the virility of the Nordic male but female charms are cancelled out by competition. I expressed this view in an article headed " A surfeit of Beautiful Women ", which appeared in the Continental *Daily Mail* and did not increase my local popularity.

" Lovely darlings," I wrote, " if they are out for conquest, ought at all costs to avoid the fashionable Southern *plages*. For nearly four months this year on the sands of Juan-les-Pins, I basked daily in the sunshine, in close proximity to some hundreds of the world's most beautiful girls.

" For the first few days this parade of charmers, dressed in the most daring and exiguous costumes, awakened a certain natural admiration in the average male.

" But as the summer wore on, after watching them day after day oiling their backs and necks and legs and setting to work to acquire the requisite bronze tint, all interest in them evaporated.

" The good people who believe that the world will be a better place when all unmarried young men and women are like brothers and sisters to each other ought to be delighted with such places as Juan-les-Pins. The atmosphere of any ordinary country church during the vicar's sermon is more highly charged with sex-electricity than this sunbathed beach.

" In vain did the ' little women ' enter beauty competitions and receive prizes at the fair hands of ' Miss France ' ; in vain did they exhibit and parade their attractions. Physical jerks, under the direction of some professor of physical culture, were more popular with the men than flirtations ; dancing was indulged in for dancing's sake and the green tablecloth worked far more havoc than green eyes.

" Girls who might have caused a sensation at Bournemouth

found themselves lost, cancelled out, amid the crowd of bronzed beauties at Juan.

"On the *plage* one saw those lovely creatures as they really are, with no glamour of remoteness or romance to aid them, and just as hot and sticky as anyone else.   Their vapid small talk in a variety of different languages, their drivelling little dogs, their extravagances, futilities, and general lack of 'human interest' reduced male onlookers to profound gloom.

"Amid such a crowd, so jaded does it make one, even Aphrodite herself might pass unnoticed.   But when, on a memorable occasion, Mr. Bernard Shaw appeared on the beach in bathing costume, the excitement was such as might be aroused by the sudden arrival of 'the world's sweetheart' in a miners' camp. I have no idea whether personal vanity enters into Mr. Shaw's make-up.   Even if it does not, the apparent superiority of his physical charms over those of the loveliest members of the opposite sex might well, despite his somewhat advanced age, turn his head."

Shaw was fond of bathing and the incident described actually occurred, when he was staying at Cap d'Antibes.   Frank Harris was at that time engaged in writing his life and Shaw (unaccompanied by Mrs. Shaw) several times went over to Nice to see him. In the end, in self-defence, he was forced to write the best part of the book himself and to revise the remainder.

III

After a time our existence in a vulgar pleasure resort began to grow irksome.   Both my wife and I are by nature and inclination workers and in love with Life, even when Life means struggle and hardship.   Constant contact with compatriots who were idle, " retired " and dead without knowing it, was enervating. For some months before the Wall Street slump, which hit the Coast like a tornado, we had wanted to get away, but had not enough ready money to escape to London.   At last my publishers released me from imprisonment and we returned to an England in which all the bright hopes of the early 'twenties had been extinguished.   The counter-revolution had won an easy triumph, the Labour Movement had not recovered from the General Strike and the Trade Disputes Act of 1927, Ramsay MacDonald was preparing to hitch his wagon to the Tory star and sell out his supporters.   Anglo-American finance, acting through the

Bank of England, decided to get rid of the Labour " Cabinet of caretakers ", the electorate were once again tricked and deceived and the National Government of appeasers secured its monstrous majority.

Before leaving the South of France I summed up my impressions of the English expatriates who, with the rest of the Conservative middle-class, contributed so largely to our subsequent disasters, in an article printed by a Sunday newspaper.

" The permanent English population in the South of France is very different from the floating population ; and the difference is hardly in its favour.

" Of late years there has been a huge concentration on the Riviera of those rather pathetic expatriates who habitually form the ' English colonies ' of Continental resorts. The Riviera has attracted them because living there is cheap, there are no vexatious police restrictions as in Italy, flats and villas are plentiful and rents low. Five hundred a year in the South of France will buy as much comfort as double that income in London and the climate is admirably adapted to a life of perfect idleness. Moreover, tennis courts abound, there are good golf courses, and nobody need speak a word of French, know anything about the country or have any intercourse with the ' natives.'

" There is practically no intellectual life among the Riviera English ; hardly anyone who settles on the Côte d'Azur ever thinks a new thought or admits a new idea into his head. As the country supplies no stimulus of any kind to the brain-worker, little of value is produced in it except by old people and invalids, whom its deadness does not affect. For those who can say to themselves ' we have had enough of action and of motion we ' it is indeed the perfect lotus-land.

" All the English ' refugees from the invisible revolution,' all the ' lower classes of the upper classes,' all those with a little money, less brains and a sense of their own importance which their compatriots at home do not share, seem to have found their way to it.

" There, in a long chain of jerry-built garden suburbs which line the coast, they have established a little pre-war England of their own, with a social atmosphere about as stifling as that of Malta or an Indian hill-station. They regard anyone who, whether from choice or necessity, works for his living as being on an infinitely lower plane than themselves. They are ' patriots ' to a man ; and the ' war mentality ' is the only sort of mentality they have left. Yet they never tire of abusing their own country, which they say is ' quite impossible '—presumably because it has no further use for them—and take care to spend every penny of their unearned increment outside its borders. Thus they neither work themselves nor do they do anything to give employment to the multitude of their less fortunate compatriots.

" The particular ' note ' of the Riviera ' English Colony ' can be best gauged from the fact that nearly every Englishman on the coast uses a military title. The plague of majors is, indeed, almost incredible. A cynical friend of mine who lives at Nice for his health assessed the proportion of those who had ever possessed even a temporary claim to this distinction as not more than one in five !

" But titles of any sort are ten a penny on the Côte d'Azur, they are so easily come by. Many are conferred accidentally by the assistants in the circulating libraries, and I once, myself, was knighted in this way when I went to change my Edgar Wallace.

" Social struggling, manœuvring to get one's name in the local paper, and personal gossip are the principal occupations of the expatriates. As the Riviera is the recognised resort for illicit honeymoons as well as the happy hunting-ground of an unduly large share of alcoholics, crooks and drug-takers, the material for gossip certainly never runs short.

" But what a death in life it is, this futile idling in the Provençal sunshine ! How dreadfully bored the pleasure-hunters are, and what a gloom their futility casts over the dazzling brightness of the Riviera scene ! There is something rotten and demoralising about this sun-bathed coast which few of the younger residents seem able to resist for long.

" It is the coast to go and live on only when you throw up the sponge ! But certainly, winter or summer, it is an unrivalled playground in which to spend a few months' holiday. A little of it is a tonic ; too much a poison."

Had it not been for the necessity, owing to my wife's practice, of our living in towns with a permanent English population of the type described, I should probably have taken a far less jaundiced view of the Azure Coast. Other writers who either settled in Provence or paid long visits there, successfully avoided the " colonials " and were both happy and productive. Away from the English belt, roughly the part of the coast between St. Raphael and the Italian frontier, the country was enchanting. The small groups of writers and painters who collected unobtrusively, in places undiscovered by the tourists and " too French " for the "colonials", had an ideal existence. They lived cheaply, worked hard and enjoyed the company of people with similar tastes and interests to their own. Had we been free to choose our own environment, we should have spent our time recovering from the nerve-strains of the war at places like Aix-en-Provence, Le Lavandou, Bormes, Cassis, Bandol, Sanary or Toulon. Of the Eastern Riviera resorts, Nice, owing to the fact that it was a large town and could thus absorb and assimilate its foreign population, was much the most congenial. Our stay there was brightened by the fact that Mary Butts spent a good deal of her time at Villefranche, while Bill and Rosamond Mathers settled down at the back of Nice in a furnished villa in the suburb of St. Sylvestre.

The Welcome Hotel at Villefranche was a favourite hide-out of Jean Cocteau, who was particularly fond of the sailors' café at the back of the building, on the ground floor. The upper floors were extremely respectable, so much so that on one occasion Mary's high spirits became too much for the management and she was requested to leave. I was lunching with her once, in the restaurant overlooking the harbour, when her beloved " Jean " came up and spoke to her. Unlike Nina Hammett, who received a conventional pre-war education in a school for officers' daughters, Mary was brought up in a highbrow Scotch school at which manners were considered less important than Greek and Latin. As a result she was inhibited by sheer gaucherie from going through the conventional motions of introducing her guest, much to the embarrassment both of Cocteau and myself.

Mary's " goings-on " in Villefranche, which included much investigation of artificial paradises and the introduction of a young baronet to the beauties of English poetry, eventually became rather more lively than even her American literary friends could stand for. Fierce quarrels occurred and whenever we called on Mary we were conscious of tension in the atmosphere. Sometimes even the music of the *musettes* in the sailors' café was half-drowned by the altercations of furiated pansies when she appeared there.

A calmer spirit pervaded the villa at St. Sylvestre, when we called on Bill Mathers and his wife. It was a pleasure on a sunny morning to find Bill, his piriform figure clad only in a short blue shirt, at work in his garden on one of his torturing " Torquemada" puzzles. His mandarin beard, his glasses, his benign smile, his gentle voice, all suggested the poet and philosopher which, indeed, he was.   As a guest, when we invited him to dinner in our flat in the Gambetta quarter, he was apt to be uncertain. A long road punctuated with *bistros* separated him from us. As he, like myself, had a high opinion of the product of M. Pernod Fils, he used to pause, en route, for refreshment and refreshment led to cogitation.   In consequence, if invited for eight, he might as likely as not arrive at ten and fall gently asleep over his soup. As I have written elsewhere* of E. Powys Matthews I will say no more about him here except that his death, which occurred shortly before the war, was as great a loss to literature as it was to his friends.

When we first went to Nice, D. H. Lawrence was in Mallorca. I had friendly messages from him through a young artist, a neighbour of the Lawrences, who came to Nice to stay with his aunt, Mrs. W. B. Trites.   Trites, an elderly American writer who had just made a considerable literary reputation with a short novel called " The Gipsy ", had a charming flat facing the sea, on the Quai de Rouba Capeu, and we saw a good deal of him. When we heard, through the nephew, that the Lawrences had left Mallorca and settled in Bandol, I wrote to D. H. L.   His reply from the Villa Beau Soleil, Bandól, dated Monday, 18th October, 1929, was written in a sadly shaky hand, unlike the lovely bold script of ten years earlier.

" Dear Goldring,

How amusing to hear from you again !   I always asked after you and had bits of your news, so knew all, except the new wife."

(After this came sundry reference to Betty and her second husband, very flattering to myself.)   He continued :

" We got this little house for the winter, I'm hoping my health will be better—it's devilish bad.   If only I knew what to do about it.   Am miserable.

If we come Nice way—not likely, but you never know—I shall write you first—and if you come this way, do come and see us.   The house is too little for guests, but the village is nice. It would be fun to talk things over.   Must be ten years since we met.   Aunt A and Uncle F have just sailed for India, where he is to sit in the chair of Arabic at Delhi.   But since *Lady C* we are not on writing terms.   But I feel I *must* make the peace.   I *must*

---

* " Facing the Odds," by Douglas Goldring.

Q

hear Aunt A on Delhi !   Do you remember them ? Hermitage ?
If only I was well I'd come to Nice for a week.
    Greetings from both.

D. H. LAWRENCE."

Alas, this letter arrived just at the time when my wife and I
were passing through one of the worst of our temporary financial
crises.   If only I had possessed the few hundred francs necessary
to take me to Bandol and back, to enjoy the fun of " talking
things over " !   The reference to " Hermitage " is to a time when
Betty and I stayed with Lawrence and his wife and met the rich
uncle and aunt who had gone out to Delhi.   It was not until
the spring of 1930, when I raised enough money to return
to London, that the journey to Bandol became possible.   I wrote
to Lawrence, telling him our news, and mentioning the day when
I would stop off at Bandol in the hope of seeing him.   I took
the letter down to the Café Gambetta (our " local") to post, but
before buying a stamp I bought the evening paper.   In it I
read that Lawrence had been hurried to Venice in a dying
condition and that there was no hope of his recovery.

The news stunned me.   In spite of the evidence of the shaky
handwriting, I had not realised that his illness was so serious.
On the day of his death, which occurred a week or two later, I
happened to enter an Anglo-American bar in Nice which was
frequented by " Riviera correspondents " of English and American newspapers.   One of these unfortunates, who could scarcely
be described as an ornament to his profession, had a much-
thumbed copy of " Lady Chatterley's Lover ", extracts from
which he was reading aloud to his friends in the shocked tones of
a Sunday school teacher.   When I came in he buttonholed me,
supposing (rightly) that I might have known Lawrence but not
realizing that I had no desire to discuss him with a Riviera
gossip columnist.   " Look here, damn it all," said this brother
of the pen, " this is the sort of stuff 'e writes.   Sheer muck, I
call it."   I lost my temper and told him that if he and his colleagues sent obituary paragraphs describing Lawrence as a
pornographer they would disgrace their profession and the papers
which employed them.   I think his story was watered down a
bit as a result of my outburst, but he adopted an attitude of
outraged virtue and did not forgive me.   A day or two later I
left for London and found on my arrival that most of the " literary " papers were taking much the same line about Lawrence as

the Riviera correspondents. I had left the Riviera with a bad taste in my mouth, but what I found in London did nothing to dispel the gloom.

IV

The Riviera English, colonists and tourists, as I soon discovered, were no more than a representative cross-section of our Conservative class, conveniently segregated for study. What was true of the Côte d'Azur specimens was equally true of the main body. They regarded themselves as " England ". They still do. And since they have had sufficient power to switch a people's war against Fascism into a financiers' war (with the City of London subservient to Wall Street) against democracy in revolt, they may for the moment be right. What then is the duty of the sincere patriot ? It has always seemed to me to be his duty, in and out of season, to protest that the Conservative class is no more the " real " England than Vichy France, to take a current instance, is the " real " France. No one likes " running down his own people " or "fouling his own nest", but the true patriot has no choice but to discriminate between the class and party whose actions are rapidly undermining what " England " has meant to the world for at least four centuries, and the masses who are determined to rebuild and save it. Although our easy-going national temperament and our vast, inert, slow-moving, slow-thinking bourgeoisie act as a useful shock-absorber, the cleavage between the able, progressive, industrious and enterprising section of our people and the rich ruling class which still frustrates their efforts and misdirects their energies is essentially as unbridgeable as it proved to be in Spain. There is little to choose between the mentality of the expatriate property-owner, retired colonel, admiral or Indian civil servant who lounged on the Côte d'Azur in the 'twenties and that of their active counterparts who infest Whitehall and New Delhi in the warring 'forties. The plutocrats who idled on the Croisette and threw their money about at Monte Carlo, still dominate the House of Commons and are still at their old game of wrecking the hopes of our long-suffering and gallant sons in order to make profits out of their blood and toil. In these circumstances, class loyalty and loyalty to one's country and its best traditions—the only real patriotism—are incompatible. I have seldom met a " privileged person " who was capable of grasping this point.

After the General Strike, when the *Daily Mail* identified the phrase "King and Country" with the interests of the coal-owners, it fell into general disrepute among the intelligent. So much so that in 1933 the Oxford Union, after a spirited debate, voted that "this House will not fight for its King and Country." Recently, during a B.B.C. Brains Trust séance, Mr. Quintin Hogg, M.P., a young Etonian Tory, flew into a passion with that wicked "old man" Dr. Joad, and upbraided him for having taken an active part in this bygone ebullition of undergraduate revolt. Yet "King and Country" in Yugoslavia, in Italy and in Greece is synonymous with Court intrigue, appeasement, and financial "spheres of influence". In England, its accepted connotation is still the coalowners, the Bank of England, I.C.I., the Prudential, the Railways, the Gas Light and Coke Company, etc., etc. Fond as we are of our Royal Family, no one, except the Old Guard of reactionaries, supposes that this is a dynastic, national, or imperialist war. Probably most of the men who took part in the Oxford Union debate are now fighting, but they are certainly not doing so for "King and Country."

My Riviera experiences provided what may be termed a "pre-view" of the underlying causes of our subsequent disasters, and it at least aided the always difficult process of clarifying principles. It is all very well to enjoin others to "clear their minds of cant", but by no means as simple as it looks to clear one's own. The cant of "unity", where there is basic divergence, is cant in its most insidious form, especially when it is cloaked by an appeal for loyalty to the country, to the Party, or to "Christianity". Theoretically, it should be possible for Dr. Negrin, General Franco, Senor Alvarez del Vayo and Count Jordana, aided by Sir Samuel Hoare, Mr. Harry Pollitt, Mr. Oliver Lyttelton, Stalin and President Roosevelt to get round a table and apply their respective intelligences to working out a plan for the good of Spain. Theoretically, Socialists like Aneurin Bevan or Sir Richard Acland, capitalist collaborators, and power politicians, should be able to sink their differences and work together "loyally", as "patriots", for the ultimate salvation of their country. On examination, such theories are cant, and such attempts can only fail. In spite of the tears and prayers of Lord Halifax and the airy assertions of Winston Churchill, the world *is* divided into "ideological blocs", and the most ardent patriot and the most loyal citizen-soldier cannot escape the decision as to which of the two great conflicting principles he is prepared to fight for. All the rest is cant.

In England we can expect no more last chances. If what is termed the "swing to the Left", which is in reality the will to live, is again frustrated by the profit-seeking business magnates who caused the second global war, then another generation of English-men will be sacrificed to Moloch. There is no discernible alternative. Another twenty years of the Tory rule which, in spite of all the sacrifices of the British people, has left " England" without a real friend in the world, will see this nation reduced to a third-rate satellite power, composed of a handful of Masters and a horde of slaves. We have on the one side the example of Russia : on the other, the example of " Franco " Spain. (Not for nothing have our reactionaries called in the aid of the Vatican to hide their Mammon-worship under a cloak of Christianity.) Our internal enemies are often charming people—nice chaps, decent fellows. But unless like Sir Arnold Wilson, Lord Lothian, and other repentant Tories, they see the light before it is too late, it will be their lives or ours. It will be their England—an England of hunger, desolation and despair for the masses and opulence for the few—or the resurgent, democratic, progressive and regenerated England for which so many of our sons have died. The patriot must make his choice and be prepared to face the fact that those of his own class who have chosen differently will call him " anti-British."

CHAPTER THIRTEEN

SOLD AGAIN

I

THE atmosphere of the London to which I returned in March, 1930, was about as exhilarating as that of a city under foreign domination. Flaming youth had grown as sullen as an un-seasoned toper on the morning after the night before, while " idealists " had turned into cynics, and the burden of their political comments could be summed up in the words: "Sold again ". The " invisible revolution ", which so many millions

believed to have triumphed in 1924, had petered out in disillusion.
Ramsay MacDonald's secession to the enemy, in the following
year, merely registered a collapse which had already occurred.
The 1917 Club, which had decayed into a cheap lunching place
for civil servants and minor Labour Party officials, was dreary
beyond belief, and obviously on its last legs.   All the excitement,
all the hope, all the seething life and vitality of the early 'twenties
seemed to have been smothered under a concrete layer of
frustration.   The angry child's complaint : " What's the good of
anything ?   Why, nothing !" was almost justified.

Even the old friendliness and good fellowship of London struck
the returned native as being temporarily in abeyance.   Those
who had been lucky enough to secure jobs were terrified of losing
them, and slammed their office doors in the faces of less fortunate
colleagues.   Rents, judged by Continental standards, were
fantastic, and the cost of living in proportion.   In 1931, Ramsay
MacDonald, now a mere puppet manipulated by the astute
Baldwin, got his " Doctor's Mandate ", with such a colossal
majority as to render Parliamentary government a farce.   He
seemed more in need of a doctor himself than any of his patients.
His orations went on and on and on and up and up and up in
clouds of woolly verbiage, and even the tactful editors of *Hansard*
found difficulty in reducing his sentences to order and in infusing
any meaning into them.   When he was succeeded by Baldwin,
who, whatever may have been his political faults, was a master of
English rhetorical prose, many of us experienced a faint sensation
of relief.   If Baldwin never meant what he said, at least he said
what he meant to say in impeccably constructed sentences.

Dismal as was the political outlook at the beginning of the
'thirties, there did not, at first, appear to be any war clouds on the
horizon.   However discouraging the internal situation might be
from the Socialist standpoint, it seemed possible to trust Baldwin
and the bankers not to involve us in avoidable catastrophe by
re-arming our former foes.   If they were not re-armed, how could
they attack us ?

With the peace of Europe not in danger, so far as the ordinary
citizen was aware, there seemed little point in worrying one's
head about the squabbles of the Labour bosses and the intrigues
of the professional politicians.   I had seen too much of the inner
working of the Labour Party in the early 'twenties to have any
faith in it as then constituted.   The complicated and hopelessly
undemocratic constitution of the Party, which gave far too much

power to the platform, made it impossible for the majority of the rank-and-file either to force their leaders to stick to their principles or to kick them out if they refused.

I believed in 1930, as I believe with greater certainty in 1944, that only a United Socialist Party, broad enough to include both Communists and middle-class Radicals and free from the domination of the Trade Unions, can provide an alternative Government to the Bankers' Coalition. In 1930 the political vacuum created by the moral disintegration of the Liberal Party remained unfilled, and caused the disfranchisement of millions of voters. History, when it does not move so rapidly that it jerks everyone off their feet, usually proceeds at a snail's pace. Few political dreamers ever live long enough to see their dreams realized. Perhaps, in the aftermath of the present war, those who still call themselves " Liberals " will realize that if they are not Socialists they are only " Conservatives with a conscience ", and therefore vote-splitters. It is a hopeful sign that just as Fascism in this country is the offspring of Tory Imperialism, so Common Wealth is the vigorous grandchild of Gladstonian Liberalism. A young Socialist phœnix has thus arisen from the Liberal ashes. Such at least, as a Tennysonian optimist, is my belief.

In the early 'thirties, when there was little sign of spiritual regeneration, little trace of any uplifting cause or movement to which a descendant of Victorian Radicals felt prompted to adhere, I engrossed myself, not without relief, in normal literary activities. There was no market, anyway, for any form of journalism in the vein of Peter Porcupine. The Cobbetts of the day remained mute, inglorious and unpaid, with little chance of letting off their puffs of steam and showers of sparks.

Only in matters concerned with civil liberties and in defence of what are loosely referred to as " amenities ", subjects which are outside the sphere of party politics, did I find it possible to write the sort of articles which the national newspapers accepted.

After the personal freedom and ease of Continental life, among the first things that struck me about England in the new decade was the numberless restrictions and controls which the Tory plutocracy, in close association with the worst elements in the Labour Party, had managed to impose on the dispirited common people. As a " Radical ", by instinct and temperament, it was borne in on me with considerable force that if the average man could not stand up for his rights on minor issues, he would never do so on major ones. Owing to the enormous number of unemployed, those who had jobs were naturally terrified of losing them. As a result, the ease with which anyone who " made a noise like a boss ", even if he were only an unauthorized busybody, could interfere with his neighbours' private lives seemed to me positively degrading.

On this point, Harold Monro and I, having inherited a libertarian tradition, found ourselves once again in close accord. We had worked together in 1919 to protest against the " Black-and-Tans." From a note dated April 25th, 1931, I see that by then we were once more collaborating.

" Dear Douglas,—I am sending you a letter which appeared in Thursday's *Daily Telegraph*, and also one from myself which appeared today. Here is an opportunity to make a noise. It is everyone's vital concern that the Puritan and Prohibitionist should not be allowed to get the upper hand. You are just the person to follow the matter up. Please do not fail. I shall expect to read a letter from you in *The Daily Telegraph*." Throughout the 'thirties, I wrote letters, articles, and pamphlets in defence of civil liberties, convinced that the only way to get the man in the street to take an active interest in world politics was to persuade him to make a start by protesting against the minor tyrannies which he could understand. The campaign was fun, even if the results were not encouraging.

It should have been the business of the Conservative " public, school-and-university " class to rally round A. P. Herbert, E. S. P. Haynes, Harold Monro, myself and other stalwarts in defence of the freedom and happiness of the people. Even from the vote-catching standpoint, it would have been a wise move on the part of the political wire-pullers of all parties to stand up for civil liberties. Unfortunately, the Conservatives of the Carlton Club, like the Conservatives of Transport House, detested the idea of the people enjoying any freedom. Freedom was reserved for the well-off, in particular the monopoly capitalist, who, protected by our libel laws, was free to control—and harass—the citizen consumer. Their argument was that if the restrictions imposed as a " war emergency " were relaxed, even in regard to beer-drinking, " Bolshevism " might result. Joynson-Hicks, later Lord Brentford, was the leading " Wowser " of the 'twenties, and had many Labour supporters. In the miserable recreation ground, in the borough from which " Jix " took his title, I was amused to notice a board displaying the characteristic injunction : " All Games Strictly Prohibited." Anything that could possibly be done by the authorities to annoy, exasperate and degrade the masses who had won the war for them was indulged in *con amore*. No doubt they will behave in the same way when the present war is over, if they get the chance. Even unofficial and self-constituted " authorities " such as the Lord's Day Observance Society, the Public Morality Council, and similar bodies, preyed upon the spiritless populace, prevented the children of the poor from playing games on Sundays in public parks and gardens, closed " lovers' lanes", prowled over commons with torches, and generally carried on a ruthless warfare against the few pleasures of the helpless and inarticulate poor. Not "*panem et circenses*", but, "here's your dole —idler and parasite—and mind you don't spend it all on beer ", was the Tory receipe for Merrie England.

The middle and upper classes, instead of making common cause with their unfortunate and downtrodden compatriots, rather enjoyed restrictions which they could so easily evade. " Class " legislation thus fostered " class " arrogance. The 'twenties were the heyday of night clubs and boozing in prohibited hours, with the resulting, indeed inevitable, corruption of a section of the police, became one of the outstanding features of the social life of the decade. The " Queen " of the night club racket, the famous Ma Meyrick of the " 43 " Club in Gerrard Street, was a woman of indomitable courage, determination and resource. Had she possessed any political sense, had she had some modicum of public spirit and conducted her operations with some worthier object than that of making money, she might have enjoyed the fame and nation-wide popularity of a twentieth-century John Wilkes. She was constantly prosecuted and finally sentenced to a sharp term of imprisonment. Unfortunately, instead of becoming the leader of a libertarian crusade, she only achieved the status of a " criminal " who aroused much good-natured public sympathy.

A friend with a car used frequently to drive us out on Sunday mornings to lunch on bread and cheese and beer in a particularly attractive pub in a Berkshire village. One Sunday, in winter, we found no fire in the usually cosy saloon bar.

" I'm sorry," said the landlord. " But it's not worth while lighting it because *they've closed the piano*."

" Who's ' they ' ? " I enquired.

" Why, the magistrates, of course."

I asked if he could tell me the names of these individuals who had had the impudence to close his piano, and he reeled off the usual list of retired Colonels, rich spinsters, and local busybodies who " sat on the Bench."

" Well, you've got a horse pond in the village," I remarked. " Why on earth don't you introduce them to it, the next time they show their noses in these parts ?"

" Oh, Mr. G., you will have your joke ! How should I earn my living if I lost my licence ?"

To this there was, of course, no answer. It would have been useless on this particular issue to say, " if you don't like the Tories, why do you vote for them ?" because the Opposition parties were equally prohibitionist and puritanical. George Lansbury, the only politician of Cabinet rank who ever sympathised with the people's desire to enjoy their simple pleasures unmolested, was out of office, and few of his Labour colleagues shared his views. The Liberals were even more prohibitionist than the Tories. Had not Lloyd George, the father of Dora, observed during the war that we have " three enemies to fight, Germany, Austria and beer, and beer is the worst of them " ? The Tories, at least produced the stuff and grew fat by selling it, even if they abused their power to bully the consumer.

Another rampant evil which flourished unchecked in the 'twenties and reached its apex in the 'thirties was the destruction by speculators of the natural beauties and architectural heritage of the country so many had died to defend. Vandalism for its own sake, not merely for profit, was freely indulged in not only by the commercial plutocracy and avaricious ground landlords, but also by Government departments and municipal authorities. Destroying architectural masterpieces, hacking down trees, defiling rivers and spreading ugliness and squalor all over our pleasant land became a mania, a contagious moral disease, like Fascism or anti-Semitism and, as we are now aware, closely akin to them. Public opinion, on this matter as on every other, was for the most part apathetic or in abeyance : indeed, the whole country seemed in a kind of trance. Fortunately, there was a small group of enthusiasts, mostly despised Left Wing intellectuals, who still ardently cherished the traditions of humanism. These champions of decency, aided by the gallant army of " hikers ", fought during the Armistice years with unrelenting zeal and, eventually, with some small measure of success, against the onslaught of the " octopus."

II

With the Bankers' Crisis of 1931 and the formation of the National Government on August 3rd, the period with which this book deals came to an end in a confused welter of treachery, fraud and, for the working classes, despair. The people had indeed been " sold again ". The " dole ", always represented by the Tory press as charity, conferred upon lazy people, too idle to seek work and only anxious to live on a comfortable wage without earning it, had been bad enough, but the addition of the Means Test aroused fierce anger in those subjected to it. The National Unemployed Workers' Movement held public meetings, and organized a Hunger March from the provinces to London. The general unrest was made the excuse for savage retaliation by the Tories, which took the form of police raids on working-class tenements and arrests, often of quite innocent people.

The excuse for forming the new Government was the alleged necessity of keeping the pound on gold. With shameless dishonesty, MacDonald had himself photographed holding up a letter, posted in Germany during the inflation period, bearing stamps costing millions of marks. This terrorized the gullible public who were also told that their savings in the Post Office Savings Bank would be raided.

On September 9th, the new Government brought in an Economy Bill, forced upon it, as many believed, by the Wall Street bankers from whom loans had been obtained, which involved a ten per cent. cut in all wages paid to Government servants, including the Navy. The resulting Naval strike at Invergordon led to the suspension of the gold standard. There was no inflation, the pound kept its internal value and the export trade immediately improved.

On October 6th, the General Election was held at which the " National " Government made its famous plea for a " doctor's mandate ". All the most prominent Liberal and Labour leaders ratted to the side of the bankers, and joined in the appeal for " united action ". The Government secured 554 seats. The Opposition consisted of 16 Liberals and 52 Labour men, led by George Lansbury and Arthur Henderson.

Put in a few words, the " Bankers' Crisis " of 1931 was the result of borrowing money at low interest for short terms and lending it at high interest for long terms.

Mr. Hilaire Belloc can hardly, in view of his Roman Catholic

bias, be accused of being in any sense a " Red ". His account of
the operations which led to the crisis will, therefore, with some
readers, carry extra weight. " The Bank of England," he wrote,
" and with it those who control the issue of bank credit in England,
saw in the impoverishment and exhaustion of the Reich through
war and defeat an opportunity of placing great loans to Germany
at enormously high interest. It never occurred to the money-
lenders—more accurately the credit-lenders—that, unless they
occupied territory they could have no security for the repayment
of the vast usury which they expected for the advances made.
To take an example out of a great number : the City of Berlin
borrowed from London at 10 per cent. for municipal purposes.
The 10 per cent. was really more like 12 when all the frills and
commissions had been allowed for." He goes on to say that
" the usurers did not doubt for a moment that the promise of the
City of Berlin to pay £12 a year for every £100 worth of credit
extended would be kept. . . . We all know what happened.
In a very short time the Germans refused to pay the interest, while
keeping the material goods and services, which were the product of
the credit extended to them. One of the main uses to which they
put this advantage, which had been given them with such
enormous lack of political judgment by the English banking
monopoly, was to set about building a new fleet. Today, the
taxpayer of Great Britain has to find usury on vast new sums of
credit extended to Germans by his own English banking monopoly
in order that the Germans may build a new fleet. The Englishman has to pay all right ; the banking monopoly is sure of its
money in his case ; but the English money advanced in German
loans has gone down the wind. It will never be recovered. The
English banks have rebuilt a new Germany rather than a new
England."

The choice of the banking monopoly, which then as now, controlled our foreign policy, for the office of Secretary of State for
Foreign Affairs was Sir John Simon. A few months after his
appointment, by refusing to follow up Mr. Stimson's proposal of
combined action against Japanese aggression, he pressed the
button which let loose the avalanche in 1939. Today, hundreds
of thousands of English parents can add the words : " which
killed my son."

THE END

POSTSCRIPT

I

THIS book was completed in June, 1944, and at this writing (March, 1945), it seems probable that production difficulties may postpone its publication for a further nine months, if not longer. By the time it appears, therefore, if current indications are to be relied upon, a General Election may have revealed the extent to which the average voter has taken to heart the lessons of the past. It may also have revealed how far the wave of optimism created by the Crimea Conference was justified.

While it would be the height of folly, at this juncture, to indulge in prophecy, certain comparisons can be drawn between the position of Thomas Atkins Senior, on his demobilization in 1919—and that of Thomas Junior in 1945—which must remain broadly true, no matter what the future may have in store for us.

The common soldier who joined up between 1914 and 1918 was a political simpleton compared with his successor, regarded the fighting, with grumbling philosophy, as a necessary job of work and assumed that victory over the German aggressor would be followed by a lasting peace. Like his ancestors at Agincourt, he fought for " King and Country ", and the necessary crusading spirit was generated by such simple slogans as, " Brave Little Belgium ", " A War to End War ", " A War to make the world safe for Democracy ". " National Unity " did not have to be ceaselessly proclaimed : it could be taken for granted, because it really existed. Apart from a handful of political pacifists and religious " objectors ", Britain was a nation in arms, and there was unanimity of purpose between the leaders and the led. Whatever Sassoon's " Harry and Jack " may have thought about the professional competence of some of their generals, at least they never suspected the Brass Hats of being secretly in sympathy with the enemy. The predominantly Liberal House of Commons, elected in 1910, contained a high percentage of able and public-spirited men, and the War Cabinet, under the inspiring leadership of a Radical democrat at the height of his mental energy and physical vigour, was, by comparison with the present Cabinet—Mr. Churchill excepted—a galaxy of talent. Every soldier was aware that one of Lloyd George's first actions, after displacing Asquith, was to break the stranglehold of the naval and military mandarins, who, by their opposition to tanks and convoys, had so nearly brought about our defeat. When the " cease fire " sounded, therefore, the Welsh Wizard's prestige was at its height, and even " old Contemptibles " were prepared to concede him the title of the " Man who won the War." His record as a champion of the people's rights, combined with his humble origin, made Atkins Senior believe that the would not only " win the peace ", but be able and willing to implement his promises to the millions who, under his leadership, had sung their way through mud and blood, through Terror to Triumph.

The soldier who returned in 1919 was treated as a hero, rapturously welcomed for a few hectic weeks, patted on the back by his former employer, and encouraged in the assumption that as he had gallantly " done his bit ", *they* would now do theirs. Had he not been offered the prospect of steady employment, a decent home, a fair share of the land he had fought for, a peaceful and prosperous future ? To the relief of getting out of khaki and saying " goodbye to all that " were thus added all the Pleasures of Hope. Disillusion quickly followed. When he started asking for a job, his popularity waned and the police grew watchful and attentive.

Most civilians, whether employers or organized workers, had not only done very well out of the war, but had suffered no worse privations than those due to restricted rations. There was a housing shortage, due to the cessation of normal building operations, but very few houses had been destroyed by enemy action. No great intelligence was required on Atkins Senior's part to enable him to realize that there was an abundance of wealth and man-power available to make good all deficiencies. If the Government could spend £100 million on expeditions to Russia, in the attempt to restore the Czarist tyranny for the benefit of London bondholders, the plea that " we can't afford it " was hardly a valid excuse for not building the houses so urgently required. In 1919, as in 1945, the provision of a roof was the first demand of the ex-Serviceman and the apparent inability to comply with it was the first intimation he had of the all-round betrayal which so quickly followed. In 1919, however, Atkins Senior was still hopeful, still unaware of what was in store for him in the near future. The crusade against " Bolshevism ", the return to " Sound Finance ", the savage treatment of the miners, the deliberately-provoked General Strike and its suppression, the uncleared slums, starvation in a world of plenty, the dole, the Means Test—all these lay ahead. It was in the atmosphere of poverty, frustration and despair, resulting from the Conservative class-war against the common people, that Thomas Junior grew to manhood.

The " Thomas Junior " we have in mind, who in the past five years has proved himself the backbone of the fighting Services, has not only, in most cases, received a better education than his father, but his intelligence has been sharpened in the school of bitter experience. He knows perfectly well " what happened last time ", he has no illusions, is not easy to fool, and in the course of years has become allergic to "dope", whether put out by the press, the B.B.C., anti-Soviet generals, or " Government spokesmen ". Even his alleged " apathy " may prove to be no more than a conservation of mental energy against the time when it is needed.*

When the call came to him, in September 1939, to repair the blunders and treacheries of the " guilty men " he had a pretty shrewd idea of the issues at stake and a pretty clear realization of the peril into which the politicians had plunged both his own future and that of his country. Unlike the civilian, the Service man has not forgotten Norway, Dunkirk, Singapore, or similar regrettable incidents, for which he holds the collaborationists of Munich to blame.

It was not until the phoney war ended and Chamberlain at last made way for Churchill that Thomas Junior began to develop any measure of confidence that the " high-ups " in the War Office were really on his side.   At least the old Bull-Dog, with his cigar and his V-signs, was a " resister"!   There were to be no more surrender, no more Fifth Column treachery, no more appeasement, no more personal letters to enemy dictators. Britain was now, at last, united in her will to survive.   Miracles were called for and miracles were accomplished.

After June 22nd, 1941, when the War Office experts' confident predictions that Russia would be overcome in a fortnight proved to be as veracious as Sir Walter Citrine's reports on the campaign in Finland, the war began to make ideological sense.   Unfortunately, when Pearl Harbour added the United States to the Grand Alliance, there came a renewal of doubt about its political direction at the highest levels. " Survival " was assured : what about liberation ?   There was, of course, no question about the Premier's determination to beat the " Narzis ", nor was his loyalty to our Russian allies, in so far as they had this end in view, open to suspicion. There was, however, a widespread and deep-seated distrust among " other ranks " of the men by whom the Premier was surrounded, and of the Party whose leadership he had accepted.   The presence of Sir Stafford Cripps in Moscow had done little to neutralize the aroma arising from Sir Samuel Hoare's activities in Madrid.

In November 1942, events occurred which renewed the suspicions of Atkins Junior that the war was becoming, once again, phoney. The double-crossing of de Gaulle, under American pressure, the collaboration with Darlan, the failure to seize Bizerta, the revelation that the long-awaited Second Front against Fascism was, in reality, more like a Bankers' Front against revolutionary democracy, provided a moral shock to the intelligent soldier which, while it in no way impaired his fighting qualities, increased his already profound cynicism.

---

* The Labour landside which has occurred while these pages are going to press confirmed this prediction.

The invasion of Italy, which might have been crowned with swift and dramatic success if directed with political intelligence, was sabotaged before it started. Lord Cranborne, replying to criticism in the House of Lords, made the astounding excuse that " if we had called on the Italian nation to rise [after the overthrow of Mussolini], it might have produced chaos." To avoid " chaos "—the word used by reactionaries to denote the democratic alternative to Fascist " law and order "—the Italian quisling monarch and his henchman, Badoglio, were accorded British and American support, Fascist officials were maintained in power by Amgot, patriotic partisans were refused admission to the " Royal " Italian Army, the Black Market flourished, and apathy, misery and starvation followed in the wake of the " liberators ". Military " intelligence " had not apparently discovered that sunny Italy was subject to icy and ferocious winter gales and that its picturesque mountains made almost unscaleable barriers, easily defensible by comparatively small bodies of experienced troops. Of the large number of Englishmen who had an intimate knowledge of the country and spoke Italian fluently, few seemed to have been called in for consultation. Thus the dreary process of " inching " went on month after month, year after year, and in spite of the heroism and endurance of the common soldiers, and the professional competence of their commanders in the field, the " liberation of Italy ", owing to a confusion of political aims at the highest levels, degenerated into one of the most disappointing and long-drawn-out campaigns of the whole war. What Thomas Junior thinks of it, what he thinks of the way in which the patriots of Yugoslavia, Greece, Belgium, and France have since been treated, is revealed by the significance given to the word to " liberate ", in soldiers' slang. The reasons for the breakdown of U.N.R.R.A. are better understood by the intelligent " other ranks " than they appear to be by complacent Members of Parliament.

Thomas Junior is above all things a realist. In spite of the Gestapo-like efforts of " Security ", M.I.5, and the hated S.I.B. to discourage the expression of progressive opinions, his letters home indicate that he has by no means abandoned his right, as a democratic citizen, to think for himself. Particularly is this true of the forgotten men who for the past four years have formed part of our huge inactive armies in the Middle East. These " sand-happy old-timers ", whose precise function has never been enquired into by a worn-out Parliament, have, indeed, nothing to do in their spare time except reflect. The suppression of the pamphlet on the Beveridge Report, the suppression of the Cairo soldiers' parliament and victimization of its principal organizers, and the petty persecution of the *Daily Worker*, told their own story. Like the anti-Soviet speeches of reactionary generals, these clumsy attempts to regulate opinion did little more than make converts to a vague form of " communism."

The lines on which many overseas soldiers have been thinking, though familiar to most of us who have contacts with men in the British (and Canadian) armies, would perhaps surprise Transport House almost as much as the Carlton Club. The unanimity with which the average soldier takes for granted that the conduct of the war has been interfered with by pressure groups of Anglo-American financiers, cartelists, monopoly capitalists and Catholic Fascists, is astonishing. Many hold the view, quoting both Stalin and Hitler in support of their opinion, that the war in Europe could have been ended by the spring of 1944, had it not been for these sinister " influences."

Atkins Junior though his sources of information may be scanty, is nobody's fool. He is aware that at all the conferences which have affected his own fate and that of the world, Labour has been left outside on the mat. Among the crowds of experts and underlings, flown now to Casablanca, now to Quebec, now to Teheran, never has a name been mentioned which could be identified as that of a Socialist, a " worker ", or even an anti-Fascist. If, occasionally, a democratic voice is heard over the B.B.C., it is always promptly followed by the announcement that the speaker, for mysterious reasons, has been muzzled or dismissed. Throughout the Army promotion has always seemed to overlook those men who have been incautious enough to admit their democratic sympathies and anti-Fascist " ideology " ; and Thomas Junior, is alert enough to realize that the same discrimination has probably been at work at home, in all the Government offices.

When the " Cease Fire " sounds in Europe, Atkins Junior would be dumb indeed, if, after all the anti-Bolshevist dope to which he has been subjected, he refrained from instituting comparison between the Russian plans for post-war reconstruction and the collapse and chaos which he will find awaiting him when he returns to inquire for his prefabricated home.

One reason why, until a General Election produces a change of Government, there is no possibility of Atkins Junior securing the home to which he has been looking forward for so many weary years is as obvious to every intelligent soldier as it is to every intelligent civilian. Homes, whether permanent or temporary, have to be built on land. Rivers of blood have been shed, in two prolonged and exhausting wars, to liberate the soil of Britain. So far in vain. Most of it still remains in the grip of a small number of landlords, whose interests are represented in the House of Commons by the huge Conservative majority. It is this majority which forced the shelving of the Uthwatt compromise and has since sabotaged all municipal planning and hamstrung every large-scale building programme. The blood of our sons is not enough for the landed gentry. They demand in compensation more than the pre-war value of their land before they will permit one home to be built for one hero, or one historic English city to rise again from its ruins. What they have they hold.

The political record of this clique of landlords, a few of whom also own a substantial part of the nation's coal supplies, does not appreciably differ from that of members of the same privileged class in Spain, Hungary, Poland, Italy and other European countries. They fawned on Hitler before the war, cringed to Mussolini, supported non-intervention, hailed Franco as a " Christian gentleman ", and have since made a petulant effort to wreck the Crimea agreement. In some of the liberated countries the large estates have already been confiscated and their " collaborationist " proprietors put on trial. This precedent in no way disturbs the British landlord, whose tenants, by their blood and guts, saved the nation from servitude to the dictators whom he formerly admired.

So it happens that if Thomas Junior picks up a Labour newspaper he can still read items like the following : " If a wealthy Sussex landowner does not change his mind before tomorrow, an expectant mother, her husband—a wounded, shell-shocked Dunkirk hero—and their two children, will be turned out of their little home into the street. Major——, of —— Park, is the landowner. He lives surrounded by an almost feudal atmosphere in a palatial mansion overlooking a lake, on a large estate complete with seven cottages and extensive stabling. He has several servants to wait on him." The major denied that the ejection order was made because his tenant " is an active trade unionist and member of the Labour Party."

Among news items in provincial papers, Thomas Junior will find similar cases of working-class families being evicted from " tied " cottages and forced to seek refuge in the workhouse, owing to the inability of local authorities to provide alternative accommodation. In the advertisement columns of the same papers he will discover eye-opening appeals like the following, which appeared on March 10th, 1945. " Wanted, by a widower, without children, for a country house near— ; 38 miles from London and near bus route, a thoroughly experienced COOK ; used to best service ; good references essential ; house-parlourmaid and between maid kept, also excellent daily woman for rough work ; house with every comfort and convenience ; home farm with eggs, milk, fruit and vegetables ; liberal dietary ; good wages ; safe area ; fare paid to view."

When Thomas Junior returns from Burma, Belgium, the Mediterranean, the Middle East, and, in due course, from Berlin, to see how the country has been faring in his absence, how his dependants have been treated, how far the Government has got with its much advertised plans for Education and Public Health, how it has safeguarded the young of both sexes and maintained the principle of equality of sacrifice, it is improbable that he will feel inclined to accord them "three hearty British cheers."

He will have other shocks in store for him besides such anomalies as the fact that a good cook, or even an unskilled charwoman, can earn twice as much as a highly-qualified school-teacher, nurse or " medical auxiliary ". If his home is in a rural area, he may be surprised to discover how easily the middle-class " lady ", especially if she is an officer's wife, has managed to evade Mr. Bevin's compulsions. Perhaps she may have consented to do a little unpaid work for some charity (under Royal patronage and run by really nice people) or to serve once or twice a week in a canteen, with a petrol allowance as a reward. The rest of her time has been devoted to leisurely shopping, while her less fortunate sisters, those who are not " ladies ", are busy on the job to which they were directed.

Mothers working in factories, whose husbands are in the Army, have, for obvious reasons no chance of keeping a watchful eye on their growing boys and girls. Without being a moralist the soldier has the ordinary man's decent feelings about the welfare of children.

When he comes back to discover what has been happening to his own and other soldier's kids, it may surprise him that the unemployed " ladies " were not called on to help keep them out of mischief. Hordes of young girls, as we are all aware, have been allowed to run wild between puberty and the calling-up age, in districts congested with overseas troops. If there was one social problem which the Government might have foreseen and provided for, this was it. After all, these girls are the future mothers of the race. In a country so weighted with professional good-workers, it may seem odd to Thomas Junior to find that his daughter or kid sister has been allowed to contract V.D., or a premature pregnancy, simply because it was nobody's business to round her up and teach her a job in her most vulnerable years. The fact that a wretched girl of eighteen, who left school in 1940, has come within sight of the gallows in 1945, has apparently made no impression on the national conscience.

Of primary importance, from Thomas Junior's point of view, is, of course, the record of the Government in regard to the pay and treatment of the fighting Services. In every theatre of war in which the British soldier has come in contact with his comrades in the United States and Dominion Armies, he has been embarrassed by his inability, through lack of money, to mix with them on equal terms. By comparison with the clubs and hostels established for the benefit of the United States and Dominion troops, the British N.A.A.F.I. is—typically British. Of all the English-speaking armies, the men of the British Army and their dependents have, from the beginning of the war, been the worst paid and the worst cared for. Proof of this is the fact that the Charity Racket, one of the most evil-smelling scandals of World War One, has again been permitted to still the national conscience by giving private aid, under humiliating conditions, to those whose necessities should be the first charge on the Exchequer. The worst feature of the war charities are the types of Mayfair harpies, toadies to Royalty, tuft-hunters and knighthood-seekers—so often satirised by comic columnists—which this form of benevolence seems invariably to attract.   No doubt many excellent persons, both paid and voluntary, have worked unselfishly to distribute public generosity on approved " Charity Organization " lines.   But the whole system reeks of class patronage, of a kind which would never be tolerated either in the Dominions or the United States.

The politically-minded soldier has, on a variety of grounds, a deep hatred of Conservative government. He is critical of Churchill's conduct of the War, revolted by his foreign policy, and has no faith in his capacity to " win the peace."

When the time comes for him to express his feelings by means of the ballot-box, he will do so in no uncertain manner.

II

In regard to the outlook for literature and the arts, which should be this writer's particular concern, the contrast between 1919 and 1945 is perhaps even more striking than the contrast between the outlook and prospects of Thomas Junior and those of his predecessor.   If more striking, it is, nevertheless, far more confused and difficult even to attempt to define.   Today, there is no apparent evidence, as there was in 1919, of any uprush of creative energy, waiting to break loose as soon as the restraints are removed.   On the contrary, there is considerable evidence, to be found in the numerous miscellanies of prose and verse which have managed to secure sufficient paper to enable them to appear, of a species of ultra-refined nihilism.   This shows itself in a rather pathetic yearning to continue what has been termed " the æsthetic adventure ", in a somewhat different form.   Eager glances have, of course, been turned across the Channel, and there has already been some alarmed scurrying from London to Paris and back.   France has too long been the recognized centre of European culture for even our most epicene highbrows to be able to ignore what is happening there. But what is happening is inexpressibly painful to those who believe that art and literature should function in a rarefied and peaceful atmosphere, above all the battles, especially the " ideological " battle. Like sex, literature ought, they think, to be " sublimated ".   Or ought it ?   Sublimated sex does not enable the race to continue.   Can sublimated literature produce the living masterpieces of the future ? Or, for that matter, a literature heavily infected with Catholic Fascism and similar mental diseases ?   Evidently, the French do not think so, Such headlines as the following : " La trahison de l'esprit est aussi grave que celle du soldat devant l'ennemi ", and " La collaboration de plume ne pardonne pas ", indicate that, on our nearest neigh bours world events have made their inescapable impact. A " purge "has. in fact, started, and a purge, though of a strangely haphazard kind still continues.   Some months before the liberation of France, critics in English periodicals of a supposedly Left tendency, went out of their way to show their freedom from " ideological " bias by boosting the works of the most notorious of French literary collaborators. These papers had nothing to say about writers of the Resistance, such as Aragon, Eluard, Maritain, Mauriac or Bernanos. That would have meant " taking sides." Instead, the creator of the " egomanical misogynist ", Costals, was held up to admiration as being "in the front rank of contemporary writers ", though one critic had the grace to admit that he " leaves a bad smell in his wake."

Apparently the French have abandoned this beautiful English impartiality, this whole-hearted devotion to art for art's sake. They actually shot traitors without the least regard for their literary merit. They even imprison Academicians, like the elderly and almost sainted Charles Maurras. Collaborationist newspaper owners and the heads of pro-Nazi publishing firms have had punishment meted out to them in Paris no less drastically than the journalists they employed and the authors whose books they sponsored. Even painters, sculptors and musicians have been made answerable to their fellow-craftsmen and to the public conscience. Astonishingly, the French seem to have realized that between the Arts on the one hand and Fascism on the other, there can be no quarter and no compromise. The complication caused among English converts by the fact that the Catholic Church comprises both political Catholics—of whom Göring, Göbbels, General Franco, Dr. Salazar, Mr. Robert Murphy, Mr. Byrnes, Mr. Ivone Kirkpatrick and His Holiness, Pius XII, are among the most conspicuous examples—and religious, or " Christian ", Catholics, has failed to confuse the issues in a country where Catholicism has been indigenous throughout the ages. To the French mind, Catholic " Satanism ", the philosophical basis of which was so ably expounded by the Marquis de Sade in Juliette's famous dialogue with the Pope, has long been familiar ; so also has its opposite, Catholic Humanism. Religious French Catholics have never forgotten the Jansenists, the tradition of Port Royal, or Pascal's denunciation of the Jesuits in *Les Provinciales*.

In the age-long struggle between the great opposed abstractions labelled for convenience, Life and Death, Good and Evil, Progress and Reaction, Civilization and Barbarism, the French writers and artists seem now to be emerging once again, with some unity of purpose, as defenders of Civilization. From their present " passion of the mind," it is at least permissible to hope that yet another great period of artistic creation may eventually result.

Meanwhile, the violence of emotion which has found vent in treason trials, and has even disturbed the classic calm of the French Academy, is viewed in London with mixed feelings, with a certain excitement and a considerable amount of apprehension. " They can't do that there 'ere " : or can they ?

For a variety of reasons, the chief of them being that the French system of State Education is far more democratic than our own is likely to become for another twenty years, the grounds for anxiety seem few. No English " collaborationist " author, publisher, journalist, or newspaper proprietor need glace at a lamp post with a shudder of apprehension. Indeed, it is far more likely that the outspoken anti-Fascist " resisters " in our midst may be " disciplined," like the Greek professors and intellectuals who declared themselves in support of E.A.M.

From 1938 onwards several reputable English publishers have taken upon themselves to exercise a private and unofficial censorship of the political views of authors whose works they were under contract to produce—always in the interests of Appeasement and to prevent any criticism of our attitude towards Hitler, Mussolini, and Franco appearing under their imprints. To my knowledge, there is no case on record of any Fascist sympathiser having had his freedom to express his opinions similarly denied to him. The majority of English authors are, and always have been, as strongly anti-Fascist as the majority of their French comrades : a great many of us were violently opposed to Munich and to Non-Intervention. I know of at least four cases, all of them " fully documented ", in which publishers repudiated their contracts rather then allow the writers concerned to say openly what they thought about these national issues. There may have been others. The repudiation of a contract, for an author, has exactly the same financial consequences as a refusal to pay his salary, at the time it is due, has on a person normally employed. It means that he cannot meet his household obligations, pay his rent or feed himself and his family. That being so, what may have appeared to the French as a guilty silence on our part, a " trahison des clercs ", is at least partly accounted for.

Another reason for the paucity of comment by English men of letters on questions of life or death for the art they practise—a reason which has nothing to do with any secret censorship—is the fact that, like clerics, they are told that it is not their business to descend into the political arena. This view is not only upheld by almost every English literary critic of consequence, but is also, for more questionable reasons, adhered to by most of the professional politicians of the Left. In the eyes of the pundits, propaganda novels, except, of course, those which, like the admirable works of the late Charlotte M. Yonge, are propaganda for the virtues and Christian principles of the landed gentry, are not " good literature " and should, therefore, be discouraged. Good literature, in their opinion, is the literature which appeals only to the few who have received the specialized education which can enable them to appreciate it. Nothing, therefore, dealing with current events, intended for consumption by the masses, can be worth consideration unless put out by an " expert " duly recognised in Bloomsbury. The author, as citizen, has neither rights nor duties: the author, as artist, must preserve his detachment, even when the skies are falling. So, roughly the argument runs and, prior to, say, 1935, there was something to be said for it. Today it is exploded. The time when a literary pontiff could declare that he cares nothing in the world what a man writes about but is concerned only with the way he writes it, has gone, if not for ever, at least for a generation.

"Literature", Ford Madox Ford once observed, " enters with an unparalleled intimacy into French life." If one were to find a French concierge absorbed in the works of, say, Marcel Proust, the discovery would occasion no particular surprise. If, on the other hand, the caretaker of a block of London flats was noticed to be reading a work by Virginia Woolf, Edith Sitwell, or E. M. Forster, it would at once be assumed that she was a " decayed gentlewoman."

On the day that Proust died, Ford records that a taxi-driver said to him as he paid his fare : " Parait qu'il est mort ! C'etait bien inattendu !" Paris " was a stricken city. In every house, in every café, on all the sidewalks people said continually : ' It seems that he is dead. . . .' " In London, if a dozen of our most eminent writers, painters and musicians were to expire on the same day, no one, outside a very restricted circle, would take the slightest notice of it or feel any conscious sense of loss.

Compared with the potential public of any first-rate French author —a public which extends to Cairo, Istanbul and Damascus and embraces many thousands of readers in the South American capitals—that of an English author of corresponding status is now extraordinarily small.

Thirty years ago it required the continuous boosting of an organized *claque* of influential critics to push even Conrad's novels into second editions. Today, the position of the " highbrow " novelist is even more precarious, even more dependent on the patronage of such members of the privileged classes as concern themselves with culture. These number a few thousands, at most. As these thousands exercise far-reaching influence on the opinions of those immediately beneath them in the social scale, it follows that neither authors nor publishers can afford not to play up to them. This may account for the fact that so many of our ablest novels still overflow with hints and asides designed to indicate that the author is almost as much at home with the " best people " as was the late Henry James. The action takes place in an atmosphere of synthetic gentility, from which all dangerous thoughts and all intellectual vitality are alike excluded. But " good " literature, which is without the animating spark, soon becomes dead literature. It certainly does not enter with any sort of intimacy into the national life, nor does it matter a row of pins to anyone whether those who fabricate it are " collaborators " or " resisters ". That is one of the reasons why the conflagration in France is unlikely to spread across the Channel.

Nothing is, of course, static. If the literature of the élite, the poetry and prose fiction produced by, and for, ladies and gentlemen who have enjoyed the advantages of a liberal (and expensive) education, has become increasingly precious, increasingly etiolated, more and more confined in its appeal to those inside a particular social *enclave*, this does not mean that the " reading public " has diminished in numbers or enthusiasm. The contrary is the case. The appetite for books, among the vast " non-literary " public, has become positively voracious during the war years. Roughly speaking, the demand seems to be divided into two categories. In the first are volumes of *reportage*, informative books, books which deal with current problems and stimulate thought. In the second are those books, mostly detective stories and light fiction, which have as their sole, but praiseworthy, object the provision of entertainment. The authors of books in the latter category have already shown themselves sensitive to market changes. The peerage has now lost its former popularity, thanks to its excursions to Nuremberg and its associations with Appeasement; country houses, replete with butlers, titled bureaucrats and Mayfair lovelies, no longer have their old appeal, thanks to Mr. P. G. Wodehouse. Crime has become tougher, has decended in the social scale. Quite ordinary middle-class people now get murdered in easily recognisable surroundings. The fiction writers have begun to grasp that their new public is no longer anti-Bolshevik, but anti-Fascist, and faint Left-ward tendencies are even sometimes observable in response to the new demand.

Meanwhile, there are signs that a great many young men, now in uniform, have much to say and are impatient to say it. They are not concerned with " creative " literature or even, consciously, with literary form, and their books will be written for the new non-literary public which has so recently taken to reading. Assuredly, in due course, art " will come creeping in " for those who have something which they feel a strong urge to express are usually the ones who find a new and arresting way of getting it over. Thus, for the beginnings of a new and living literature, strong enough to break the layers of concrete imposed by class prejudices, it seems to me that we shall have to rely, at first, upon *reportage*. Later on, some towering creative genius like Dickens a century ago, may arise to herald a new era. If some such Great Figure appears, his work will, in itself, supply all the requirements of a "purge". It will be democratic and anti-Fascist in spirit, revolutionary and propagandist in its implications and effect.

In the interval it will be the duty of those writers who have been eye-witnesses of world conflict, who have seen our young men die for a cause in which they believed, to defend that cause with all the strength and courage of which they are capable and, in defending it, to lash its betrayers. The Fascist beast, whether he hides himself behind a blasphemous misuse of the Sign of the Cross, or takes refuge in his position of prestige and power in an acquisitive society, must first be expunged or rendered harmless, if any new standard of moral values in which alone a new art and a new literature can be built, is to emerge from the bitter experiences through which we have passed.   We must , therefore, hope that the days when nothing means anything and everything means nothing will eventually end and that, with the restoration of the meaning of meaning, will dawn a brave new age. The fact that, in spite of the epicene squeals of " henna'd hermaphrodites ", *reportage* has already developed into a recognized and appreciated literary form, is perhaps the most hopeful indication for the immediate future. *

---

* Since writing the above I have read " A Soldier Looks Ahead," by Captain " X." Besides confirming my view of the general attitude of the politically adult " Atkins, Junior ", this book contains several passages of *reportage* which are simple, direct, inspired by a passion for " decency " and, in consequence, deeply moving in their effect.   The author, a professional journalist in civilian life, is evidently quite unconscious of any " literary " intentions.   He has set himself the task of making a plain statement of what he honestly feels and believes.